I0124680

Recalling Childhood

Edited by Nicholas Tarling

WITH THE ASSISTANCE OF
OOI KEAT GIN & RUPERT WHEELER

Hamilton Books

Lanham • Boulder • New York • Toronto • Plymouth, UK

Copyright © 2017 by Hamilton Books
4501 Forbes Boulevard, Suite 200, Lanham, Maryland 20706
Hamilton Books Acquisitions Department (301) 459-3366

Unit A, Whitacre Mews, 26-34 Stannary Street,
London SE11 4AB, United Kingdom

All rights reserved
Printed in the United States of America
British Library Cataloguing in Publication Information Available

Library of Congress Control Number: 2017942138
ISBN: 978-0-7618-6946-7 (pbk : alk. paper)—ISBN: 978-0-7618-6949-8 (electronic)

♾️™ The paper used in this publication meets the minimum requirements of American
National Standard for Information Sciences Permanence of Paper for Printed Library
Materials, ANSI/NISO Z39.48-1992.

Contents

Introduction

Nicholas Tarling

"The human brain has one hundred million neurons, and recording a memory requires adjusting the connections between neurons. Neurons send messages to one another across narrow gaps called synapses. While short-term memory involves relatively simple chemical changes to the synapses, long-term memories require neurons to produce new protein and expand the synapses to transform short-term memory into a memory that lasts days, months, or years. Neuroscientists have long believed that once a memory is built, its content becomes stabilized. The memory is, in their terms, "consolidated", and cannot easily be undone. Recently, however, researchers proposed a new theory about how memory works. To put it simply, every time a memory is being recalled, it involves building protein at the synapse, and the memory has to be re-formed in a process known as reconsolidation. The point is that memory becomes unstable every time it is recalled."[1]

"The life-writer who draws on memory does so in full awareness that the temporal position he or she occupies is the present moment of the past and that an excursion into history can begin only with a backward reading from that point." Readings of experience are performed though memory "and its repetitional, restorative capacity", as James Olney puts it, "but repetition and restoration always with a difference, in part due to the most immediate previous repetition."[2]

Some at least of what memory records must be hearsay, particularly in one's early years, certainly so far as the circumstances of one's birth are concerned. Asked by my brother-in-law, who has shared with his brother the authorship of a book of recollections on the part of his family members, to do rather more than I did in the rather career-oriented *History Boy* (Dunmore, 2009) and still more work-oriented *Eighty Years On* (Dunmore, 2010), I no doubt set my synapses a demand for protein, and may have re-consolidated memory in the circumstances of my immediate environment. That, aside from Rupert's urging by phone and e-mail, is at least at the start of this project a quiet room on a windy Auckland day in a country physically as far as it is possible to be from my birth-place where, well into my 80s, I am confiding my memories to a MacBook that also patiently gave birth to or borne with those earlier books and several others of a different nature.

For a few weeks before that, however, I had been jotting down recollections of my earliest years, and thus, I suppose, already re-consolidated them, whether or not they were already re-consolidated in *History Boy*. This is disconcerting for an historian who has necessarily relied so often on the written word. But, though not everyone takes their word for it, historians, at least since the nineteenth century have treated the written word with some scepticism, 'relativised' it, as some put it. Letters are written for a purpose, memoranda composed to persuade. Even diaries may be less than honest – consider the asterisks in Arthur Sullivan's or Gladstone's – and autobiographies are often, perhaps unavoidably, self-protecting. When writing those earlier memoirs, I used letters I sent to my mother for most of the time I was away from her (she lived into her hundredth year), and diaries I had started keeping in the mid-1970s. Those stirred memories – or prompted the synapses to seek protein – but that also reminded me of things I had left out of the letters and even of the diaries. And when writing the autobiographies – which I called memoirs, at the suggestion – if I recall correctly – of the publisher – I engaged in some self-censorship. I did not want to offend people I loved, nor rake over too many quarrels with those who could no longer respond.

I have, however, few if any written records, mine or others', of my earliest years. But trying again to recall them at Rupert's behest, I found, as I found when writing the memoirs, that, as in some conceptions of history, one thing led to another. I am not sure what neurons or synapses were responsible for that, but it does seem that memories are recalled in some kind of context, and stimulate what seem to be recollections of elements at least of that context. Perhaps that is more interesting in respect of one's earliest years, now so remote. My lectures on the inter-war period to first-year students in the 1980s and 1990s covered the Manchurian crisis of 1931, and I used to say *sotto voce* for the benefit of those kind enough to fill the front rows, even though they were in spitting distance, that it was an important year for me, too. Slow laugh. What sitting outside in the healthy Buckinghamshire air in my perambulator I then knew of all this, and indeed of the subsequent sequence of disasters in international relations, was, of course, nothing, though the surviving photograph of me at six months does capture waving an arm as if trying to make a point.

The 'fact' that I was born in a blizzard at home in a house in an estate recently planted next to the village of Iver, and that the midwife had difficulty getting through the snow, was established only later on the say-so of my parents, who were indeed in a better position to know and so remember. I liked mother's other story, that I was conceived as a result of a rather good bottle of sparkling burgundy. Could my elder brother Michael beat that? But in extreme old age she denied the tale: it was, she said, a disgusting idea. It had had its appeal to an historian with his interest in cause and effect.

Recollection, I suppose, is associated with consciousness: no doubt neuroscientists and psychologists, and indeed experts in many other fields, have plenty to say about that. My neurons, drawing on what protein is available, seem to bring back from the early years more of the context than the self. That perhaps makes it perhaps more interesting to the historian, though it runs the risk that the knowledge he subsequently acquires in his profession will complicate the re-consolidation. I have also found it difficult to recall sequence, though more or less aware of the dates of such transitions as moving up the educational ladder or such striking events as the annual seaside holiday that a far from upper middle class family took for three weeks each year.

The early years are thus rather blurred, resistant to the call of chronology that is fundamental for historians. But the contexts stand out the more, and I have had some fun from considering how different everyday life was from what is now taken for granted. Last year I read the recollections of childhood written down by a former colleague, an authority on Auckland's history now in his 90s (his mother lived to 103), and wrote some marginal comments on it. He was struck by the similarities of context between his childhood in an Auckland suburb and mine in a dormitory estate twenty miles from the financial centre of London. What he had assumed must be distinctive in a remote part of the empire was not in many respects not so very different. The empire in a way was a family in itself. Not many cars were on the road. Children were enjoined to read the same books. We hankered after the same sweets. And in Iver we knew about Canterbury lamb, though I suppose it was not called that in Auckland, and drank Kia-Ora squash as well as Tizer the Appetizer.

It was, I think, this exchange that led me to the idea that our childhoods could be recounted in a wider context. How had others – in the Commonwealth or outside – experienced it? What, persuaded to cudgel their minds, could they recall? What was similar in their surroundings, what was different? The time periods would be different as well as the locations, even if, as I decided, we had to confine our invitations to contribute to those who were senior enough to have to make an effort to recall the past or to try to surround what memory made vivid with what seemed quotidian. My later profession meant that those I persuaded to contribute were more likely to be academics than otherwise, though it did increase the geographical range covered, and Rupert persuaded some non-academics to join the venture. Academics are not always ready to put pen to paper or pound their laptops, and historians are reserved about relying on memory. But the contributors were all ready to have their writing or computing arms twisted into shape and their neurons and synapses put to work. I rather hope that our example will be followed by others. Memory itself is worth preserving as well, we hope, as memories.

Going over the contributions, I found an expected diversity, but also a not entirely unexpected commonality. The fears and affections of children are apparent: more than one contributor narrowly escaped drowning, for example. The contexts widely differ, but the lack of motor transport and TV, let alone the internet and the cell-phone, are common. The recollections appear both remote and close.

Perhaps they qualify the view Shostakovich allegedly expressed to Solomon Volkov. 'For some reason no one writes about the humiliations of childhood. They reminisce tenderly, I was so small and already independent. But in reality they don't allow you to be independent when you're a child. They dress and undress you, wipe your nose roughly. Childhood is like old age. A man is helpless when he's old, too. And no one speaks tenderly of old age. Why is childhood any better? Childhood injuries last a lifetime. That's why a child's hurts are the most bitter – they last a whole life.[3]

NOTES

1. So writes Xiaofei Tian in introducing his translation of The World of a Tiny Insect, Zhang Daye's memoir of the nineteenth-century Taiping rebellion in China and its aftermath. (Seattle and Washington: University of Washington Press, 2013, pp. 26-27).

2. James Olney, Memory and Narrative. The Weave of Life-Writing, Chicago and London: Chicago University Press, 1998, p. 344.

3. Testimony, London: Hamish Hamilton, 1979, p. 5.

Memories of My Childhood in the Black Forest

Elizabeth Arndt

I was born in the Black Forest in September 1942 at a time when my father was drafted as a doctor into the German Army and was sent to Russia. My little sister was born in February 1944.

Bombing started in earnest in 1945. Pforzheim, the "World's Gold and Jewellery city", named Goldstadt Pforzheim, was only 30 km to the north. This city was mostly flattened, even the hospital where my sister was born. People tried to jump into the river Enz to escape the raging fires and flames but this was in vain as even the water was on fire, ignited by the phosphorus bombs. The bombing was carried out by the Royal Air Force (RAF) on the evening of February 23, 1945. About one quarter of the town's population, over 17,000 people, was killed in the air raid, and about 83% of the town's buildings were destroyed. I could never make out why the Spa town Bad Wildbad was bombed. Could it just have been to dump deadly surplus loads?

This is the background of my earliest memory. As I was delving into my memory I realised more than ever that your identity starts with your family. I remember clearly, even being only two and a half years old, that I was standing in my cot and screaming in utter panic. Tears running down my face. Hearing the piercing sound of the air raid siren and seeing my mother grabbing my baby sister and rushing downstairs into the cellar. She could not carry both of us. I can still see her face and shouting: I will be back. Don't cry.'

Later I remember seeing black/brown faces (Algerian and Moroccan) for the first time. They were, as I later found out, the front soldiers of the French Army. I recall the stories being told that they raped and looted. In our garden I saw holes being dug, lined with duvets from the house which they used as sleeping quarters. The French Army occupied my home town and due to the fact that my grandparents spoke French the first floor of my grandfather's pharmacy, a very large building, was commissioned for the French commander and his family. We were allowed to stay on the second floor. As a child, I guess you trust and just do what you are being told. Nothing made sense to me. Why are these strangers living in my grandparents' home? It seems they all got on well as they became friends in later years. Or were they frightened that my Granddad might poison them with pills from the pharmacy? My dad who was still alive had been taken prisoner of war by the British and was sent to a POW camp in England near Manchester. Boxes full of buttons started to arrive from England to the delight of us children. I still remember the fun we had with them. Much later when my father returned I found out about the "mystery boxes". He told us that he was well received and was "installed" as the local GP as the village had none. The local industrialist (button manufacturer) even asked him to live with his family in their very big villa. They could not understand why my father wanted to go back to Germany, a totally destroyed country.

The pharmacy of my grandparents also had a wonderful magical garden situated on the mountain side. It seems to have been the saviour of my family and their many friends as they could feed themselves from the fresh produce. It also had a little garden house with a balcony and a pear tree with the most wonderful pears creeping up the wall. And the huge cherry tree I loved to climb. There were chickens too. Eggs must have been such a rarity as I remember there was always a little celebration when we found eggs in the chicken coop. Having enough to eat and to make the best with what we had was a challenge. I still have in my possession the handwritten war recipe cook book of my Gran!

This part of the Black Forest is not an agricultural area. One had to trek (no cars) by foot and handcart for many miles to the plateau where there were some farms to barter for flour, milk, potatoes, butter, cheese; oh, those luxuries. We loaded the cart up with Persian rugs, clothes, books, jewellery etc to exchange for food. I remember one farmer having at least six rugs on top of each other which must have been just funny from a child's view. I think that we survived on potato pancakes, called Kartoffelpuffer, with apple puree. This was our daily food and years after the war I felt just sick just smelling them.

Despite the lack of food we were healthy thanks to the garden and having a pharmacy in the family. I remember in the mornings we had to line up and my grandfather administered pure Cod Liver Oil. No father present, my grandfather stepped into his role. He also was my moral guidance and a role model with his deep well of kindness and forgiveness towards anyone he met. Granny was a stern teacher in manners and how to behave.

During the war my dad came home on the occasional leave from the front. The name 'front' had no meaning to me. What was it? During one of those leaves we travelled to the Starnberger See, south of Munich, to visit his mother, my other gran. It was a different world to me. She looked really old compared to my other Gran. She was the mother of 11 children and the smartest of them all went to University. I recall the place being beautiful, with a big garden and lots of rooms. I spent quite a lot of time with her in the kitchen and on one occasion, with a swift move, she removed her front teeth to clean them under the running water. I was absolutely fascinated and even tried to remove my own teeth. We went for walks in the village and I recall that people collected horse manure for their gardens.

When I was older I asked my father about his brothers and sisters as I only met one. Three of his brothers were killed in the war, shot down over Russia. I did not understand what war was. Why did people get killed? Were they so bad that they had to be punished?

He told me that he being the brightest was destined to become a priest, then the tradition in Catholic families. He was educated by the Jesuits. The night after he received his exam results for his Bac/Abitur he scaled the walls of the seminary and escaped. He paid for his medical school in Munich by giving German lessons to Chinese students and earning money with his photography and paintings.

My father returned from England in 1948 and my mother hoped he would settle down as a GP. Not so. His ambition was to qualify as an orthopaedic surgeon (probably due to his horrible war experiences). He settled for the Uni Clinic in Heidelberg which was untouched by bombing raids. Why? As it happened one of the US commanders studied in Heidelberg before the war and it later became the US HQ in Europe.

My grandad was generous enough to pay for his training - which was common then –as well as for our upkeep. In 1949 we, my mother, sister and I moved to Heidelberg. My father rented a nice flat in the centre for us while he had a flat in the clinic. I started elementary school which was an adventure. People spoke with a different dialect and I made many friends. I broke my collarbone falling from high railings while playing circus. Still remember the horrific pain.

Sadly, the marriage of my parents experienced difficulties, a so called "war marriage" I guess. And a divorce was on the horizon. Did I really understand what was happening? As a 7 year old? All of a sudden the "new found dad" became a stranger. Despite this upheaval we were very lucky as we returned back to the Black Forest and my grandparents provided a wonderful home where we experienced much love and protection.

In 1951 they started to build the most wonderful house on the mountainside, overlooking the town. A true paradise on the edge of the vast pine forest where we spent most of our time playing hide and seek, Indians and Cowboys, cops and robbers until it got dark. We were a mixed bunch. Boys and girls. When I look back now we did not know any fear. Collecting the wonderful blueberries and raspberries: we had it all. In the summer, when it got very hot, we went skinny dipping in the River Enz, looking for deep pools. Sometimes the older boys brought homemade fishing rods and we tried to get some of the famous trout. It was great fun but I can't recollect that we caught any.

My grandfather being a hunter had a love for hunting dogs and he bought one for me. A beautiful pedigree Münsterländer (Pointer in English) with the name of Sellmann of Zavelstein. I nicknamed him Selly. He was a true friend, walking the 2 km to school with me and accompanying us to our various ski excursions in the winter with my mother who was a former ski champion and member of the Olympic Team.

Occasionally my granddad took me with him, especially in the winter to lay out food for the deer. There was a special place, a clearing, from where one could observe them, unnoticed.

It was specially constructed called "Hochsitz". Chestnuts were their favourites which we carried in big bags to the clearing. I never actually witnessed the killing of a deer and my granddad explained to me that it was necessary to control the "herds" as they would damage the trees too much and no natural predators were present.

Sadly Selly was also fond of chicken, actually anything with wings, and raided various chicken coops which could end us in tricky situations. I clearly recall an incident when a man came to the front door and accusing our dog of murdering his precious chicken, all pedigree naturally. I denied it and then my dog whisked past me still with some feathers sticking in his fangs. Stupid dog!

Back in the Black Forest I joined the Primary School and the classes seemed to be me quite big. In Germany it is a big event. When you start school at 6 or seven you get a gift. A huge cornet shaped coloured cardboard filled with sweets and little presents given to children in Germany on their first day at school. I guess to sweeten education?

Armed with our Schiefertafeln (a plate of slate in a wooden frame) and Griffel (slate pencil) we were taught the ABC and to write. Never will I forget the screeching sound of so many slate pencils in the hands of so many kids. The good thing was that you could easily erase your efforts with a damp sponge when something went pear shaped and start again. I guess that paper was also in short supply even though Bad Wildbad had a paper factory. I remember the very patient teacher and his reassuring voice, the singing lessons and the days on the nearby sport grounds or when it rained in the huge sports hall.

My school organised twice a year school outings called "Wandertag" which meant a lot of walking, visiting museums and castles on the way. I only know that each time my classmates and I returned home we slept very well and nurtured our blisters.

One of my loveliest memories—I must have been about 10 years old—my sister and I snuggled up to my Gran early on a Sunday morning and listened to her childhood stories. She was such a great story teller. The people in her stories really came alive: her friends, the hotel staff, the hotel guests and her father. A totally different world. The clothes they were wearing were just amazing. Thankfully I inherited the old family photo albums which give an understanding of the world they inhabited then. Like skiing in long skirts and the enormous hats of the ladies.

She grew up in my great grandfather's hotel and had to pull her weight at the age of 14 as her mother died. She told us about horse-drawn coaches arriving from St Petersburg with a huge entourage including the tutor to the heir of the Tsar's throne. I still have the leather-bound Guest Books to prove it.

Fresh salmon from the river Rhein was delivered in huge wicker baskets packed with ice.

The cooks, all 20 of them, were mostly French and worked in the winter season in the hotel in Nice as the hotel in the Black Forest closed down until late spring.

I had one special friend called Monika who also had a bike. We did a lot of biking together. As my town did not have at the time an open air swimming pool we had to cycle to the next town. One of the trips did not end well. On the way home my satchel got caught in the front wheel and I was thrown over the handle bar and landed on gravel. The result was a gaping wound on the inside of my left hand which is still visible even today after so many years. We managed to make it home and I kept it secret as I did not want to worry my Mum. In hindsight it was really stupid as it should have been sutured.

Where did I learn swimming? With my dad in the river Neckar which flows through Heidelberg. He was still in his doctor's garb taking a break from his hard shift.

My grandparents were one of the first to acquire a car in our town after the war. A beautiful black Borgward. It ran so smoothly, too smoothly, as I got car sick. It had weird number plates FW 21-4891, meaning French Württemberg 1948-53. Sunday drives in the Black Forest were finished off with a lovely dinner. One of those excursions brought us to the University City of Freiburg im Breisgau, the very southern tip of the Black Forest, near the Swiss border.

In autumn 1953 the time came to sit the entry exam for the Gymnasium (Lycee). I remember that we were all stressed out as we heard scare stories that it would be very hard. But in the end it was all fine.

The Primary School on the first floor and the Gymnasium on the second floor were in a large building, quite impressive on a hillside reachable by many very wide stone steps.

I never forgot the joy in the autumn when apples were delivered to the cider factory and press which was to the left of the bottom stairs. Apples were pressed and large carpets of the pressed apples were stored in huge brownish coloured piles on the bottom of the stairs. They were like trampolines and stank to the heavens. After school my friends and I jumped from the stairs, about 10-12 meters above, into this smelly, warm and soft cushion and afterwards walking home covered with the stuff! Such fun, indeed, but my mother was not amused.

Our extended family lived all around us. Aunts, uncles and cousins. It was a bit of a bummer at Christmas as we usually made the presents ourselves. One uncle, the brother in law of my Gran, then retired, was a very interesting character indeed. During his working life he worked in the hotel business and had travelled far and wide. He told stories from France, Switzerland to Greece, Syria, Egypt, Turkey and Armenia: faraway places with photos and coins to match. My sister and I sat spellbound at his feet. This was our "Thousand and one nights". He certainly whetted my appetite for visiting foreign lands.

Winter was a sheer joy and we spent as much time outside as inside. There is a saying you learn to ski before you can walk. Something very interesting developed about 120 years ago and is totally unique to Bad Wildbad. People come from afar to watch the competition. The German name is "Fassdaubenrennen", in translation "Race on staves", the staves being made from cider barrels and used as a very short "Ersatz-Ski".

In the early 1900s skiing was a sport only for the privileged. Proper skis were very expensive. A rich watch manufacturer from neighbouring Pforzheim who had a house in Bad Wildbad, had the idea to use the "staves" as skis and the first competition was organised in 1923. The first prize was a pair of brand new "real" skis.

I took part but I never won. Thinking back and looking at my own performance, I treated the whole affair as a joke and I felt that it was solely to the amusement of the spectators. I told one of my teachers that we should get paid for that which did not get down too well.

We even had to jump over a smallish ski jump. Later I made up for it with real skis.

My grandparents were involved in creating the first Ski Club and fostered my mother's career as a competition skier ending up as a member of the Olympic skiing team. Later on they organised skiing trips to Switzerland and Austria.

Childhood in Iowa

Jake Dailey

These are the memories of Donald Duane Dailey, better known as Jake. I was born on 25 November 1921 to Roy and Gertrude Davis Dailey, the sixth of their eleven children, the middle child of a large family. The brothers and sisters older than I were Harold, Howard, and Marion, Darlene and Margaret. Born after me were brothers Frank and Merle and sisters Donella, Dorothy and Joanne.

I was born on a farm in Ringgold County, Iowa, near Mount Ayr, the county seat, in the rolling hills of the southern part of the state. I have a few memories from approximately three years old. My younger brother Merle fell on the scythe my older brother Harold had been sharpening on a foot pedalled and granite sharpener and cut his chin to the bone. Being the resourceful person that she was, my mother put flour in a dish pan and put this on to stop the bleeding. Also I remember going to the Waterston country store and the wonderful sweet aroma there.

We lived in Section 7, Lots' Creek township. The house was on the north side of the road and the barn on the south. That was still standing in 1999. The hill has been cut down. When we lived there it was level from the house to the barn.

I didn't start school when we lived there, but I remember going to school at Lots' Creek Number 4, better known as Stansbury. Harold, Howard, Darlene and Margaret went there, too. I also remember going across the road south to Jake Funkhauser's in 1923 or 1924 and listening to their radio.

We moved to Liberty Township in Section 13 and went to school at Liberty Center. I remember going to church there called High Point. It was in Section 12 of Liberty Township. We next moved to Section 10 in Liberty Township and went to the school of Kolorami. Then we moved south to Section 2 in Poe Township where we went to school at Leesonville and also to the church there. Then in 1931 we moved to Mount Ayr where my folks both lived till they passed away.

My father, who I think went to school until the eighth grade, farmed and ran a steam threshing machine until he went broke and moved to Mt Ayr. He worked at the county road crew and then the State Highway Commission.

My mother was a home maker: that was enough with this large family. She had gone to Morningside and taught school before marriage. She was a good musician. She played the piano, both at home and at church, and she had a great influence on all her children's lives. We used to sing and play church music at home. This was the only music my mother would play on the piano.

The schools when I was growing up were country schools situated two miles apart. In my thinking the people in this country valued education from the beginning, and when the pioneers first came to the area education was started in the home where the person of learning was teaching the best they could. Then came the one-room school houses two miles apart, wooden structures fired by wood or coal, with two outhouses and a coal shed. The toilets were outdoors, one for boys, one for girls. Catalogues were used for toilet paper.

With 10 to 30 pupils in each school, one teacher taught all eight grades: reading, writing, arithmetic, history, geography, spelling, music and so forth, as well as keeping discipline. Sometimes this was most difficult because some of the boys got pretty big before they graduated from the eighth grade.

Most of our teachers were girls who had taken what was called a normal training course in high school and were about 18 years old. When the girls got married, they had to quit teaching. A lot of them only taught one year. After World War II they could be married and start teaching in a country school and some started by going to college in the summer and getting a teacher certificate.

Transport to and from school was mostly walking. Some rode horses or a horse and buggy. School started at 9:00 and ended at 4:00. Lots of boys started school in the fall bare footed and we would take off our shoes as early in the spring as our mothers would let us.

Before the older ones could graduate from eighth grade and go to town school—usually in Mt Ayr, unless they lived closer to some of the other towns in the country—they had to go to town in the spring of the year they were in eighth grade and take two days of tests. If they did not pass these tests, they did not go to high school. I don't feel this was fair as most of the town kids did not have to do this, but that was the rule.

We had a county superintendent who visited the school two or three times a year. I can remember we had two ladies as superintendents when I was in country school, Miss Dolacheck and Miss Dickens. We would spruce up the school and clean it all up if we knew they were coming. Sometimes we knew when they would be there and sometimes we didn't. They would just come in unannounced and stay for two or three hours to see how the teacher was getting along and how the students behaved.

All the roads were dirt until the early 1930s when the river rock was used on the highways. All other roads were still dirt in Ringgold County. The only hard surfaces were the bricks around the square in Mount Ayr and one block off the square and going north from the square down to the railroad depot. Part of Highway 2 was paved in the late 1930s.

Kerosene, a very thin oil also called coal oil was used in lamps and lanterns for light. There were also gas lamps which you would fasten to a light with a pump. When these were put in there was much more light and it was cleaner. Kerosene smoked up the chimneys and they had to be cleaned every few nights. There was also a Delco system. This was a wind-charged electricity stored in batteries and the used somewhat as we use electricity today except that the lights were not as bright.

Perishable food was left in cellars, dugouts in the ground that were lined with bricks and had concrete floors. Also most of the houses had wells into which food was lowered into the water in waterproof containers. There were also some ice houses made from cutting ice in the winter and storing it in sawdust.

Heat was from coal and wood-burning stoves. Most houses had just one heating stove plus a kitchen stove, with sand at the bottom so that the heat would not burn through, for heat and cooking. The stove in the kitchen stove was too small to hold a fire overnight. Water froze in the kitchens. Fires in the living room got very low. Most of the bedrooms were cold. We would hurry behind the heating stove to dress when we got up. Most baths were taken in wash tubs behind this stove. Can you imagine all the family using the same bathwater? It is difficult for my generation to believe that the standard of living will improve in the next eighty years as it has in the past eighty years.

Most families had pets to keep mice and rats away. Some had house cats and cats that stayed outside. Most had dogs, some to protect livestock and others to hunt with. Most had ponies or riding horses. Some had canaries in the house. But that is about the extent of pets in those days: people did not have money for exotic pets or anything of that nature.

Most families had their own meat and we always had milk, butter and eggs. Some had orchards with fruit of many kinds. We had big gardens in which we grew potatoes, onions, lettuce, green beans, peas, and strawberries. My mother baked bread, rolls and cinnamon rolls. She sewed on a treadle sewing machine, cooked three meals a day for a large family, and always had room at the table for one more.

Food other than what we grew ourselves or purchased at the store included wild animals and birds—rabbits, squirrels, ducks and geese—fish, fruit, nuts—walnuts, hickory nuts—and mushrooms. There were many different types of mushrooms, some of them poisonous, so you needed to know what you were looking for. Green weeds were also harvested and cooked and were called greens.

The fish in this area were bullheads, channel cats, blue gills and croppies. They were harvested in rivers and farm ponds. Most of the fishing was done with fishing poles rather than rods. In those we didn't have too many fishing rods. We made the poles ourselves, mostly from gunny sacks with weights on the bottom to hold them down and also from throw lines. Thrown lines were a bunch of hooks on a line strung across the river or pond. This type of fishing was illegal, but it was done anyway, as we needed the food.

Radio came to our area in the early 1920s. A teacher took us across the road to see and hear the first one. Most of the people had telephones, but the lines were go grounded and had so much static that it was hard to hear for more than a few miles. Messages of any distance were telegrammed. Lots of letters were written. My mother read almost every letter she received to us children. We all sat and listened very carefully and quietly.

I worked most of my life beginning in the summer we moved to town in 1931 when I was eleven. We mowed yards with a hand-pushed lawn-mower in the summer, scooped walks in the winter with a number 14 scoop shovel. We picked fruit for neighbours. Almost everyone had fruit trees in their backyard: apples, cherries, and peaches, as well as strawberries. Needless to say, we ate while we were picking. Farm work could be had part-time for 50 cents a day or less.

H.P. Leeson had a dairy and delivered milk door to door to his customers. Cars had running boards in those days and I stood on the running board with my head inside the window to keep warm in the winter. I would run to each house to take milk and cream. Everything was in glass bottles, quarts of milk and half-pints of cream.

When I was a junior and senior in high school, I worked for the Pure Ice Company in the summer time for Leo Hacker. We worked from 7 a.m. until all the customers had gone, normally about 6 p.m. My pay was one dollar a day. The ice came to us in three hundred pound cakes, and was then cut into 100, 50 and 25 pound chunks to be put in ice boxes in the top section where the freezer part is today. Customers had a card which was put in the front window for drivers to see and it told them how much ice they wanted. The sign said 100, 75, 50 and 25, and they turned these over to where what they wanted was on top.

In 1942 I worked at the Rexall Drug Store. John or Barney Horn and Bertis owned an operated this establishment. Later in life, when I had my own business, I tried to treat my employees and business associates with the same respect and consideration, patience and so forth that Barney showed to use. These were true, great people.

Many farmers moved from one rented place to another in those days. Once when we were moving, my father and brother were pulling a wagon full of hogs and pigs and poultry, followed by horses and cattle. I followed for about half a mile, and then my father sent me home. The distance they moved these things was nine miles. Wood had to be moved and stoves removed and reinstalled each time.

One Christmas we went to a nearby church for a Christmas program and a play, travelling in a farm wagon the wheels of which were replaced by sled runners. The coupling pin came out and scared the horses. They ran off home. My father and elder brother went to get them. We were wrapped in blankets and sitting on bales of hay and did not get cold. We sang Christmas carols while we were waiting.

In 1928 all seven children got the measles. One brother who suffered from sugar diabetes passed away at this time. I was six and remember distinctly the sadness in the home and in the neighbourhood. He was 14. Another brother was to be lost, also at 14, on the practice football field in Mount Ayr, in 1940. Perhaps he suffered a heart attack.

I never realised what a shock and loss this was to my parents until I lost loved ones of my own. My mother told me many years later that that old fellow, my father, was never the same after losing his sons. That, going broke in 1929, starting again in 1931, and having four boys in combat in the second World War, were the hardest times in my parents' long lives.

Altar Boy

Recollections from a Catholic Childhood

George Dibley

ET INTROIBO AD ALTARE DEI.

The Latin Mass, used in my childhood, started by invoking the Trinity and then the priest would announce to the congregation, *Et introibo ad altare dei: and I will go to the altar of God,* to which as altar boy, I would respond, *Ad Deum qui laetificat juventutem meam, to God the joy of my youth.* These recollections record something of the ethos of my childhood growing up in a large Catholic family in 1950s New Zealand.

One of my earliest memories is from my sixth year, my first year at school. It was spent at the convent school in Thames, a small town, south of Auckland, the site of a gold rush in the 1860s and still oversupplied with pubs.

My older sister came running down the convent path behind me, "Sister says you can come back and help, it's all right," but I was already taking my indignation home. Sister had breached the bond of friendship between us and while Jesus may have taught humility and forgiveness, with back straightened and lips pursed I was off home. Sister would not be given a second chance to display her lack of judgement. I'd been staying after school on Fridays helping one of the younger nuns prepare the altar area of the church for Sunday mass, vacuuming, flower arranging, linen etc. I can't imagine that I was much help, but perhaps some fetching and carrying and the company lightened the routine of the tasks for her. On this occasion however, she decided to take me to task for not paying attention in church. She had seen me the previous Sunday turning around, perhaps even talking to one of my brothers or sisters. I had confided that I wanted to be an altar boy when I grew up but she said this was not the behaviour of an altar boy or even of a little boy who assisted in the preparation of the altar. I was indignant. She understood nothing of the principles which forged the basis of the friendship I had offered her. I had offended her religious ideas and she, my ideals of friendship. I maintained my visits to the convent and sat on the veranda with the elderly nun who told me stories of the saints and with whom I exchanged cards once we left Thames to live in Auckland. But I never returned to assist the nun who prepared the altar.

Despite her predictions and my occasional inattention in church, I was to become an altar boy. It involved me in experiences which, aside from their religious content, opened my mind to prospects beyond the nest of my family and the confines of our raw new suburb at the edge of a city at the ends of the earth.

SURSUM CORDA: *LIFT UP YOUR HEART*

My father woke me with a hand on my shoulder, no words were spoken so as not to disturb my older brother in the bed under the window or my younger brother who was in the bunk bed below mine. I dressed quickly, careful not to disturb my four sisters in their room. My mother waved us a smiling, wordless goodbye as she sat in bed feeding my new baby brother by the light of the little clip-on Bakelite bed-lamp.

Gently closing the door my father and I set out in the dark to walk "up the hill" to church for the six o'clock mass. No breakfast, as we would both take Holy Communion and you needed to fast from the night before. I treasured these times where I had my father to myself, we would chat about this and that, he would teach me the names of the planets and I'd try to find the Southern Cross. He was deeply committed to his religious beliefs but not doctrinaire or restrictive. His approach was one of "finding" God. He accepted all my questions openly and treated them respectfully. He didn't like the disciplinary side of fatherhood and preferred to put aside adult authority and just talk. We'd walk the two miles as the light broke and I like to think, though I can't specifically recall, that he helped me learn the Latin mass and the responses I would make on behalf of the congregation when I was an altar boy. He was a shy man in some respects. We had a memorable but mysterious conversation one morning that revolved around the moon, the length of its journey round the earth and a mysterious connection to the moods and changing temperaments of my mother and sisters which I should be prepared to treat with tolerance. Later I found out from my mother that this was his contribution to my sex education.

Eventually I walked to serve the early mass by myself. Mum's little alarm clock under my pillow, I was up, dressed and out the door with my surplice and soutane over my shoulder by half past five. The soutane is a long black coat-like garment that goes on over your clothes before you put on the surplice, a loose white top that reaches your hips. It has a square yoke and full half sleeves. Mine was plain and had come from another boy who had outgrown it, or outgrown being an altar boy. My mother brought out the old chocolate box with the roses on it where she kept her most precious things and found in it a rolled length of crocheted lace. It was about three inches wide and in what I now know as a Greek Key pattern. I liked its craft and its manly geometry. It had been crocheted by my father's aunt for his surplice when he was an altar boy. This aunt was his mother's oldest sister who had come from Ireland as a teenager. In her old age she still retained a brogue that my mother couldn't understand. This aunt had recognized my father's religious feeling and saw in him the wider family's best chance of that highest of ornaments of the Irish family, a vocation to the priesthood. My father's marriage at 23 was seen by his aunt as my mother's willfully pitting her seductive wiles against God's designs for my father. She had headed him off from his higher calling even as he'd been preparing to set off to the Seminary.

I was proud to receive this special garnish to my surplice. I would iron it myself, sometimes using a little cold-water starch to get the crochet to lie flat. I'd carefully hang the soutane on a coat hanger with the surplice on top. Many of the boys had a little suitcase to carry the surplice and soutane to church, but I did not. My mother offered a suitcase, but a combination of piety and vanity meant that I preferred to carry mine over my shoulder the two miles to church through hostile territory. It was my modest Way of the Cross. I would be taunted and ridiculed from time to time by neighbourhood boys and occasionally adults, but I was undaunted. As Catholics we had always known we were outsiders. I'd made friends with a boy my age in the street we lived in, but was ordered out by his mother who told me the sight of Catholics made her sick. Our world was divided into two groups, Catholics like us, and Publics, the rest. Since we went to Catholic schools and the rest of the children in the neighbourhood went to Public schools, this seemed a clear enough marker for us of the primary social divide. Baptist, Presbyterian, Anglican were all subsets of Publics. It worried my younger brother, since there were Catholic Schools and Public Schools, but Public libraries, pools, buses and hospitals with no clear parallel provision for Catholics who must therefore have access only through the sufferance of the Publics.

My hair was in sharp contrast to the carefully prepared surplice. One of the advantages of growing up in a large family was that you didn't get overly close adult supervision in small matters. My mother would tell me to comb my hair before I went out, but I could ignore her without further reproach. I didn't comb my hair regularly until I was about thirteen, when I started noticing that all the mirrors were looking at me. Then I started dipping my hair in a hand basin of lukewarm water, combing it wet and letting it dry in place. This was before the time of daily showers, ours was a routine of daily wash and weekly bath often sharing the water with our siblings.

My hair stood straight up at the crown unless plastered flat and as I didn't even attempt to comb it, it stood like an Indian chief's feathers. The priest asked me to comb my hair but I could never remember. When I arrived in the sacristy to help him put on the holy vestments for mass he would greet me with a reproachful look and put his fingers behind his head Indian-feather style.

I loved walking through the waking streets, some houses still in the dark, others with a woman's face lit at a kitchen window, chickens beginning to stir in people gardens, a door opening to pour light on to a front path, a garden or back porch where a man pulled on work boots, or put on bicycle clips before riding off to work. These glimpses into other families' worlds as I walked past in the dark intrigued me. I liked the comfortable, orderly unfolding of a day in the wider world outside the little circle of my family. It was dark when I started out, the sun rising behind me, sending my long shadow ahead to mark the way and exaggerating my unruly hair. The church stood on its hill above the tidal lagoon. If there was enough water, it fixed the first light in its silver-gilt surface. But there were terrors to be overcome in the last hundred yards of my journey. At the intersection where the convent school sat opposite the old two-story hotel, two roads lay ahead. One led past the school grounds, obscured behind a high monkey-apple hedge which blocked the low light. Beyond the hedge was the graveyard where the light broke through to illuminate the high marble crosses with their garlands of marble flowers and two life-sized angels set high on plinths. Both had their backs to the footpath on the street. Beyond the graveyard was the high wooden church. The prospect of passing the graveyard quickened my pace, but a further hazard lay in the second street which dropped away from the school and the hotel down the hill toward the lagoon. The narrow triangle of land between the two streets was covered with high open gum trees which reared up above me in the early light. I approached cautiously always on the far side of the road but still too often, managed to disturb the pheasants which roosted in the grass at the base of the trees. They shot into the air with a startling clap and I'd break into a run, surplice and soutane flying, past the graveyard and the marble angels to the vestry door to catch my breath before I stepped into the comforting smells of beeswax and incense.

A VOCATION: THE TROUBLES

Our neighbours over the back fence were an elderly couple. She was tall with thick veins in her thin arms, grey hair pinned loosely on the top of her head.

He was heavier set and worked a large potato garden on a site up by the church. He was not forthcoming and barely greeted me. Perhaps he had no time for little boys who liked to hang around the kitchen listening to an old woman's stories. Standards of appropriately male behaviour were narrow in those days and I was already aware that my interests positioned me poorly in this regard. It was to bother me later in adolescence but not at twelve. I'd lean on the bench in the kitchen or perch on a stool while the old woman told me stories of growing up in Ireland, of altar boys grown to fine young men who brought salvation to themselves and honour to their dear mothers by becoming priests. She was gently encouraging my vocation as it was called in the Catholic community. She told me stories from the time she called "the troubles," when she was a young woman. I had no knowledge of history but the Black and Tans I came to know were about as bad as bad guys get. One day she brought out a small broach to show me. It was about three inches long and one inch wide and was carved and pierced in a rough pattern of flowers. She said it was mutton bone and that when the boys were imprisoned by the British, girls in the village would smuggle the bones to the prisoners so they had something to do. By rubbing the bone against the edges of the stones of their cells the brave boys would make what she called love tokens and this was hers. I was astonished. I looked again at her lined sallow face and thin corded arms persuaded by the evidence of the love token, that she had once been a girl courageous enough to smuggle bone to the prisoners under the eyes of the savage Black and Tans. The beloved of the brave boy who had carved the bone. Was her solitary old man, the brave boy?

The old couple had a daughter, a young woman in her late 20s or 30s at any rate not a girl. She was the object of gossip and censure among the local women whose conversations in lowered voices I wasn't supposed to hear. Their conversation hinted at so many mysteries and wonders that I always took to opportunity to listen if I could. The young woman was not married and past the age that she should have been. She was a journalist and there seemed to be a consensus that this was not entirely respectable and certainly didn't put a woman in the way of the marrying type of man. The rumour was that she was involved with a married man. I had no idea what that meant but the tone of the conversation made me sure that this meant being daring as her mother had been daring. Some weeks after the overheard gossip I finally met the daughter. I sat at her mother's sink listening to stories while the potatoes were peeled. She spoke to her mother from a room beyond the kitchen where she was preparing to leave and came in to kiss her mother goodbye. She was fair skinned with dark wavy hair topped with a jaunty little hat, bright lipstick and a swing coat. She came to where we sat at the sink and bent down to kiss her mother's forehead. She leaned toward me and the coat swung open, the perfume and warmth embraced me, an initiation that, despite her mother's hopes for me, would contribute to eventually confound my vocation.

Q. Who made me?

R. God made me.

Q. Who is God?

R. God is our father in heaven.

These were the first of the questions and responses of the children's catechism. I had a father on earth who left all the disciplinary roles to my mother, he wouldn't use physical discipline on us as was common in our friends' families. He said he didn't have a large family to spend the day at work and then play the "bogey man" when he got home. My mother, when pushed to her limits, would claim she had nine rather than eight children to manage for all the use he was in an adult role.

In my mid childhood my mother used meal times as her quiet time. She ate her dinner standing at the bench in the kitchen with an ear cocked to the discussion in the adjacent dining room where my father was ringmaster of the circus he conducted with us at the dinner table. Stories were told, jokes shared, new tricks demonstrated in a noisy clamour for attention. My father beaming over the chaos, shared the time out on two criteria, fairness, everyone should get a go, and skill, if you'd worked on the story, if the joke was slick you'd get the time to tell it to the end. After this chaos we'd go to the living room to lie on the floor in front of the radio to listen to our favourite programmes. Dad would take out a book to read, quietly marking the margins or underlining the text, sometimes scribbling illegible notes which he always screwed up and threw away. His theory was that this physical effort focused his attention while reading. It worked well enough, while we were growing up he got a BA, LLB and LLM from the University of New Zealand and a BSc in Economics from the University of London, at that time the distance education university for the Commonwealth. He studied while we squabbled for prime floor space in front of the radio, the drama of Coast Road unfolded, Dexter faced life and the advertising jingles rattled on. We were organised to bed by our mother fairly early and he had the rest of the evening for more focused reading. Not much company for my mother I expect. She would come from her labours for a relax and a chat, he'd look up from his book, "how about a cup of tea love?" "I used to think I must look like a teapot," she told me latter.

There was a lot of love in our family. My father was probably no more demonstrative or articulate in his affection for our mother than most men of his generation but it was plain to me that he loved and admired her. As we all lined up, tidy in our Sunday best he'd run his eye over us and look at her, "you're a marvel Marie." As small children if we came upon our parents standing, having a cuddle in the living room, a cry "we all love each other" would be announced. It was an event. A "we all love each other" was an occasion when we clambered around our parents legs as they embraced clinging to them as compactly as we could and singing our good fortune as we rocked back and forth chanting, "we all love each other," "we all love each other."

When I went to intermediate school I caught the train with my father into the city. He had his train pass in his wallet and opposite it a photo of my mother. When he'd opened his wallet so the guard could see his travel pass, he'd look at my mother's photo there and tell me with a smile "lucky boy, mother like that." It was a bit embarrassing, but then I'd had to harden myself to it. They held hands when they took me to the enrolment night for my intermediate school. I was obliged to walk ahead and pretend they weren't with me!

ET LUX PERPETUA

We were told at school that our church was nearly a hundred years old. People said that if you stood at the back and rested against the wall in windy weather you could feel the wall move. It was to be demolished, cut into pieces by a steel cable. It would be replaced with a new one to cope with the increased population from the government-sponsored subdivision that was filling with new families in the 50's baby boom. The new church would be large and bright and would have a "crying room" where parents could take fractious infants. They would see and hear the mass without disrupting others. There would be new classrooms for the school as well, even though the government didn't give the Catholics money for this as we felt they should. The old church had a dark wooden interior with two gold lettered tablets that listed the men of the "Imperial Forces who fought in the Maori War," and were buried in the cemetery. I went to school with the grandchildren of these men but we had an Irish perspective on the conflict and were on the Maori side.

Sometime before the old church was destroyed I was called from my class to be altar boy at a requiem service for an important person, a bishop perhaps. I crossed the grave yard past the marble crosses and the two angels with their disappointed expressions and into the church vestry which I found crowded with clergy in black vestments. Some were in full length copes which were decorated with embroideries and fringing in silver. I was overwhelmed to find myself part of this splendid tableau. The liturgy was not one I knew but our parish priest while not very communicative, guided me firmly through my role. I handed the smoking thurible and the little bucket of Holy Water with its aspergil. The service was sung in plain chant and I found myself quite heady with the drama, the press of the splendidly vested dignitaries in the cramped sanctuary of the altar and the strangeness of the Latin. It seemed a doorway to another world.

At the school fair some weeks later I lingered over how to spend the little money I had. I settled on a little white vase for my mother and a set of art reproductions, American cigar cards I think, that someone had carefully mounted onto larger backing cards. I pored over them, Murillo, Whistler, Delacroix, Rubens and Raphael. But one stood out, it confirmed my place in a wider horizon. It was El Greco, the Burial of the Count of Orgaz. The armoured body of the dead Count was being supported by richly dressed priests and above with just a simple cloth to maintain his modesty, he was presented to Christ and the Saints. And in the foreground looking directly at the viewer, the mediator of the whole splendid spectacle, was a boy, the altar boy? His gazed directly at me, we recognized each other, we at the edge of the drama knew we also had our place.

ACCIPE SAL SAPIENTIAE -RECEIVE THE SALT OF KNOWLEDGE

There is only one photograph of all ten of us together. It was taken by a professional photographer who visited our home. It is a record of the achievement of my mother's ambition to have a family of eight children. An ambition that had taken hold, she told us, when she saw a photo in the newspaper of an elderly couple with their eight sons. She was fourteen at the time. She had been happy to settle for four daughters and four sons. Nothing was surer to stir her indignation than the assumption by non-Catholics that she had a large family because she couldn't avoid it. While not all of us arrived as far apart as might have been ideal, it had been uncertain that she'd reach her goal. The eighth pregnancy had ended in miscarriage. It happened while we were home on school holidays and to my mother's ongoing guilt and distress my eldest sister, then 15 had to cope with the initial consequences. The ambulance arrived and mum was taken off to hospital. For us she was cheerful and we filed into the ambulance to kiss her goodbye. There were about thirty children in our little cul-de-sac of 13 houses, many of them our playmates. As the procession of children continued to file into the ambulance I remember the ambulance driver saying to my mother, "jeez, missus they're not all yours are they?" She'd been treated for pernicious anaemia for the three years since the birth of my youngest sister. She remembered the doctor in the delivery room saying "my God this woman's blood is like lemon juice". They'd put the baby to sleep in the womb and given my mother blood transfusions before it was safe to deliver it. She was forty-one, with anaemia and the cause of the miscarriage was uncertain. The doctor advised her against further pregnancies, but she had only seven children and was sure the fated number was eight. She was delighted when she found she was pregnant again. She was told she had to take it quietly to ensure the baby went full term and with her usual energy and imagination communicated to the younger children who were most demanding of her time, the excitement that awaited us with the new baby and how fortunate we were to have been singled out for this privilege. In that spirit we were set to prepare for the baby.

She taught us skills appropriate to our age. I was seven, my closest sister six, and we were each taught an embroidery stitch. My sister Lazy Daisy and I French Knots. Over that winter before the baby's arrival my sister and I worked progressively through the layette. Little singlets, smocks and nighties were all garnished with circlets and swags of colourful daises and French Knot rosebuds and leaves. Even the four corners of two dozen nappies. Our youngest brother and sister chose their favourite characters from picture books. We traced the images and mum cut out the figures in coloured felt. One of my older sisters blanket-stitched the figures onto a little dressing gown. Meanwhile my mother knitted and crocheted and we all admired the wicker cot dressed in pale yellow cloth with little drawn-thread patterns in it like casement windows. Yellow because we didn't know if it would be a boy or a girl. When she did go into the annex as we called it, to have the baby, she reported to us with pride that the staff had never seen such a layette and certainly not for an eighth child.

My birthday was close to the expected arrival date and when I was asked what I wanted for my birthday I said that I wanted a budgerigar and a baby brother. The baby brother arrived home a few days before my eighth birthday. And eventually I got a bright yellow budgerigar in a blue wooden cage. But to my annoyance no one seemed to recognize the priority of my claim on the new baby. I had wished for him, he was there. I deserved some credit and some precedence. Mum had provisionally baptised the baby at the annex with water from the tap because babies who die before they're baptised can't go to heaven, they go to Limbo. To clear the threat of Limbo, Mum came directly from the annex to the church on her way home, to have the baby baptised. Dad was there with the little ones who weren't at school and those of us at the Convent School across the cemetery from the church were called over for the baptism. We stood at the baptismal font at the back of the church, the prayers were said and the water poured. The name bestowed was that of the patron saint of safe deliveries, towards whom mum's prayers of intercession had been successfully directed. The priest asked the baby to renounce Satan and my eldest brother and sister, as his sponsors renounced Satan and all his works on the baby's behalf. The baby's clothes loosened, the priest traced a cross with his thumb on the baby's little chest and on his back between his shoulders and salt was put on his tongue, "receive the salt of knowledge."

I kept tapping the priest's arm asking to hold the baby but was ignored. Finally the baptism over he announced that we would go to the front of the church to the little side altar with the coloured statue of Our Lady, where he would say the prayers dedicating the baby to the Virgin Mary. I took my opportunity and tapped him on the arm again. This time he bent down toward me. I took the baby quickly and firmly and started walking toward Our Lady, my mother anxiously beside me, "be careful, don't drop him."

Drop him! He was my birthday present. I'd be careful. We got to the little altar and I handed him over, irritated by the adults' relieved laughter.

The one photo of us all together records that, five months on from the baptism I was still aggrieved. My father holds the baby, he and my eighteen year old brother are wearing ties and jackets, the younger children are more informally dressed. I have insisted on wearing one of my father's ties, it covers most of my chest. I am in my usual posture of grievance, straight-backed and grim-mouthed. It's my birthday baby and even for the photo I am not allowed to hold him.

ET VERBUM CARO FACTUM EST

"In the beginning was the word ....and the word was made flesh" I heard this often and it seemed a very satisfactory idea. I liked words. I especially liked words that seemed directly to invoke what they named. Words that God must have used to call things into being at the Creation. I liked words too that were coy, that hid aspects of the things that were named. Words that might spill their meaning only gradually. Training as an altar boy there were many words in this category. The sacred vessels, chalice, paten, monstrance and the vestments. I would assist the priest in the vestry before mass, the white linen amice first, tied across his shoulders, then the alb, the long white over-garment with a deep lace border, cincture around the waist, stole around the neck crossed over the chest, chasuble over the top of all and the maniple like a little drape over the wrist. Each had a special meaning that was to be learned. The chasuble, stole and maniple were of a colour appropriate to the feast of the day. Red for martyrs, purple for penitential times, green and white, and black for funerals.

My favourite ceremony was Benediction. It was in the early evening and was full of theatre. It included the mysterious Litany of the Blessed Virgin, Mirror of Justice, Seat of Wisdom, Tower Of Ivory, Gate of Heaven, Morning Star, Refuge of Sinners, Help of the Afflicted.

On the altar, in addition to the usual six tall candlesticks there were two ranks of candles held in decorated candelabras of polished brass that caught the light. They stood either side of the tabernacle where the Hosts were kept. These candles stood highest near the tabernacle and sloped away left and right. Under the eye of the congregation the altar boy lit the wax taper and put it into the brass fitting with a little conical cap at the end of a long rod. The cap would be used to extinguish the candles but the challenge first was to find the wick of each candle and light them quickly. Our new church had come with an innovation. To ensure the six principal candles were at the same height, the beeswax candles were not inserted directly into the candlesticks, but inside a cream enamelled tube with a brass cap. A spring held the candle against the inside of the brass cap with the wick protruding. It was satisfying to have the candles in an even rank and economical as the candle could be burnt right to the end. But if the altar boy struggling with his taper stick to reach the high candles broke the burnt wick, then very little of the wick remained proud of the brass cap. It was almost impossible to make it take fire, the priest standing at the vestry door impatiently, the children tittering in the congregation.

The centre of the ceremony was the elevation of the consecrated Host, the Real Presence of Christ, displayed in a glass lens at the centre of a golden sunburst. There was incense, which was swung in a cloud, up, two clicks against the chain, down two clicks, as the priest held the golden monstrance high above the congregation. There was a little brass boat for the grains of incense with a spoon. The thurible was an exotic brass lamp on chains with a lid that could be raised on the chains to add the incense to the glowing charcoal and renew the fragrant smoke, up two clicks, down two clicks.

A boy a few years older than I taught me how to do this and helped me with the words of the Latin hymns that were sung. His father was at the university and his family had many strange ideas. They had a house that was specially made for them. It was not like other people's houses. Some of the walls were all books, behind which his father hid. His brothers and sisters each had a very small space to sleep and a shared play room. This was for privacy he said. This was an idea I did not recognise and whatever it was, it was no compensation for the stories told in the dark of our shared bedroom and my little brother climbing into my bed to cling to my back on the nights he woke from his nightmares. This boy also told me that he knew where babies came from and what the proper names of the private parts were. I had no interest in the babies, but the other information I was eager for. I'd looked in my father's massive leather-bound Latin dictionary, I found the Latin translation for the words I knew and then looked them up in the Latin to English. This was no help, "in sensu obsceno," it said "the male organ of intromission." The mystery remained. My new informant said that his father told him that it was silly and humiliating for children to have no words for these parts, other than baby words and slang, so he had been told the proper words and he gave them to me. It was plain to me straight away why these names hadn't caught on. They had no substance, no familiarity with their referents. They were words without flesh.

The humeral was a vestment worn by the priest for Benediction, but rarely otherwise. It was a length of rich fabric with, at its centre, a panel of embroidery and beadwork of holy symbols. It was carefully laid out on the altar rail by the nuns who prepared the sanctuary, with two set of folds either side of the central panel. The art of the altar boy was to pick up the humeral at the top edge of these folds, holding it compactly before raising it to the priest's shoulders. The released folds cascaded the fabric down the priests arms to cover his hands. With his hands wrapped in the humeral he would lift the golden sunburst as I swung the incense. Humeral was a very satisfactory word, its sound suggested the unfolding at its release and it stood aloof from ordinary words as its role required.

THE TEMPLE VEIL

The Palm Sunday of my sixth year was a warm autumn day and the small church was very crowded. St Matthew's version of the Passion of Christ was read in full. It was a long and gruelling reading in an already long ceremony. *"Now from the sixth hour there was darkness over the whole earth, until the ninth hour when Jesus cried with a loud voice; Eli, Eli, lamma sabacthani, that is My God, my God, why hast though forsaken me. . . And Jesus again crying with a loud voice yielded up the ghost."*

This was the climax of the mounting horrors of Christ's ordeal. I was appalled, a hollow feeling in my stomach. We knelt in silence for some time, then the priest broke the silence, *"and behold the veil of the temple was rent in two from the top even to the bottom; and the earth quaked and the rocks were rent; and the graves were opened, and many bodies of the saints that were dead arose, and coming out of their tombs ..."*

The rending of the veil of the temple struck me with great force. I recognised it as the place where uncertainty and distress might pour in and where love and meaning might be sucked out. My older brother's recent time in hospital that had so worried my parents, mum's illness when she had my new baby sister, dad walking at night up and down the hall waiting to hear from the neighbour who had a phone that the hospital could ring to report on how she and the baby were progressing. All of these things that breached the warmth and love of our family came through the gap in the temple veil I felt sure. Latter in my adolescence, it seemed, if not an explanation, then a powerful figure for life's uncertainty and loss.

But at six I was not without resource. Again I remember the straight-backed, grim-mouthed determination that took me home to search out all the crucifixes in the house. I remember at least three pairs of rosary beads, and my oldest brother's crucifix. My mother's pearl rosary beads were important to her, a gift that had sentimental value. My brother had gone to the Junior Seminary to train as a priest and his crucifix was about a foot tall, wall mounted with a bronze cast figure of Christ. With cruel detail there was a single nail through both feet. I set about my task with a small screwdriver that belonged to my mother's sewing machine. I levered the pressed metal Christ figures from the rosary beads and the bronze figure from its wooden cross, breaking the right arm near the elbow. My father was no gardener at that stage and beyond the clothes-line our garden was overgrown with blackberry. I chose what seemed a difficult spot to access and dug a small hole. From the place on the damp side of the garage where the gutter dripped I collected the emerald moss, lined the hole and buried my collection of Jesuses. Let that be an end to it.

I was discovered. The rosary beads could not have the figures restored, but the bronze figure was replaced on its cross and mounted once again on the wall. My mother would tell the story of what I'd done as evidence of my tender nature. I was happy enough for the praise but uncomfortable with the fraud. I was removing an affront from sight. I was going back to before the Palm Sunday awfulness to the time when the temple veil was intact and protected us all.

JESUS' ARM AT HALF PAST SIX

In the sole photograph of all ten of us together, the photographer has arranged us in front of the fireplace. The gilt-framed picture of a fishing port at sunset that hung above the mantelpiece has been taken down. But two pictures remain, to our left the image of the Sacred Heart of Jesus and to our right the Immaculate Heart of Mary. Behind both images are dried fronds of cypress. These were blessed on Palm Sunday in memory of Christ's triumphal entry into Jerusalem and distributed to the congregation. The cypress fronds with their resinous fragrance were taken home and placed behind the Holy pictures that hung on the wall. The only photo of all ten of us together places us between the two Holy Picture decorated this these mementos of Palm Sunday.

My brother's crucifix also had a Palm Sunday cypress branch behind it. The arm that I had broken on the figure of Christ was never repaired. When the nailed palm and forearm section of the broken arm was raised and lowered onto the fixed upper arm and shoulder it stayed in place. Doors slammed in argument, running in the hall, the general boisterousness of life in a large family would dislodge Jesus' arm, which though regularly restored, stood, in all but the quietest times, at half past six.

It stood at half past six that June night. The ambulance attendants had difficulty maneuvering the stretcher in the narrow hall to take my father to hospital.

He was 46, I was 12. He didn't return. I got his watch.

Memories of Childhood

Paul G. Halpern

I was born in a hospital in Manhattan on January 27th 1937, a date I eventually learned was Mozart's birthday.[1] I was an only child but my parents both came from large families. As a result my life was full of aunts and uncles not to mention cousins. To confuse the issue, close friends of the family seem to have been designated honorary "aunts" and "uncles" and it was a long time before I figured out who were the real relatives. My father was the youngest in a large family and my mother was in her thirties when she married. Consequently I was somewhat of an intermediate generation. All but one grandparent were gone and my first cousins were all years older while their children, my second cousins, are years younger. After a few days—I was a premature baby and had been in an incubator—I was brought home from the hospital to my parent's apartment in Brooklyn and this was my residence until I went off to college in Virginia at the age of 17. From then on I was only back on what were essentially visits until my now widowed mother moved to Manhattan in 1972 after 41 years in the same building. As this was the location of my childhood and early teens I should begin by describing the setting.

We lived in a six story apartment house that was one of six similar buildings of varied architectural styles on the block where Ocean Avenue split off from the main artery Flatbush Avenue, curved and then ran parallel with Flatbush for several miles until it reached the inlet from the Atlantic at Sheepshead Bay. The rear of the building overlooked the Prospect Park Station of the Brighton Line—a branch of the subway which emerged into the open here and ran in a deep concrete lined open cut or an embankment all the way to Brighton Beach and Coney Island. The subway was destined to play a considerable part in my early life. The location of the station, just a few minutes away, was very convenient for my father as he could be at his office in lower Manhattan in less than 30 minutes.

Our block was purely residential. Shopping was done on the main artery Flatbush Avenue or Lincoln Road, the street that connected to it. There was also another entrance to the subway station on Lincoln Road and in the plaza around its entrance a candy store that sold sodas and other treats as well as a range of newspapers. It also sold comic books which is why I mention it. Obviously an important feature when just learning to read. The commercial establishments were all relatively small. Today we would call them "mom & pop" operations. There were no supermarkets or chain stores until the mid-1950s. About a block away on Flatbush Avenue there was the Bond Bread Company, a large bakery. The building had a landmark clock tower but its most memorable feature was the aroma of bread which was quite noticeable whenever the wind came from the east. There was a popular saying that when one could smell bread it would rain. I am not sure an east wind bringing rain would stand up to scientific scrutiny—most of the weather systems seemed to come from the south or west, but that was the common belief in the neighborhood.

The major feature of the location and one that undoubtedly kept my parents there was the fact that Ocean Avenue at its beginning ran for close to a mile alongside Prospect Park, one of the major parks in New York City. My parents moved into the building when it was new in 1931 although their first apartment was a smaller one in the rear of the building. About 2-3 years after I was born a larger apartment with two bedrooms on the fifth floor overlooking the park became available and my parents moved into it. Consequently, although in the midst of a large city when looking out the front windows I saw nothing but trees. Initially I had the smaller bed room facing an interior court, but around my tenth birthday my parents decided that since they were at work during the day and only used the bed room to sleep, I should have the larger and brighter front room to sleep and play.

The apartment had two bed rooms, a kitchen and small dining area, a living room, bathroom, and foyer at the entrance where a small alcove provided a convenient place for a table with the telephone. The living room with my parent's precious antiques was off limits to me. I think I remember at one stage one of those small portable gates to keep me out and prevent me breaking things in my curiosity. The result was I never spent much time in that room even after I had grown out of the toddler stage and the gate disappeared. The living room was a place for company, not everyday living.

There were five apartments of varying size on each of the building's six floors. This meant 30 families or residents in the building although the left rear apartment on the ground floor was reserved for the "superintendent" and his family. The "super" did minor maintenance in the apartments, kept the downstairs lobby clean and, most important of all, tended the furnace used for heating and hot water. Superintendents were of varying ethnicity, my earliest memory is one of German background and my parents talking about a visit by the FBI concerning the super's brother in the early years of the war. Our next super was Greek and after his death an Irishman and eventually a Columbian, a prime example of New York's diversity. An annual duty of the superintendent was to put screens in the windows and attach awnings on the west (sunny) side of the building. They would be removed in the Fall. This was an age before air conditioning. The practice of using awnings ended during the war, too much labor, air raid precautions, possible liability. I do not know the reason they disappeared but it was interesting to see a few years ago that many apartment buildings in Paris resumed putting up awnings. My parents had another technique to combat the heat. When away from the apartment during the day the windows were closed and shades drawn against the sun. Then after sunset windows were opened to catch a breeze.

Until 1947 or 1948 the building was fueled by coal and I remember the big bull nosed coal trucks whose bodies could be tilted to send the coal down a chute into the bunkers in the basement of the building. I distinctly remember the loud clatter that came with the process. Our conversion to fuel oil brought by tanker trucks may have been cleaner and quieter, but was much less picturesque.

There were concerts in the park during the summer and if the wind was right the sound of music would fade in and out. In addition, the Prospect Park zoo was near the entrance to the park and when the hum of traffic died down I could often hear the seals sounding off. Not many city residents could claim that.

On the opposite side of Ocean Avenue on the edge of the park were a series of benches where, especially in summer evenings, neighbors from the building might gather. During the day it was occupied by mothers or nannies with the young children. There was a fence between the benches and the park. Fortunately the top rail was flat—no spikes—and the fence relatively low. By my 10th birthday I was able to climb over it with ease. Until the eve of my 11th birthday a trolley (tram) line ran alongside the park. I remember once racing the trolley on my tricycle. Yes, I had a tricycle. I never had a two wheeled bicycle, the urban environment was not conducive for it and there was no one to teach me how to balance. I am not sure if either of my parents ever rode a bike. Consequently, I never really learned how—a matter I now love to throw in the face of local environmentalists who assume everyone could ride one.

I also had one of those little pedal cars, bright red and marked "Fire Chief." I do not know what happened to it, I either outgrew it or it was collected for a wartime scrap metal drive. One of the neighbors took a picture of me in it ostensibly giving another neighbor's little girl a ride. Alas, the negative given to us has been lost. Those neighbors and their daughter moved to California and I like to think it would be a long time before I would have another red convertible! In this case a Triumph TR-4 in 1963. The population of our apartment building was relatively stable or so it seemed to me. There were even one or two families I had always known still living there when my mother moved out.

Either friends of the family or relatives passed on a sled for me to use in the winter months. There was no room for it in the apartment and it had to be stored in an area reserved for tenants in the basement so retrieving it could be a problem for the area was naturally kept locked. Nevertheless I made good use of it when it snowed since the park was across the street. Snow can be fun when one does not *have* to go anywhere.

My father had a wholesale stationary business in lower Manhattan and my mother worked with him handling the book keeping. This meant some-one had to take care of me and at some point there was an Irish nanny named Katherine, I have only vague memories of her for I must have been very young. I think she was the only one you could call a nanny. The rest of my "babysitting" seems to have been accomplished by my parents, relatives or friends of the family.

I have an early memory of being taken to the New York World's Fair. This must have been during its second somewhat curtailed season because of the war in 1940. I am not likely to have remembered the first season in 1939 when I was only two. I can remember "Elsie" the Borden's cow, a talking robot, and best of all, General Motor's "City of the Future" with miniature cars moving along the super highways. That exhibit was a source of frustra-tion, I wanted to see it again and only slowly came to the realization during the next year that the fair was over and the exhibit gone.

The idyllic life ended in September 1942 when I started kindergarten at P.S. 241. From then on the arrival of fall would be associated with "back to school", and though I did not realize it at the time this would be true for the next 60 plus years since I had a career in the academic world. Autumn would be associated with dying leaves, chill winds heralding the approach of winter and "back to school work." I was destined to spend the next eight years at P.S. 241 (grades K-8). P.S. 241 at this time was a reasonably new school in what was basically a middle class neighborhood where children came from families with a wide range of accommodations. Some might have lived in modest apartments above a store while others came from fairly wealthy families with large apartments overlooking a Park, the Botanical Gardens or the Brooklyn Museum. I remember going to a children's party in the 6th grade in a building where, on a recent trip north, I noticed an apartment featured in the *New York Times* with an asking price of $1.9 million.

Kindergarten gave me a lesson in government. That is, I remember a school official proudly showing my mother and I the kindergarten class room. It was very large and included a play house. All very good, except during my semester in kindergarten I was never one of those picked by the teacher to play in the house. This may have been the first step turning me to a conservative—government does not always deliver on its promises! The school was not that far away but I lived at the very edge of the school district boundary line. The kids on the next block south of ours went to another school. The majority of P.S. 241 pupils lived in walking distance. There were none of the traditional yellow school buses—they were not needed. However, between school and home there were a few difficult and dangerous crossings, including Flatbush Avenue. At 5-1/2 years old I was not trusted to do this myself and it was a good thing I wasn't. In the 7th or 8th grades when I would occasionally walk with friends from the block I clearly remember having a very close call from a turning car when I was caught in the middle of the street when the light changed. The solution was the subway. The station was around the corner and the first stop on the Franklin Avenue shuttle (which also ran above ground) was called "Botanical Gardens". The southern entrance to the latter station was almost directly across the street from school. I obviously did not take the trip alone in the early grades and I do not remember all the arrangements that were made for me. Sometimes one of my parents would walk me, someone else would meet me after school—at one time I seem to remember it was my father's secretary. I also remember sometime in 1943 when my mother and the mother of another little girl on the block staged an expedition, that is riding the Brighton line all the way to the terminus in Brighton Beach and then back again.

Eventually, and I cannot remember exactly when, I was considered old enough to make the trip to and from school by myself. I then became what is now called a "latchkey child", that is I let myself into our apartment, took required milk, went out to play and then awaited my parents return for supper. The term "latchkey child" was not in use at the time. The subway was therefore part of my life at an early age. I also remember being given a lift to school by one of the neighbors. This was noteworthy because he then had a LaSalle, a make of car that had gone out of production a few years before. I believe General Motors folded the brand into Cadillac, but it is not everyone today who can claim to have ridden in a LaSalle.

Although the war was far away, P.S. 241 conducted air raid drills during my first year or two. There was no shelter and I do not remember being taken to the school basement. The drills (at least as far as I could remember) consisted of leaving the class room with its large glass windows and gathering in the corridors where we sat on the floor with our backs against the wall. Aside from protection from flying glass, I doubt if we would have been very safe. Fortunately the Germans never developed at weapon capable of reaching New York.

A few years after the war I had a male science teacher, rather unusual in an elementary school at the time. He had been a fighter pilot in the Marine

Corps and had a picture of his F4U Corsair in his locker in the class room. You can be sure he had our respect. I will never forget one of my classmates piping up and asking: "How many did you get?" Male children are indeed blood thirsty.

P.S. 241 did not have any kitchen facilities. The majority of pupils either brought their lunch or, if they were only a few blocks away, went home for lunch. My mother would pack a lunch for me and I remember being asked sometimes by friends to go home with them and eat in their apartment. Incidentally, we had little brief cases and/or lunch boxes. We did not have the back packs children seem to be afflicted with today. As I grew older, say 11 or 12, my parents if delayed at work, would telephone and have me meet them at a neighborhood restaurant. There were occasions when my mother would not have time to cook a proper supper and this was an era before frozen meals and convenience foods were available. Cooking was done on a traditional gas stove, microwaves had yet to come. I also do not remember any "take out" restaurants. There were two Chinese restaurants within walking distance but they did not do "take out".

At some time in 1948 the New York Transit System raised the fare from 5¢ to 10¢. School children were allowed to buy a monthly (unlimited) pass for $1. It was valid on all buses, trolleys and subways in the transit system. The pass was a different color each month and all one had to do was show it on entry. By the time I was 12, I was allowed by my parents to travel about the city. This meant "expeditions" to Manhattan with friends to visit museums, stores, etc, on Saturdays. One knew the dangerous areas and neighborhoods to stay away from. It was a glorious feeling to have the city at your fingertips.

There is now the question of "play." There was a play ground near the entrance to Prospect Park about a block away from my apartment house. Here there were the usual objects, swings, see saws, a sand pit and "monkey bars", that is an assemblage of pipes meant to simulate a house. I can remember climbing on this. However, the playground was really for small children and their mothers or nannies. Once we were a bit older my friends and I would play in a small grass field outside of the playground.

I am not naturally "good at games" but tried to do what I was expected to do—but nothing more. At school we had the obligatory "recess period". Here I seem to remember we played a game based loosely on baseball that was called "punch ball". The ball in question was a "Spalding". It was a pink soft rubber ball manufactured by the Spalding Company that would be familiar to any boy in the city at this time. It was roughly the size of a baseball, but was soft and the game was played without any special equipment. The "batter" would bounce the ball and then hit it with his hand or fist, hence "punch ball." The game proceeded much like baseball. I do not remember the specific rules. There was also a variant known as "stick ball", played with the

Spalding but using a broom or mop handle in place of a bat. There was also an occasionally more formal game of "Soft Ball". This was basically baseball but with a larger and presumably softer ball played with a regular bat and gloves. The big difference is that pitching was underhand rather than overhand. I remember participating in the game organized by the school after classes. It was not often in my case as special arrangements had to be made since I lived "on the frontier" of the school district.

By the time I was 8 or 9 there were no children close to my age in the building. There were about 7-8 boys close to my age on the block—I cannot remember any girls. Occasionally someone would come from "across the frontier", that is the block south of us. The games we played were loosely organized, essentially baseball, but with rules made up as we went along and fitted to the numbers playing. It was a far cry from the highly organized and structured games one sees today. I do not think any of us took the thing very seriously. I should also add that I do not remember football making much of an impression. There might have been "touch football" games played in the school yard but I do not remember them. People in my circle were essentially baseball fans. Very different from today when football is king. There were news reels in the cinema of the highlights of football games but I remember these as mostly involving colleges, not the professional teams that dominate today.

The first apartment building at the beginning of Ocean Avenue did not have any windows on its north side, probably because it was anticipated that another building would eventually go up close to the property line. At this time was an open space with a gas station and parking lot in the empty space. The blank wall served another purpose for us, a natural site for a form of hand ball. In this game the "server" projected a rubber ball against the wall and the other player had to return the serve with potentially exciting volleys developing. Once again, it was a game we played with minimum equipment. A building eventually went up where the gas station and parking lot had been but that was after my mother moved from the neighborhood.

My close friends and I had another activity. This was "exploring" or "scouting." That is, we had an entire large park to investigate. It was relatively crime free in those days but one still had to be wary of marauding gangs of older boys possibly up to no good. The park was actually located in part on a battleground during the Revolutionary War. The battle of Long Island took place around my neighborhood. There were a few historic markers, I particularly remember a large one dedicated to Lord Sterling's Maryland Brigade, credited with saving Washington's army after the notable British victory. When I was a few years older in High School I was able to establish that it was the Hessian Regiments and Black Watch in the left wing of the British army that probably advanced through my neighborhood.

Rainy days when one could not go out were not a problem for me. In fact, I rather liked them. I had a fairly basic electric train set and an "Erector" set. The latter consisted of metal parts of varying sizes and shapes that could be used to construct things. It was widespread and rather like the Lego sets of today. I do not remember Lego being around. I did not follow or attempt the often elaborate constructions in the instruction book. Instead I used my imagination to build forts and castles which took part in games I played with toy soldiers. Eventually I started collecting better models in earnest (W, Brittains) and a friend from P.S. 241 had the same hobby. On selected Fridays we would combine forces and bring our collection over to one of our apartments in a suitcase. I still collect model soldiers, having graduated to better made, beautifully painted connoisseur (and expensive) models—as did my friend. We still keep in touch and try to meet for lunch whenever I go north to NY. You know the old saying, "The difference between men and boys is the price of their toys." I also collected stamps and a neighbor whose business included many overseas customers kept me supplied.

By the time I was 11 or 12 "play" was not my only or even major activity when not outdoors. Reading occupied an increasingly important role in my life. Some time—and I cannot remember exactly when—an aunt presented me with a carefully preserved collection of *National Geographic* magazines. They ran from the late 1920s to mid-1930s. I devoured them and probably learned as much about the world as I did in any of my school classes. I also found the advertisements fascinating, especially those for automobiles (naturally) and travel.

P.S. 241 was ideally located. The Brooklyn Museum was only a few blocks away and an entrance to the Brooklyn Botanical Gardens was even closer. Naturally our class had field trips to both fairly often. The Botanical Gardens even had a scheme where children could cultivate small plots of their own. I was not tempted—agriculture was not my thing. The main building of the Brooklyn Public Library was about a mile north of my home. It was a pleasant walk alongside the park or only a few minutes by the Flatbush Avenue trolley, converted to bus after the spring of 1951. By the time I was 11, I had a library card and made frequent use of it. At this time I had progressed far enough in my reading to handle "adult" books. I remember reading *Gone With the Wind* and the whole series of historical novels by the author Kenneth Roberts. One of them, based on Roger's Rangers during the French and Indian Wars, was made into the movie "North by Northwest." I did not discover C.S. Forester and Horatio Hornblower until I was in High School. I am, however, mystified by the current section in book stores labelled "Young Adult." We went from the children's book category to so-called adult novels without any intermediary stage.

There is another feature of New York life that I remember. This was the Macy's Thanksgiving Day parade with its giant balloons based on cartoon characters. One of the people my father did business with had an office overlooking Broadway, the route of the parade. I remember being taken there and the big balloons. It must have been 1941 when I was 4 for the parade was suspended after the U.S. entered the war and I would have had much clearer memories after the war when I was older.

This brings us to the subject of the Second World War. I was really too young to have any memories of the early part of the war and, unlike a few friends. cannot say I had any memory of Pearl Harbor. I am happy to say that the first large color (professional) photograph of me at the age of four shows me in a little jumper with a Union Jack clearly visible. The date on the photo is June or July, 1941, months before Pearl Harbor. My parents were certainly not neutral. Churchill and Roosevelt were heroes in my family. As far as I was concerned, the war was something one could say I "grew into". That is as time went by I learned there was a war on, that my country was fighting it, that there were allies and enemies. Learning to read helped and by 1943/44 I was able to follow events, especially with flags on maps. I also learned about events earlier during the war, especially the battle of Britain, I also became fairly knowledgeable about ships, tanks and airplanes, especially the latter. One event I particularly remember was looking at a map and asking my father why we did not attack Japan from bases in Russia? I soon learned the complexities of diplomacy and that there were Allies and then "Allies." I remember listening to radio reports and direct broadcasts. One was the launch of the battleship *Missouri* at the Brooklyn Navy Yard. I also clearly remember the on-the-spot broadcasts of D-Day—in fact I still have the same radio stuck away somewhere. Non-functioning but surely an antique for collectors. I was across the street alongside the park when my mother came down and told me President Roosevelt had died. I remember the ceremonies broadcast over that same radio. FDR had been in Brooklyn during the election campaign of 1944. He spoke at the nearby baseball park Ebbets Field and some of my class mates cut school to see him. It was a nasty day and I am sure the weather did not do the President's health any good. I remember the principal delivering a stern reprimand to those who skipped school.

My father had been too young for the First World War, he had just received the notice to report for his physical when the Armistice took place. Uncles on both sides of the family were in the Army in 1917-1918 and two of them were wounded in France, one of them badly. He showed me the torn jacket he was wearing when he was wounded and gassed. He also worked as a civilian for the Navy during the Second World War. My father was old enough not to be subject to the draft in World War II but he did volunteer as an Air Raid Warden and post 1945 I remember playing with his warden's helmet and gas mask. Various cousins were in the military and one cousin in the Navy met and married a girl from San Francisco in 1943. The wedding took place in Brooklyn and I remember being put to bed for a nap before being taken to the wedding, the first one I ever attended. Cousin Jack moved to San Francisco after the war. I believe his sister was in the WAACs. As my father had been the youngest in a large family, most of my uncles were also too old to be called up. Fortunately, as far as I know there were no war causalities among family members (cousins) who were in the service.

Of specific incidents during the war, there is one that has been fixed in my memory. This was the burning and subsequent capsizing of the former French liner *Normandie*. We drove by in the family car up the West Side Highway and I can still picture this great ship and superstructure lying on her side. Shortly afterwards they put up a wooden fence to mask salvage operations from the highway.

I made my own contribution to the Allied War effort. Old tin cans were collected and I was given the job of stamping (rather gleefully I understand) on the cans to flatten them. On a more serious note, I remember War Bond drives with solicitations taking place in the cinema during intermission. I remember being with my parents when my father bought a bond. My parents eventually bought a number of them and some were in my name. I happened to go to my safe deposit box in the local bank a week ago and noticed there was a paper wallet that must have come with one of the bonds. It had a picture of General MacArthur and the slogan "Victory". At the moment other papers are in it but I keep it as a souvenir.

My arrival tended to curtail the travels of my parents. They were not the type so common today who would drag an infant or young child everywhere they went. I was not taken places until I was at least reasonably "civilized" and could be expected to behave. We did have a car, my parents had always used one for business as well as pleasure and had a habit of buying relatively low priced Fords which they traded in every two years. Consequently, the first car that I remember was a 1940 green Ford (standard) four door sedan. It cost new $900. There was a manual column shift, heater but no radio. Seat belts and child seats were unknown at the time. I usually rode up front with my parents and I remember my father holding out his arm to restrain me when there was sharp braking. Pre-seat belt, pre-air bag. My father for some reason named the car "Suzy". I do not recall subsequent cars being named. I was fascinated by everything about automobiles and could recognize the different makes and models. Cars seemed to have an individual character, unlike the majority of today's cars that all seen to look alike.

The first long trip that my parents took me on was by train to Florida in late winter or spring of 1940. More than half my father's family had settled in Florida from Jacksonville south to Key West and there were numerous relatives for me to be presented to. The journey was by train, I have vague memories of the compartment in the train and being fascinated by glimpses of steam locomotives out the window. Again, I can remember looking out of a high rise hotel window at a park in Miami with palm trees—an unusual sight for me.

In addition, we used to go to an old fashioned hotel for a period every summer in Asbury Park on the sea shore of New Jersey. One trip was with my mother in a train drawn by a steam locomotive, other trips were in the family car. As we did not take long trips and the car was used only once or twice a week, gas rationing during the war was not a problem. Asbury Park was only about 50 miles from New York. It is well known that gas rationing in the U.S. was not primarily to conserve petrol but really to conserve rubber since the Japanese had seized control of so many of the sources. I do remember in what must have been 1943 or 1944 a heavy cloth screen between lamp posts on the boardwalk to cut the glow that would silhouette coastal traffic so conveniently for German submarines. I also remember armed sailors or coast guard patrolling the beaches.

When the war ended there were a series of homecoming ticker tape parades for leaders. This was a well-known New York tradition. Unfortunately most of them took place during school days. Consequently, I got to see only two which passed on a street near my father's office. One was for General De Gaulle—and I was given a small tri-color pin to wear. The other was for General Eisenhower, an interesting combination since both men were destined to become leaders of their country.

We resumed trips to Florida shortly after the war in 1947 and 1948. They were by train—still heavy stock rather than stream liners—in compartments aboard "The Florida Special" of the Atlantic Coast line. I was apparently a good traveler and rarely grew tired of looking out of car or train windows at the passing scene. By some means my parents were able to finesse things with the school authorities so a week or two absence from class would be excused and combined with regular school vacations. The only other long trip I remember was a weekend visit by car to Boston in 1947 to see business friends of the family. It was the last long trip for the faithful Ford for in the summer of 1948 my parents got a new car, a '49 gray Ford. With American manufacturers, "Model Year" did not always correspond with calendar year. This was the first truly re-tooled body style, the cars in the first two years after the war were pre-war models with trim changes. The car seemed very modern with "black light" instruments and, wonder of wonders, a radio. Business prevented my parents from taking long trips but in the late '40s and early 50's we also made a number of weekend drives to Atlantic City where there were good friends of the family—another pair of honorary "aunts" and "uncles". Atlantic City was about 100 miles from New York and famous for its boardwalk and the Steel Pier where General Motors had a permanent exhibit of their automobiles. I had a wonderful time trying out the cars for size! The DuPont Company also had an exhibit and demonstrations with the slogan "Better living through chemistry." People were more optimistic about that then than they are now.

The closing months of the war corresponded with a new adventure for me. My parents had the problem of what to do with a child during the summer months when schools were closed. They solved it by a common middle class solution. I was sent to a summer camp for eight weeks. This began in 1945 and became an annual experience for the next eight years. In those days summer camps were not all that expensive. Today, a full eight weeks would cost a fortune and most of today's camps are two weeks if not shorter. The camp, about 50-60 miles north of the city, was not particularly rural. That is, we did not sleep in tents, We had wooden "bunks" which housed 8-12 "campers" with their "councilor", the latter a college student seeking extra money during the summer or very often a teacher supplementing their not very generous salary. In the first few years after the war some of the councilors were veterans and as such a source of war stories. Some were also from different parts of the country, I remember one from North Carolina who introduced me to all sorts of colorful southern expressions. Summer camp was in many ways a learning experience. There were fairly rigid schedules for the week for "activities" which were mostly sports, although there were some which had "nature" related subjects and also amateur theatricals. I endured the sports but rather enjoyed the "nature" part, especially the occasional "hikes". The famous "Appalachian Trail" passed near to the camp. The trail was a near thousand mile path which ran along the mountains of the east coast. There were camp "inspections" and bunks had to be made neatly. In some ways the camp was good preparation for the army although I would later learn few of the "jocks" (athletic types) ever served in the military while I did—and had my experiences of sleeping outdoors which I am not in a hurry to repeat.

The highlight of camp was the week of "Color War." The camp was divided into "Red" or "Green" teams with names like "Highlanders", "Smokies" (fire fighters), "Gremlins" or "Gauchos". There was a week of intense competition in sports with activities awarded points which eventually led to a "winner." People became awfully excited over color war.

There was another activity I enjoyed, the camp field trips. These could be to other camps—with competitive sports, or best of all historic places. I remember going to the Roosevelt home in Hyde Park and, especially interesting to me, West Point where I toured the military academy museum. The majority of my fellow campers came back year after year. We knew each other fairly well but lived in different neighborhoods and did not see each other between summers. Campers as they aged could become waiters and junior councilors and eventually regular councilors, not having to pay and even receiving remuneration in the form of traditional tips. I had no desire to do this and by 1953 I was in the midst of high school and most of my friends were in the city. So my camp days ended.

For a few summers starting in 1948 I did not return to New York with the rest of the campers. My parents picked me up at the camp and we drove north to the southern portion of Maine where an aunt and uncle from Florida had a summer place. This was probably the longest trip by automobile I took with my parents before college. On at least one occasion we stayed overnight with business friends of the family in a suburb of Boston. On another occasion, when my mother was not present, we were on the Maine Turnpike and my father decided to see "what the car could do" and we reached close to 90 mph which was fast for the old Ford. Driving was beyond the horizon for me as in New York City one had to be 18 and probably could not get insurance until one was 21. When I went off to college in Virginia at 17 I was probably the only one in the dormitory who did not drive.

The cinema was certainly a far bigger part of my life than it is today. There were many more cinemas than there are today. They ranged from grand palaces in extravagant styles dating from the 1920's to small theaters which showed older films. They were also a place to cool off during the summer as they were air conditioned at a time when small units suitable for apartments did not exist. I cannot remember the first film I was taken to by my parents, but at a fairly early age I saw and thrilled to the Disney cartoon film "Snow White and the Seven Dwarfs." When I became a bit older, there were the Saturday afternoon specials, that is the local theater would show films geared for children along with 30 minute serials which left one in suspense until the next week. The entrance fee for children was very low and there was a certain amount of pandemonium from a theater full of kids. Again, as I got a bit older I preferred going to the small theaters which showed re-runs, usually films that had been out for a few years. For example, "Casablanca" came out in 1943, I saw it in 1948 and when it was on TV last month it seemed as good as ever. There was one memorable afternoon in the Fall of 1948 when my soldier collecting friend and I went to a double bill, "Four Feathers (1939 version with Ralph Richardson and C. Aubrey Smith—the best of the many versions) and "The Drum".

The medium that played the biggest part in my young life was not the cinema. It was, rather, the radio. I was a radio child. TV sets began to spread when I was 11 or 12 but my parents were not "early adapters." We did not get a TV set until early 1950 when I was already in High School. I thrived on the radio, knew the comedians like Jack Benny and Fred Allen, followed the classic serials like "Captain Midnight"[2], "The Shadow" or "The Lone Ranger" or was frightened by the horror shows like "Inner Sanctum". We dared each other to listen to the latter alone in a dark room. The show "Escape" had some of the greatest dramas I have ever heard. Radio also had a great advantage over TV. It forced one to use one's imagination, one of the most powerful things around. When home sick during the day, the radio was on and I listened to the traditional "soap operas" like "Stella Dallas". There was also a NY disk jockey named John Gambling who had been in the Royal Navy during the First World War and I would march off to school with his signature tune, the World War I classic "Pack up your troubles in your old kit bag."

There was another feature of growing up in Brooklyn. That is, the importance of "lines of communication." By the time of adolescence I roamed fairly far from home but it was on a north south basis (roughly) thanks to the existing subway and trolley/bus routes. On the other hand, areas just a few blocks to the east or west were a complete mystery. Of course the park was to my west, but I do not remember ever reaching the western fringes of the park and to this day I do not know the street that runs along the western edge of the park the way Ocean Avenue does in the east.

The return of peace also brought the resumption of ocean liner traffic. It was always a great treat for me when my father drove up the West Side Highway and I could see the *Queen Elizabeth* and *Queen Mary* and other great ships now resplendent in their peace-time liveries. Our Atlantic City friends were the first of our circle to resume touring Europe and in 1949 we saw them off on the Holland America Line's *Nieuw Amsterdam*. This beautiful 1939 ship had survived the war and was the first large ship I was ever on.

In addition to ships I was also intensely interested in aviation and in those days one could go to the observation deck at La Guardia airport. Security concerns preclude that sort of thing today, but in the late '40s the observation deck was a pleasant place for a Sunday afternoon. We also went to Idlewild airport (later to become JFK) to see the international flights and I remember the quaint custom of airliners flying flags after landing. The pilot would open the cockpit window and affix a small national flag.

My love of aviation did not always go well with sports, the sound of a plane overhead caught my attention—not the ball. I can still remember being thrilled once by the sight of the famous Pan American Airways Boeing flying boats. I once cut school and joined a friend on the roof of his apartment building—two "illegal" acts for children—in order to witness a scheduled mass flight by B-29 bombers. Probably my outstanding example of undetected crime. I was normally a "good boy"—but a mass flight of B-29s was worth the risk. I also enjoyed visiting relatives who lived in Belle Harbor. This is located in the Rockaways, a distinctive split of land visible when you land at JFK. The trip passed the now closed Floyd Bennett naval air station and I therefore got a good view of Navy aircraft. I apparently had a reputation for this sort of thing. About 10 years ago I had lunch with a friend from Camp days whose wife had gone to P.S. 241. He mentioned meeting another old 241er who remarked when my name came up, "Oh Halpern always knew a lot about warplanes and ships."

I thought I had an excellent free education in the New York City public school system but in retrospect there was one area that was lacking. We did not study a foreign language: that would only begin in High School when I was almost 14. When I asked the woman in Vienna who had translated my book into German where she had learned to speak English so well, she replied, "Oh, they start us in kindergarten." I wish they had started me on French when I was five, the results might have been better.

In concluding this memoir I have the feeling my life sounded more interesting and exciting than it really was. One only remembers the high points—after all they are memorable. It is hard to remember what I did most of the time. Routine days have faded from memory. In September 1950 I started school at Erasmus Hall High School, a sharp break with the past and my movements were now a mile south in the opposite direction from P.S. 241. Work became much more serious and intense, but that is another story.

NOTES

1. It is also the birthday of Kaiser Wilhelm II, a less attractive anniversary, although had I been a resident of pre-1914 Germany I might have been pleased to see buildings decked with flags on "my" birthday.

2. I was a member of Captain Midnight's "Secret Squadron" and in one of my drawers I still have the wings, something that will no doubt cause considerable confusion to military historians after I am gone.

The Java 'Podiyan' of Maligawatte

My Early Life

B.A. Hussainmiya

HUMBLE BEGINNINGS

The earliest childhood memory I have was the ecstasy I experienced when I witnessed eggs laid by a toy hen given to me by one of my uncles. It was an age when a child would not have distinguished between the real from the unreal.

The house number 399/32, in Jumma Masjid Road, Maligawatte, was the unit in which we lived. It was situated in Ward no 10 in the heart of Colombo Municipal Council division (which consists of 15 wards). My whole childhood, in fact until I passed out from the university, was spent in that house. Despite being situated in the capital city of Sri Lanka, our little rented unit built of bricks and mortar at the end of a row of houses lacked basic amenities including water and electricity. It was called a *'mudukku'* (in Tamil) house as it was a little more than a hovel, but something better than the thatched or tin roofed shanty homes, commonly found in the poorest living quarters in urban cities. Such dilapidated shacks in the Indian city of Mumbai was so movingly depicted in the award winning Indian film, *Slumdog Millionaire.*

My home was divided into two portions, one in the front and the other in the back. The front measuring some 10 by 8 feet served as the sleeping quarters for my aunt's family and my younger uncle who slept on the mats. During the day it would become my playpen. The rear section also was used as the sleeping area for my grandmother and me. At day break cooking was done on this side on cooking mud pots fired by chopped wood sold in the corner of the street.

Maligawatte was divided into two areas. We lived in the area called Big Maligawatte situated south of the Jumma Mosque while the northern part was known as Small Maligawatte. More often than not there took place gang wars fought on the streets between the Chandiyas or thugs on the opposite sides. And as a child I had witnessed people being stabbed and hands get chopped off during such mini-wars by the unruly elements. But living in our area was comparably better than the misfortune of living in other bad suburbs of Colombo, especially Wanathamulla, notorious for its share of thieves, drug pushers and prostitutes and so on then.

Maligawatte was preponderantly a Muslim suburb, inhabited largely by the Tamil-speaking Muslim Moors. However, I belonged to a Malay family, one of the few who lived in the area. My peers called me somewhat pejoratively a 'Java Podiyan' or a Java Boy which indicated the Javanese origins of my ancestors. I was Malay from my mother's side whereas my father's ancestors referred to as 'Banggalis' had come from South India. However, it was the Malay identity or affiliation that was strong in me and I was listed in my official birth certificate as Malay. At home we conversed with our elders in a kind of creole Malay, but our common lingua was the 'Moorish' Tamil spoken in the area. Very little Sinhala was spoken despite its being the national language of the majority population. In fact, there was but one tenement section which we used to call 'Talaratne' gardens situated right across our garden where only Sinhalese lived. The notable family in that garden belonged to the Dhoby or washer men caste. They washed and ironed our clothes with the help of a cast iron box heated by charcoal.

We used kerosene lamps to light up our homes and I studied under poor lighting conditions provided by bottled kerosene lamps, a fire hazard indeed. Due to lack of space inside the house I used the little veranda outside for reading and relaxation. There were no attached toilet facilities. The squatting latrines built adjoining my house were meant for common use for the residents of nearly ten or more households. Sometimes, especially in the morning, we queued up to use the latrines which had no running tap water. So we carried buckets of water for cleansing. The garden had only one common water tap again close to my house. We used water from that tap for drinking, cleaning and bathing. In between the common tap and the toilets, there was a mound on which people simply threw garbage. So my surroundings were in squalor though we strove to keep the inside of our home as clean as possible. The little house just in front my home had a large family of a father, mother, their brothers, and above all about 10 children. The lady of the house used to give birth to a child every year in succession and the final count was I believe 16 or 17. The worst part was the kids were allowed to defecate just outside our shared frontage which annoyed me immensely.

As children our main play area was the small passage between the opposite row of houses. We played the usual kids' games such as hide and seek and marbles. One neighbour, named Shaheed Nana, used to operate an old HMV record player with his favourite vinyl record that played the dialogues of the then popular Tamil film, *Parasakthi,* in which the great Tamil actor Shivaji Ganesan made his debut. We were glued to his record when we were not playing our kids games.

Unlike the crowded conditions today, one relieving feature of Maligawatte during my childhood was the availability of some open spaces. Nowadays the Maligawatte area is incredibly overcrowded and made worse by three wheelers, otherwise known as Tuk-tuks, parked on both sides of the road impeding vehicular traffic and even pedestrian movements. Furthermore, during the day street markets operate on the roads meant for passing road traffic.

At the time Maligawatte was a much better suburb than it is today. Not all the spaces were built up; there were still some open spaces such as the small coconut plantation with some shady trees providing much needed shade and space for outdoor activities. This area we called *Pittani*, situated not far from my home and on the way to my school. It provided us with an ideal resting place to play and relax during the day. In fact the Maligawatte Pittani served as my second home; after school I would simply drop my books at home and run to the Pittani to spend time with other children of the area. The area was used for common entertainment including mini-sports games such as soft ball cricket and soccer and we learned to form clubs among ourselves. I had participated as a young child in mini athletic meets for kids. Spending time in that area was the best memory that I still treasure in my heart.

At one time in a corner of that 'Pittani' my friends and I were playfully engaged in building in mud a model dam and irrigation system of canals. Suddenly I remember receiving a pat on my shoulder by a tall looking gentleman who had been silently watching us. He happened to pass by in a bid to familiarise himself with the people of the area for political propaganda purposes. He was Mr A. Aziz, a famous trade union leader who was involved in many Islamic welfare organisations and activities. Much later on, when I took an active role in community service matters, we became good friends. He used to recollect the day he had first met me as a child and thought he had witnessed a potential 'hydraulic engineer' then.

EARLY SCHOOLING

My first school was a preparatory school situated within a walking distance of about 300 meters from my house. It was called Denham English School, named after one of the pre-Independence period British expatriate school administrators. It was a mixed school adjoining the main Jumma mosque. The school building was one large hall subdivided by temporary divisions for the class rooms. The only closed room belonged to the Principal's office. It was not an ideal environment to study or teach in because the teachers had to virtually scream to impart lessons to avoid being disturbed by the adjoining class rooms.

In 1951, when I was first enrolled in the LKG, there was a major policy change under the Kannangara reforms of education when the Government of the day decided to switch the medium of instruction from English to swabasha (indigenous languages), either Sinhala or Tamil. I was thus in the first batch of pupils island wide to pursue our education in the vernacular right up to the university. The English medium instruction pursued during the colonial period, it was felt, did not help the rural and underprivileged children in the country. As might be expected, only certain well equipped schools of old vintage, especially in the urban town ships such as in Colombo, Kandy, Galle and in particular Jaffna where Tamils were preponderant, benefited mostly from the old form of instruction. My school which had classes only up to Junior Certificate level and situated in a backward area of Colombo hardly produced any noteworthy educational achievers even though it was English medium.

My medium of Education was Tamil. I began learning English as a second language only from the third standard. That too was only for one or two hours in a week. Hitherto the English educated pupils from my area had some prospects in getting employed in agency houses or as shop managers and government clerks. But only a few prospects were available for the Tamil medium students. A handful of them at best could become untrained teachers if they completed the senior certificate or 'O' levels whereas many of my peers, having become drop outs, ended up doing petty jobs as peons, sales assistants, municipal labourers, or pavement hawkers.

I consider myself lucky. I survived this drastic change in the education system. When I look back I could say that I was helped by many to survive within the disadvantaged circumstances. I owe a lot to my teachers. God helps those who help themselves is a saying: my teachers saw how much I strove to educate myself and they took upon themselves an onerous task in nurturing me, though they too were struggling to retrain themselves in a new system and themselves were preparing themselves to enter vernacular teachers' training colleges. Some were aspiring professionals using the teaching occupation as a stepping stone. One of my English teachers, I think his name was Mr. Renganathan, later became a prominent lawyer in Sri Lanka.

I distinctly remember my first teacher, the late Mrs. Rajadurai. From the beginning she took it upon herself to groom me. This awkward looking stick of a boy had somehow managed to grab her attention. Wonders have no reasons and likewise I seek no answers. Mrs. Rajadurai created the opportunities for me to excel. I on my part needed no prompting I must confess. Nothing succeeds like success: another saying. During the periodical inspectorate visits to our school, I was put forward by her to answer questions posed by the visiting school supervisors. If there were any contests outside the school such as for good driving manners etc., sponsored by the local police department, I was selected by her to represent my class. Furthermore, she enrolled me in children's programmes on Radio Ceylon (National radio). She offered me opportunity and I grabbed it with both hands (feet as well if I could have). Most importantly she tirelessly coached me to succeed in the 5th standard competitive government scholarship examination.

Another teacher I would never forget is one Mukhtar A Mohamed who hailed from the southern coastal city Weligama. He became my class teacher during the 2nd standard. Besides being a smart student, I and four others having been tutored by both Mrs Rajadurai and Mohamed Master received double promotions. That is from the 3rd standard we went to the 5th standard.

It was Mohamed master who inculcated the reading habit in me. He exposed me to the Tamil periodicals and magazines imported from South India. My reading knowledge was further reinforced by my interest in reading books on "General knowledge." These books I received during the annual prize-giving in the school. Besides, I borrowed books from the school's mini library. I was very fond of reading the tales describing the exploits of Alauddin and forty thieves, 1001 Arabian nights and so on. Through my avid reading habit, I developed comprehension and a good command of language in Tamil which came in handy in my later education in Tamil at the University level.

Since my early younth I had developed Tamil Oratory skills. I never knew stage fright. Besides I had that desire and drive to want to stand out among my colleagues. Mohamed Master introduced us to the Tamil Literary Club held every Wednesday afternoon where I learnt the art of public speaking in addition to getting some leadership skills. I even became the secretary of the club. Furthermore, toe other persons who exercised greater influence in my early life were my uncles, namely S. Basheer Haladeen, and S. Basheer C. Thassim who were my role models. Both of them were involved in the local branch of the Young Mens Muslim Association, founded in 1949 by Mr A. M. A. Azeez, a distinguished retired Muslim public servant who became later the principal of Colombo Zahira College. In Maligawatte, I became the founder President of the Junior YMMA in 1962 by following the path of my uncle who became the President of the main organisation.

Even as young boy, through my oratorical skills in Tamil, I became a crowd puller. I was exposed to political propaganda meetings at so young an age. In 1958, for instance, the Local Municipal Council elections in Colombo were heating up as the candidates from all the main political parties such as UNP, SLFP, and Marxist parties were contesting the elections. They were very exciting and interesting times as during the election periods whole areas of Colombo came live with party meetings, demonstrations and visiting trains of candidates who hunted votes in the areas. A young man of the area whose name was A. H. M. Fowzie, (later a senior cabinet minister) was put forward as a candidate by the main stream UNP to contest the Municipal Council elections in that year. At only eleven years of age, I joined his team for propaganda work. Apart from serving as an announcer in a moving vehicle fitted with loud speaker equipment, I got on the public stages to support his candidature. In one final political meeting held in support of him, I appeared on the stage to speak in Tamil along with the well-known Sri Lankan political leaders such as Dudley Senanayake and J. R. Jayawardene.

Decades later in August 1985 when I was the Chairman of the 2nd Malay World Symposium held in Colombo under the patronage of the then President J. R. Jayawardene, the President during the coffee break mentioned that he remembered my being on the same stage as he. I relate this story at this juncture to highlight that even at that tender age I had acted without fear and my penchant for meeting high profile persons without any reservation. Another saying: fools venture in where angels fear to tread!

SECONDARY EDUCATION

My primary school education at the Denham English School came to an end when I passed the 5th Standard all-island competitive examination. Based on a means test the scholars were given 30 Sri Lanka Rupees a month as living allowance which was a godsend to my poor family, especially to my grandmother. More importantly, the top scholars could study at the well-endowed Government Central Colleges. In the case of Tamil medium Central Colleges the best were found in the Jaffna Peninsula, equipped with reasonable facilities for science education. I would have been better off studying in Jaffna. However, my poor family could not afford to send me that far and pay extra for my boarding fees etc; In the end I just had to contend myself in studying at the Maradana Central College situated a 15-minute bus ride away from my home in Maligawatte.

The Maradana Central School was not the best of its kind, especially the Tamil medium section in which I was enrolled. Situated again in an underprivileged area, my school once earned a bad reputation in the headlines of some local English newspapers as the 'blackboard jungle' of Colombo due to the unruly behaviour of some pupils. Unlike the pupils who attended elite private schools such as the Colombo Royal, Thurstan, Ananda and other good schools, the students in Maradana Central came from much lower social and economic background. The Tamil stream was poorly managed to the extent that there was only one teacher available to teach science in the Tamil medium. Despite such disadvantages, with plenty of self-motivation, I stayed on top of my class rankings mostly through self-study.

HOME LIFE

My beginnings were mired in poor living conditions. My mother was married off at age 16 to a man many years her senior who served as policeman in the British Royal Navy. As was the case in many of the marriages in my area it was done to ease the family's burden: a kind of sacrifice they made of their tender daughters. My grandma, a widow, had struggled husbandless and penniless to bring up her four children including my mother. Her eldest son, my uncle, S. Basheer C. Haladheen, even had to leave school very young to find employment in a Colombo agency house as a peon in order to support the family.

Talking about my immediate family sometimes confuses me. But I shall try to arrange chronologically as far as possible the events that shaped my life. I was the eldest in a family of three with my younger siblings, Shaikh Fareed, my brother, and Qamarrun Nissa, my sister. My father was not particularly a responsible husband to my mother. He did not bring much relief to the family as expected. He was eternally a man in debt. A habitual borrower from extortionist money lenders, he used a main part of his monthly wage to settle his interest payments. In 1953, my father moved out on transfer to Trincomalee naval headquarters. My mother followed him with my two siblings. It must have been a difficult decision for my parents to leave me behind in Maligawatte, but they did it because of my educational needs. I can only remember that the day they left on a train leaving the Maradana railway station I ran behind the railway carriage that took them away till I collapsed with exhaustion. My memories fade for a while in this aftermath. On hindsight it was great decision by my parents to let me continue my schooling in Colombo. Moreover, my grandmother who was very fond of me would not easily have borne my separation from her. In Maligawatte I lived with my grandmother, my aunt, Janeer Muda, and her husband and my younger uncle, Saifuddin Thassim.

Looking back, I must attribute my success in life to a large extent to the sacrifices made by my grandmother, Nona Indran Cuncheer. She was my heroine. Herself a poor woman, she was dependent on the welfare handouts given monthly by the Colombo Municipal Council for the underprivileged people.

To speak of poverty at home is something too much for me to elaborate at this point. We were always in need. That is all I knew at the time. My grandma could not even pay her monthly house rent of eight rupees to the landlord. Whatever the case may be, she brought me up in a sort of luxury shielding me from all hardship, so to say. I was her life and I was her pride and joy. Perhaps if I dig deep into my psyche I was driven to succeed by my need to see the way her eyes lit up when someone praised her little grandson. She was my greatest cheer leader. And I believe that I never disappointed her. I did test her unconditional love in more ways than one especially when I expected her to replenish (I do not know how she did) the countless pilot pens that I lost almost every other week. She never disappointed me and tried to give me everything I asked for.

As a child I used to earn a little pocket money by running errands to people in the neighbourhood to bring their ration rice and other essentials from the cooperative stores. In addition, I used to assist in small business my great grandmother, Gnei Syamsuddin who lived above our garden with her other daughter Sundari Muda's family. We bought pieces of broken biscuits sold in bulk by the Maliban biscuit company and re-sold them to people in our area. At one time I also worked as a child- labourer packing match sticks in safety match boxes, in a minor industrial plant situated not far from my home. The extra income for me used up to buy gallery tickets to see South Indian Tamil movies of which I was very fond. The gallery ticket cost me 50 cents which entitled me and my friends to be seated on benches uncomfortably placed close to the screen area. Colombo had many cinema theatres screening Tamil films.

Apart from the fact that I was the apple of my grandma's eye, I brought extreme joy to her miserable existence. Not a year passed without my winning school prizes annually in public ceremonies officiated by some VIPs at the time. My grandma would proudly attend the prize giving ceremonies carrying back the books I was awarded. As my parents were living away in Trincomalee, it was my grandmother who would attend all important public events in the schools which required my participation. Thus at the Maradana Central College, once at the young age of 12, I won the best speaker prize beating all other senior students during a speech contest held to commemorate International Labour day. Our Principal Welikala, inviting me to the stage to receive the prize, mentioned in his speech that I was no rat (meeya), a pun on my name in Sinhala, but a fierce cat, a 'balalaya'. No wonder my grandma was in ecstasy to see her little grandson receiving the best complements in front of a large audience of teachers, students and VIPs, which she used to relate to all her visitors until she passed away in 1985.

During the school holidays, at least twice a year, my parents brought me down to Trincomalee. I usually travelled by night train accompanied by a naval police officer. They were some of the best days of my life. My father moved houses several times in Trincomalee. They lived first in the Dockyard and second at Love lane, and a third time in a hut house near the beautiful blue sea beach at Nilaveli. Lastly they moved to China Bay Naval quarters, a few kilometres south of Trincomalee which was situated in the midst of a thick forest and where the navy stock piled oil in specially reinforced oil tanks. Often my father gave me rides in the navy trucks he drove. I also used to watch drills conducted by him as a Crown Sergeant. At home, my mother conducted Quran reading classes for the Muslim children living in the naval quarters. Most of my time was spent on reading books. My father used to save cuttings of Tarzan comics from the Virakesari Tamil newspaper he used to subscribe to. I relished the luxury of foods issued by the Navy Commissariat including tin fruits and corned beef. In 1958 it was in the China Bay naval quarters that both my brother Shaikh Fareed and I underwent a circumcision ceremony.

The forest environment in China Bay appealed to me. I loved to accompany my father and his friends to chop wood in the forest. In the forest I came across some tasty forest fruits such as 'Palu', a favourite food of the jungle bears. In the quarters we had a pet monkey named Togo who was my friend and even bathed with me in the same water tank. It was a naughty monkey and when we were not at home turned the house upside down, including the photo frames hung on the walls. It was, nonetheless, an intelligent creature. When my parents had to move out from the China Bay quarters when the Royal navy closed its operations in 1958, Togo could not be brought back to Colombo and had to be given away to a visiting Pakistani sailor, and I was told both my mother and Togo were in tears, and Togo simply refused to go with his new master.

It was my penchant for reading historical tales since my young days that shaped my mindset and interest in liberal arts studies, I believe. Besides, I sat in awe at the feet of street story tellers near my house. There was one particular story teller whose name was Aan Sahib who lived down our lane. On the pavement steps of the main road we sat around him to listen to his tales of exploits of famous Arab and Persian heroes such as Hatim Tai. I was also fascinated by Bikramaditya stories from North India which I read in big volumes of books borrowed from a neighbour's home. I borrowed further historical novels housed in a bullock cart library which doubled as the sleeping quarter of an Indian milk seller called Asiri Appa in our neighbourhood. Later, I developed an interest in reading more comprehensive Tamil historical novels based on themes from the heroes and kingdoms of South India. Some of these novels were the serialised versions that appeared in the famous Tamil Literary periodicals such as Kalki, Ananda Vikatan and so on and written by excellent story writers.

Apart from my play time in the Pittani, I spent hours scouring various newspapers and periodicals kept in the nearby reading room run by the Colombo Municipal Council. There were other interested readers of the area who frequented the reading room, but I must have been one of the younger. I read all kinds of newspapers in English as well as Tamil. My favourite English magazine used to be the *Illustrated Weekly* of India. But I was more comfortable reading periodicals in Tamil. The librarians of the reading room especially reserved the weekly subscribed Tamil language periodicals for my first use.

Despite being Tamil educated, I was motivated enough to learn English on my own. I remember the very first word in English I learnt- 'The Sky' - from a picture book bought for me by my young uncle Saifuddin Thassim. The instruction in English in my schools was so minimal that I had to go to night schools that conducted English classes in my area. The schools were run mostly by unqualified teachers. I was not charged any fees as they were aware of my family background. In so far as the learning of English was concerned, I tried to run even before I could walk. For example, I tried to read D.H. Lawrence's controversial novel, *Lady Chatterley's Lover*, which was lying around in my cousin's home situated at the entrance to our garden. My cousin's house, number 403 in Maligawatte Road, served as my nursery for self- reading. Most of my reading notes and books for preparations for public examinations were done there. I used to sit in the sofas placed near the windows that allowed plenty of light from the outside.

With all my efforts I could not attain a desirable level of proficiency in English. I was not exposed to formal class room teaching in English and as a result my pronunciation was not up to standard. Learning mostly by my own, I could not write proper idiomatic English. I realised my weakness when I failed to obtain a credit for my only English language paper sat for the 'Ordinary' level examination in 1961. At the university I had no option but to study in the Tamil medium.

History was my favourite subject. I was fond of books of historical inter- est including biographies and historical novels. My grades in history in the school had always been high. In fact at the form 3 qualifying examination I scored the bull's eye of scoring hundred out of hundred at the Maradana Central College. Mrs Viswalingam, my History teacher, commended me especially for my prowess in history.

As I entered senior secondary level, a big decision awaited me. There were three streams to follow --in Science, Commerce or Arts. Studying sci- ence carried better prospects for professional success like becoming a doctor or lawyer in time to come. However, I had to make a tough but a viable decision in the circumstances since my school provided very poor facilities to study science in the Tamil stream. I fell back on the Arts Stream which I thought I can get by well in the least through self-study. Apart from a host of other Arts stream subjects such as civics, literature, and Hygiene and Physiology, there was a further option to choose between the History or Carnatic music offered as alternatives. The music teacher was a famous Carnatic singer in Tamil and there was always a temptation to follow his class. But I chose history. Had I studied Music instead, I used to tease my children, that I might have become a genius like A.R. Rahman, a celebrated Tamil Nadu musician, the only one in the Tamil film industry to win Holly- wood awards.

Memories of Childhood

Pradeep Kanthan

CONTINUOUS LIGHT

"Come out soon you b*****d", shouted the nurse as she and the midwife struggled to bring the baby out. The baby was pulled out held by its heels and spanked. I must have cried. I would imagine this when my mother later told me how I was born.

It shouldn't have been all that difficult for the maternity staff, considering that my mother was driven to the hospital in a *Jutka*. This was a single horse drawn carriage, with thin creaky suspensions, wobbly wheels and a hard-to-get-in passenger area covered with a tubular canopy. The yaw, pitch and roll must have prepared my mother for a swift delivery. The *Jutka* was truly mankind's gift to pregnant women!

I was born in 1951, at a Hospital run by a charity in the heart of a conservative Bangalore. India had become independent just five years ago. *Jutkas* continued to be a form of transportation right till the mid 70's, carrying an overload of passengers, moving forward on three axes drawn by a famished horse. They were slowly being replaced by phased out Fords Morris, Austin, later to be replaced by the ubiquitous, Made in India Ambassador car.

After birth and the mandatory post-natal stay at the hospital, mother and I must have travelled the same way back to my grandparents' house. Not that I remember, as the wobbly ride would have been a familiar one inside and outside the womb.

I was born in the dark night phase of the moon of *Kartik Amavasya*, heralding the great festival of lights *Deepavali!* My parents had traditional names in a syntax that had their home town, their parents name followed by their own. A child is named after its birth star, or *nakshtra.* Here they broke tradition and gave us all hyphenated first names. Naming some of us after popular film stars of the time.

Mine meant the 'continuous light of the moon'!

THE RELUCTANT PRIESTS

My parents came from the *Brahmin* community, which merely served as a social identity. They were religious in a philosophical way and cared less for ritualism. In an economic sense they came from the middle class that had laid great stress on education. So our extended family had doctors, engineers and lawyers who pursued white collar jobs. There was another reason for the high value attached to education. The Kingdom of Mysore, the region where we hailed from, was a well administered princely state, which had wisely invested in a knowledge based economy. It had several reputed colleges and schools providing free education.

We were a displaced community that had migrated and mixed into regions which technically could have been different countries. Much of the displacement was caused by famine, plague and wars. So my parents came from different regions, had a common mother tongue with different dialects but spoke a common regional language and were educated in English. They had the benefit of literature in quite some languages.

My father was the first to join the armed forces, making him a rebel of sorts. The Army gave an elitist lifestyle, which made us live in two worlds. A secular national one influenced by the British and the other we shared with our relatives, a community one which was fairly liberal.

My father held a commission as a Lieutenant in the Royal Indian Engineers. He served in the Second World War where he was involved in mine clearing operations at Bari in Italy. He returned to India in 1946 after the War. The same year he married my mother, a graduate from Mysore University. They had an arranged marriage, as was the custom, and at a time when Bangalore was under curfew due to the agitations leading to the independence of the country.

My parents came from slightly different environments. While my mother came from Bangalore a modern city of the times, my father came from Bellary a smaller town. My father was entirely a self-made person, who did exceedingly well at his Wardlaw London Mission School in Bellary. Like all self-made people he exuded confidence and pushed his way through diligence and tact. He was a polyglot speaking several Indian languages as well as Pashtu and Dari picked up while serving in the Persian and Iraq Command. He spoke fluent Italian, learnt by the need to employ Italian labour. Both my parents were great teachers. While my mother, a graduate, was my teacher for the sciences, my father was a thorough military officer from whom I learnt to swim, play tennis and all the knots and lashes that one needed to know. They both inspired me in their own ways, except for mathematics.

My father was the maths teacher; a role he was most unsuited for as he chose the path of 'spare the rod (in this case his web belt) and spoil the child' which put the fear of mathematics in me. A subject which was to form the core of my career. Alas, my mother, who was a more approachable teacher but had graduated in Chemistry, Botany and Zoology taught me subjects which I did not pursue. The irony of the wrong teacher for the right subjects eventually saw me in several schools, an idea pursued relentless by my father who supported the idea of changing the environment to improve one's academic prowess! It did work is some way! Though I learnt the real reasons for studying in many schools much later.

I must mention that my father had the gift of the gab. He was very good at striking up a conversation with any one. This got us quick admissions in schools, movie halls, trains and almost anything. Yes, he could hail a taxi with his ability to produce a loud whistle, and sometimes get the best deal through artful negotiations.

There was a great reliance on his confidence, and he never failed us. He would get his colleagues to teach him maths without letting us know, which he then took upon himself to teach us. He was a great cook, a 'know all' in some ways, much to the annoyance of my mother. So much so, my mother had to assert her knowledge of botany in which she majored, when my father tried to show his knowledge of flowers and gardening. We always had the hibiscus flower amongst others, and the banana plants and coconut trees growing side by side. I think either as a tribute or in competition to each other's love for different yet specific parts of nature.

My father also had sharp reflexes, perhaps because of his country background. He could handle snakes and animals with ease. His love for country life often saw the existence of a chicken run and cow shed where ever possible. He had an insatiable love for acquiring agricultural land, which he couldn't really capitalise on, much to the relief of my mother who couldn't imagine spending life on a farm!

I was their second child.

DUXBURY LANE BUNGALOW

By late 1951 or early 1952, we had moved to Bombay, where we lived in a Bungalow on Duxbury Lane in Colaba. The spacious accommodation had a couple of acres of land with a compound wall and a driveway that went through a portico. Along with the allotted accommodation, the occupants inherited the staff who lived in the annexed servants quarter. My mother had a lot of help ready at hand. So much so, the first word I uttered was *'Langdu'*, which means lame in Hindi, for the washerman was Langdu. Perhaps I was in his care most of the time and quite naturally learnt his name. There was my father's batman (a military valet), Sapper Dilbaugh Singh, a Sikh, who would be around the house.

While at Duxbury Lane I remember my father placing me on a coffee table and dressing me up for an Officers Mess function where children were invited. We had an Austin of England, which had steam powered wipers and indicator hands that came out from the door frame right in the middle. The steam system had a governor, which would release a valve letting out a whistle. I would be on my mother's lap sitting in the co-driver's seat and excited each time the car whistled.

We had a dog, a German Shepherd called Rover. I cannot recall much of Rover at the Duxbury Lane Bungalow and know only from my mother's narration of its alertness and great fidelity to the family.

THE ORNATE DAGGER

'Courage Conquers All,' was the title of the article she submitted to a magazine several years later.

My father commanded an engineering unit called 6 Docks Inland Water Transport Company, which was close to the Duxbury Lane Bungalow. One mid-morning, after he had gone to work, Rover was going berserk barking and pulling at his chain. My mother was alone and didn't know why Rover was barking.

Intuitively, she went in to check my crib in the bedroom. I was barely a year old then. When my mother entered the bedroom, where I was sleeping, a pair of hands crept out from under the bed and held on to her feet. She was shocked and horrified, but even before she could scream for help she heard a pleading voice asking for help. This must have been a terrible incident for my mother who came from a very soft spoken, well-mannered gentile background, absolutely unaware of how to react in such a traumatic situation.

A bearded man came out from under the bed with a dagger in his hands, but he pleaded with my mother, in Hindustani, to protect him. This must have surprised my mother and she found the courage to demand that he immediately let go of her feet. The man, a Pathan, was tall with a big turban and had a dagger in his hands. He handed my mother the dagger in submission and kept pleading for help to save his life. He said that there was a mob chasing him and might soon be near the gate. He was sure that they would kill him.

My mother got her wits around her and called up my father on the phone through the military exchange. This must have been a field telephone connected to the unit exchange, as owning a telephone was a rare thing. My father came along with military policemen to take the now sobbing intruder away.

The Pathan, who was a moneylender, was grateful for being saved from the mob. (Pathans hail from the regions bordering Afghanistan. They were known to be in the money lending business). He left the dagger in my mother's hands, an ornate one which could have been a crucial piece of evidence when it was later known that the Pathan had murdered one of his debtors. It stayed at home, till it left as a parting gift to Sapper Dilbaugh Singh a couple of years later, when my father had a slight change of plans in his career.

It was 1954 when my younger sister was born and we had moved out of the Duxbury Lane Bungalow to a modern flat in Sion in Bombay. I was now two and played with my elder sister and other kids in the compound.

I remember the dagger as a mantelpiece in the Sion flat, kept out of my reach.

PAPPADUMS AND RICE

The Sion Flat was in a building called Manohar Villa: it had a lift with collapsible doors and a balcony overlooking a busy double road. My father had taken a posting to a non-operational post to further his studies in engineering. He had brought along with him from Italy a portable HMV Gramophone as well as an Olivetti typewriter. So my childhood at the Sion Flat had some Italian songs. Of them I distinctly remember *Oui Marie* and *Trombe*. Several Indian vinyls of Hindi were added later, some for my elder sister's *Bharatanatyam* dance practice. My appreciation for music and movies may have started here at the flat.

My elder sister, and later I, would go to a school just behind Manohar Villa. Here there were no permanent servants as at the Duxbury Bungalow. My mother had three children to care for and did away with cooking, relying on the nearby Mangalorean Student's Hostel for delicious South Indian vegetarian fare, Brahmin style. I remember the tall brass tiffin carrier with pappadums stuck on top.

However, as aromas and odours go, we were an Army family and lived with the smell of boot polish, brasso and starch. An odour that kept me company even later in life.

The aroma of freshly cooked hot sambar, rice and vegetables from the Mangalorean canteen was a welcome interjection. I knew it was lunch time!

There was a ritual which my parents followed in child rearing. My father's panacea to all health issues was captured in two tablets, a laxative and a deworming tablet. The other wonder was called Vicks. They all kind of worked. One ritual was a periodic 'improving' of the children's eyesight.

Something we didn't look forward to as we had to be kept in a stranglehold, while a half cut onion was squeezed into our eyes. "Good for the eyes!"

The other much more comforting ritual was my mother's ear cleaning. Warm garlic-flavoured sesame oil was poured into our ears and plugged with cotton. "Good for the ears!" My mother had her way with finger nails, which she would peel with her hands, right through till I learnt to use a nail clipper. My father was the official hair stylist for all, including I think sometimes for my mother.

THE BLISS OF OPIUM AND BRANDY

I was a drug addict at two.

My parents in their youthful years were fond of movies, mainly English ones as Bollywood cinema was still finding itself in the 50's. I was partly in the care of an *Ayah* (a nanny), who my parents discovered would drug me with opium or brandy. Seemed like a common practice in childcare those days! I don't know how they did it, perhaps through milk, but I would sleep for unusually long hours.

Ayah was fired, and we were now taken out to the movies instead of being left at home. I remember crying and ducking my head in some horrible scenes. Movie going was a regular pastime and Bombay had several movie halls with some state-of-the-art fittings. My father would often talk of his tenure with the 8th Army and spoke of how Cairo and Alexandria were modern, with coffee vending machines and so forth. Bombay was a modern city then and had an excellent public transport system run by BEST (Bombay Electricity Supply and Transport) and an equally great milk supply. I remember the foil capped bottles of toned milk delivered to the door. One bottle was cocoa flavoured, perhaps for me, the boy child. I continued with a glass of hot cocoa every night at bedtime till I left home. It looked like a continuation of my opium days, and not really my mother's preferential treatment for a boy child.

SCHOOL AND THE RED DOUBLE-DECKER BUS

I was soon sent to school, along with my elder sister. The school was behind our Sion flat. It was a new school run by a Parsi lady, in a long barrack like building with red tiles. Sapper Dibaugh Singh would take us to school: a short walk. We would be back very early and I would enquire about our little sister. It was something my elder sister and I would come home to everyday: the baby in the house, to play!

I remember a red double decker bus, which was my favourite toy. I would spend time 'driving' around, with a greater effort on the part of my vocal chords making motor noises, than on my hands and on my knees, putting the bus through an imaginary route while also calling out the stops like the bus conductor.

There was a car with pedals, which was 'whrromed' around the smooth mosaic tile flooring. My sisters had their toys. Then my elder sister's *Bharatanatyam* dance classes started. I think a teacher came home for the lessons.

THE STORY NOT OVER

Our German Shepherd was quite intelligent and seemed to be able to respond to door bells and was very gentle with the children. Rover would sit and watch over us, while we played in the balcony. He was big and barked occasionally.

One day, Rover was not getting up despite everyone's attention, and appeared to be sleeping. Later I remember him being put into a gunny sack and taken away. He had died, poisoned by the others in the building.

At that time, I felt no grief, perhaps because of being too young and not knowing what had happened, but the incident remained etched in my memory. Poor Rover, the faithful friend of the family didn't have to die, for no fault of his or anyone.

He was poisoned by a conservative group of vegetarians living in the building, who did not like the idea that the dog was fed with meat. What a contradiction of compassions! Knowing of this incident shaped quite a few things in my life.

I had dogs later in life, and named some of them Rover.

DEPARTED SOUL

While we lived in Bombay, we made a trip to Bangalore in 1956. My maternal grandfather had passed away. They lived in a small house in the same locality where I was born. We had hired the ubiquitous *Jhatka* to take us home from the railway station. Many cousins and all my maternal uncles and aunts had come to partake in the ceremonies for the departed soul. The house, like all others, had a well and I remember peering down the well and seeing my reflection in the waters. Looking beyond it were a few tortoises which kept the well water clean. I was barely able to look over the parapet. Despite the heat of summers, the water from the well was incredibly cool and tasty. I used to run to it every time I heard the squeaking of the pulleys to get a taste of this wonderful water.

The ceremonies were a prolonged affair and food was generally served only after it. The atmosphere with the smell of burning wood and smoke accompanied our hunger. Wood was the most common fuel. My mother having moved to Bombay had promoted her fuel to gas, which was available piped at the Duxbury Lane Bungalow.

Here at the last rites ceremonies, I was introduced to marbles, gilli danda (a game played with a stick and a double conical object, which is hit with stick, calling for hand-eye coordination), tops and hopscotch and other games played along with the girls. There were cries of cheating and agreement and commitment to the game, broken only by the announcement that food was being served.

At night all the children slept together, exhausted by the day's play with no understanding of the departed soul's journey, which only the ceremonies seemed to secure. The food was great, always accompanied by sweets.

One of my uncles had a motorcycle and my ride on it was by clinging to the petrol tank! It was a horrifying experience mainly from the loud noise of the engine.

I was 5 years old.

THE GREAT LIZARD CAPTURER AND MISS O'CONNER

My father was posted to Jhansi, in Central India, a city famous for '*Jhansi Ki Rani*', the Queen of Jhansi who fought the British.

At Jhansi Sapper Chellaiah was the new batman. He had great skills and was very good at catching lizards in the garden. He once caught a large lizard, skinned it and boiled it to extract its oil, which he said was medicinal. I saw the skin nailed to a wooden plank, drying in the sun.

His quick reflexes came in handy saving my life in a miraculous escape from a road accident. Had it not been for Chellaiah, who was taking me to school on a bicycle, I would have certainly not been narrating this story. He was injured while trying to save me from a head-on collision with a truck which was apparently out of control. It must have shocked my parents. Chellaiah rode me home before going to get himself treated. My parents were indebted to him, and kept in touch with him for a while after he had gone home on pension.

Jhansi was also where our academic progress needed some disciplining. English became important and to wean us away from slang and speaking in Hindi and Telugu, my father would insist that we spoke in English at the dining table. The idea served us well in the Catholic schools where we studied.

Living in a cantonment we enjoyed weekly movies and parties. The occasional party at home was an event. I remember the cook hanging the chicken carcasses to drain out the blood. The houses generally had the cook house as a separate structure, connected to the main house through an open veranda. Most important it was that there would be other children to play, of all ages.

Jhansi had some tragic moments. One of my father's colleagues drowned in a boating accident while on a picnic. The other was when I almost drowned in the swimming pool, saved just in time by my father.

In the happier moments, it was attending Miss O'Conner's birthday. I liked Miss O'Conner, and I was the teacher's pet.

My father took me there on his bicycle, not Chellaiah.

The teachers would invite their entire class for their birthdays, perhaps to reap a good harvest of presents. This of course, was not in my thoughts, but I was groomed and taken to the event and was eager to give Miss O'Conner her present. I had memorised her address to reach there.

I stood first in the class.

LIPSTICK ON A LIP

My father's military service meant frequent postings and travel. Invariably he would go ahead and we would follow generally after the school term, in time to join the school term at the new place.

The next move was to Nagpur, South of Jhansi in Central India. Nagpur is the geographical centre of India, with the highest temperatures, orange country and plenty of mica and manganese ores. It wasn't a military station and my father was on deputation with a fledgling organisation for disaster management. We initially lived in a place called Civil Lines, our bungalow, shared by two families overlooked the Central Provinces Club. The club's members included several rulers of Princely States. We never got to see them, only hear the music on their club nights.

I was 6 or 7 by then.

The bungalow was set in a large compound of perhaps 5 or 6 acres, with a lot of bush, wild animals, snakes and berries. We would eat the wild berries and so would the jackals, hyenas and other animals. We knew this when we found droppings of these animals on the numerous trails around the house. Our first encounter with a snake was when my elder sister sat on one unknowingly, inside the house. The snake had coiled itself into one of the numerous cracks and joints of the granite slabs of the floor. I don't know who killed it, but it was burnt because they say the snake remembers who killed it. Myth it must have been, but wild life always has some wild myths around it.

The district forest officer lived not too far away, and the children of the two families sharing the bungalow trooped to his house to see the captured tiger cub. It was hardly a few weeks old, but could leap around the coffee tables. Though it was quite aggressive, we were allowed to play. Playing with Tiger cubs was not a core activity, but the forest officer's children soon became friends. The next visit to the tiger was some three months later. This time it was no child's play: the tiger was caged, huge, and we soon learnt that it was being shipped to a zoo. Tigers grow faster than children.

I learned to ride a bicycle pretty fast, without bruises by learning to ride across the main frame of the adult size bike. They call it the scissors method. It was a great achievement, but a struggle fighting for it with my elder sister.

Nagpur had some incidents. The first was when we initially arrived. We almost suffocated to death from carbon monoxide fumes of a coal burning stove. We were saved when my father came home for lunch and found us all lying unconscious. A close call.

On another occasion the school bus had broken down and we were late for school. So two of us boys from the bungalow family decided to see the movie posters and what the world could offer us. We were actually peering into the poster of Harry Black and the Tiger, when Mrs Minocha (I think that was her name) from St Francis de Sales, our school, saw us, and pulled us by the scruff of our necks on to her cycle rickshaw to take us straight to the Principal's office. This was a major incident (actually my first): parents were summoned and both families lamented the quality of sons they produced.

Mrs Minocha, a middle-aged lady used to apply lipstick only on one lip, and I was curious to know why, and would keep asking my mother. There really was no answer, but Mrs Minocha was etched in my memory for apprehending me and my friend when we were just about to enjoy a day away from school!

From the bungalow in Civil Lines we moved to a new locality. It was reasonably nice but a small place, and really didn't give us much room after our grand bungalow-style furniture had fought for space. The house faced a slum across the road. This was fun as there were more children to play with. We got a dog: actually we adopted a street dog and named it Dicky. The funny thing about Dicky was it could get on to the pillars of the main gate and perch itself on it. It was like Snoopy, Charlie Brown's pet beagle. It would howl more than bark.

Two things happened in Ram Nagar.

The first was an attempt to teach me to play the *tabla* (a musical percussion drum). I think it was my father's intention for me to accompany my sister's *sitar* renditions. However, I suspect that the real reason was for me to be a chaperone to her at the music school. (It falls upon the boy child to become a chaperone of sorts to his sisters: while I did not see it as such, perhaps parents did). I hadn't progressed much as luckily a sitar teacher closer to home was discovered, making the music school journey redundant along with my boring *tabla* training. At that time, I didn't have much interest in music. Ram Nagar we were to leave soon, but not before I got introduced to the RSS (Rashtriya Swayam Sevak Sangh), an organisation that runs training programmes for youth, generally Hindu youth.

I went to a Roman Catholic school and in the evenings played with the slum children, ate with them and saw their internally well-kept shacks and huts: shining brass utensils and welcoming mothers, who could go into a crescendo to keep their children in line. The RSS *shakha* (branch) would meet at a specific time and children of all ages, mostly boys, would assemble for the drills. It always began with a prayer; of which I knew nothing. I knew only the Hindu prayers which matched some of the RSS ones and the Angeles of our Catholic schools. The *Shakha* leader asked me where I studied and when I told him of my school, he asked me to say the prayers that we said in school. Soon I was leading the RSS gathering with my school's Roman Catholic prayers following the Hindu ones. It amused all the children and young adults, like a novelty. We did not speak English here, and our Hindi was peppered with Marathi, a language I learnt because of its common script with Hindi, even before learning to write my mother tongue.

(I do not know if the RSS has undergone a sea change and is at the centre of Hindu Nationalism, but my experience with it was a welcoming secular one. I can compare it to my later association with the Boy Scouts and YMCA).

We carried our local linguistic slangs to the next posting only to be replaced by newer ones.

MYSORE LANCERS

We didn't know that we would live in Bangalore as we had come on a holiday which transformed itself into a posting. Bangalore is a military station and a unique one as it really isn't a cantonment like most others. It was called a Civil and Military Station, the only one of its kind. One of the reasons was the historic joint administration of the city by the British and the Maharajah of Mysore. On arrival we lodged in the Maharajah's part of the area called the Mysore Lancers. It was the location of the erstwhile forces of the Maharajah. Here we lived in house belonging to my father's colleague who was off on annual leave. It was temporary. We had access to the house and the colleague's car. It could be a vintage car today, but it wasn't quite that then; a few of them similar ones were around through the 60's: spoked wheels, running board, canvas drop down hood and starting handle. The car was functional, a far cry from the Austin of England in Bombay, till it broke down pretty badly. The axle gave way and I don't know what happened to the car thereafter.

The colleague must have been a really good friend!

BENSON TOWN

From the stately sounding Mysore Lancers, we finally settled down in an area which was known as 'Little England', also Benson Town. I was by now 8 years and started life in a different India. The locality was relatively new, with modern, modest, single storey 3-bedroom houses. It was largely populated by Anglo-Indians who were mostly Indian Railway employees. Most of them had one leg in Britain and the other in the grave. Many may well have been British who had never travelled to Britain. It was the 60's and other nationalities also lived in our neighbourhood. There were two American families of disparate social class and professions, an Austrian doctor, an English aircraft engineer and several families from mostly out of state, who were domiciled in Bangalore. There were plenty of children and the three American children would join in playing with us. Not the English girl, who was reserved and occasionally spoke to my sisters.

The street was the main playground, with hardly any traffic, just the occasional lorry with constructional material. It was mostly playing seven tiles or throwing rocks in the nearby rainwater catchment areas. The girls would occasionally join in for cricket. We all soon started playing in the nearby YMCA, which was the first to be declared a family YMCA. In the neighbourhood was the Parsi Dharamshala (Parsi Rest house), which one could not miss due to the very appetising fragrance of *biryani* and *dhyanas*, besides the manager, who they said was quixotic and rode a peace shattering Indian Chief motorcycle.

YMCA was great, with basketball, table tennis, picnics, singing songs and hearing some older boys playing the guitar, particularly Nathaniel who played the Shadow's 'Peace Pipe' so well that he earned a title 'Piss Pipe' Nathaniel. I wanted to learn to play the guitar but never got to it as my parents felt that it would take me away from my studies and yes of course I'd become a drug addicted Hippy.

I had joined my 4th school, a Roman Catholic boys one and came closer to the wonderful world of settling classroom scores in the local park, shooting birds with catties (catapults), asking passing engine drivers for grease, flattening 2 Anna coins on railway tracks and making tops out of tar. St Germain School didn't do much more to my academic progress, and I soon fell prey to some greedy teachers who made a meal ticket of me through private tuitions. There was however one highlight to the schooling here, Miss Martin, the young lady who was the Physical Training teacher. Everyone loved her class especially when she bent and exposed her lungs!

THE REBEL WITHIN

We had several dogs during this period: most notable was Jigme, a Bhutanese Alsatian, a pocket dog, which got stolen from our house. Then there was Dick 2, a mongrel, two GSD's and the last one was of a shaggy dog breed, Fido, who lived the longest. Rabies and other diseases took a toll on pet dogs.

Benson Town house had a stream of vendors selling their wares at the door. Fish, bread, snake charmers all came to the door. The ones that we would love to watch were snake charmers, who had monkeys with them. All brass vessels had to be tinned periodically, so the tradesmen would come to the door, establish a furnace, digging the ground, place bellows and tin the brassware. An entertainment by itself.

There was no lack of entertainment and play and no one had heard of a TV. Records were expensive and we didn't have players: just the radio and this would be playing almost the whole day. No telephones: all communication was by a simple post card. Tops, marbles, comics and friends on the street was all we had.

Benson Town is also where I met Bubloo my neighbour. He was about the same age as I, and studied in a protestant school. I can never forget him for one day he showed me a black and white photograph. It was my introduction to Porn.

To be fair, Bubloo was my source for comics, books, aeromodelling, 16 mm family films, which his uncles had brought home from the US. He was my best friend, but somehow he never joined me when playing at the YMCA, or with the American kids.

It was here I came to know my paternal grandfather, who left a lasting impression on me. He and I shared a room, he taught me English grammar, told me stories of our ancestral lands and about the attack on the city of Madras by the German submarine SS *Emden*. He was born in the 1890s and was my link to the past. I missed him every time he left home, and cried like anything years later when he passed away alone in his village.

I failed that year at St Germain but got a competitive place after an entrance examination at King George V Royal Indian Military College. It was 1962, and my father felt the need for some discipline, a military one. It wasn't a very exciting place, but I fared better academically, till my father returned from a posting and sought my admission into yet another school, the 6th one, a Roman Catholic School.

St Joseph's European Boys High School was eventful: I led a strike and was thrown out. My father was summoned by the Principal. School annual day was round the corner and the local military band was essential to its success. My father was the commanding officer of the unit which controlled the band.

There were pleasantries and I was back in the school. Father Da Silva, the principal who had caned me, and I, soon became good friends.

I had turned thirteen.

My parents never failed me!

What Mattered Was Europe and Its Music

An Australian Childhood

Colin Mackerras

.

When I look back on my childhood, what looms largest is that my family looked to Europe and European music for almost all its inspiration. Although my career and passion have been in China, there was nothing in my childhood that prepared me for this, other than a general love of culture and history. Neither my parents nor my siblings took much notice of China or its culture. For them, and at the time me, there was a clear dichotomy. Europe, especially Great Britain, and its culture were admirable, and Australia was lucky to be dominated by Britain, British institutions, the English language and the culture that flowed from that. China and Asia and their cultures did not matter, and where they did impinge, they were the enemy or something we should avoid as far as possible.

ANCESTRY, PARENTS, RELATIONS

Both my parents Alan Patrick and Catherine Brearcliffe MacLaurin Mackerras were born in Sydney in 1899.[1] Both were highly educated, my father graduating in electrical engineering and my mother in history. My mother, in particular, had several ancestors who had contributed to Australian cultural life and of whom she was, in my opinion rightly, very proud.

The earliest of them was Isaac Nathan (1790-1864) who claimed descent, through an unknown Jewish woman, from the last king of Poland Stanislaus II. My mother wrote a book about Isaac Nathan,[2] as well as the entry on him in the *Australian Dictionary of Biography*, in the latter of which she writes: "He was certainly the first musician with a European reputation to settle in Australia, and the first to attempt a serious study of Aboriginal music."[3] His only opera *Don John of Austria*, which was premiered in Sydney in 1847, was the first to be composed and produced in Australia.[4]

I was born in Turramurra, an Australian Aboriginal word meaning "High Hill", in the northern suburbs of Sydney. Like most of my siblings, I was actually born in my mother's bedroom, as it was not the norm in those days for women to give birth in a hospital. The whole of my childhood was based in the house where I was born.

I am a fraternal twin, and was born twenty minutes earlier than Malcolm, my twin brother, who has become a very prominent and well-known election specialist (or psephologist) in Australia. We were the youngest of seven children, five boys and two girls. Of the seven, the eldest was conductor Charles (1925-2010), who went to Britain in 1947, with the result that I did not know him very well in my childhood. Alastair (1928-99), my eldest brother apart from Charles, was actually a greater influence on me in my very early years. Neil (1930-87), Joan (b. 1934) and Elizabeth (b. 1937) also influenced me strongly, and I shared a passion for music with all of them.

The date of Malcolm's and my birth was the week before the war broke out in Europe, though China and Japan had already been at war for over two years. Of course, Australia took an active part in the War and, with good grounds, was very much afraid of the Japanese threat. Nevertheless, the impact of the War on Australia's domestic life was infinitesimal by comparison with Asian and European countries. I have only two memories of the War. One was that we blackened our windows in order to prevent any potential Japanese bomber from identifying dwellings at night. The other was that when the war ended, my favourite radio programme "Kindergarten of the Air" on the Australian Broadcasting Commission was missed due to constant messaging that "the war is over" and that I was upset by this. Looking back, I cannot but feel ashamed of my insensitivity and ignorance of the suffering the war had caused so many people.

Unfortunately, I never knew any of my grandparents. I do remember being taken by my father on one occasion to meet his ailing mother towards the end of her life. But I never even met my other grandparents. My mother spoke continually about her own parents and her paternal grandfather, Sir Normand MacLaurin, who gained a very good reputation in Sydney as a surgeon, parliamentarian and Chancellor of the University of Sydney.

My mother was an only child, but my father had an elder brother, Ian. All our family loved Uncle Ian, though he lived in Brisbane and we in Sydney. Actually, both he and his wife Josephine were very distinguished medical scientists and entomologists, Josephine being quite an icon for her scientific achievements at a time when women rarely rose to the top of their professions.[5] They had an only son David, a world leader in the field of lightning research, who was a contemporary of Charles and also much beloved by all the family.

From very early I was aware that my parents did not really get on. On the other hand, they did not quarrel openly in the presence of me or my siblings. One of the main factors driving them apart was that my mother converted to Catholicism in 1932 a few years after they married. My father was agnostic and rationalist in his thinking and simply could not understand or support this change.

My parents did not often agree about things. However, by today's standards they were extremely conservative, he in a British way, she in a Catholic way. My mother was the more dominant of the two personalities. She always expressed her opinions forcefully. My father, on the other hand, was very quiet and gentle by personality. He rarely argued or got angry. If argument or disagreement emerged, as it often did in our rather boisterous family, he was much more apt to depart quietly, preferring his study and his boat to arguing his point or pointing out how right he was.

His boat was one of the centres of his life. He had a series of yachts and was in fact a very good yachtsman. In the early days of their relationship, my mother often accompanied him on outings on Sydney Harbour on his yacht. However, from the days I can remember, most of his family was rather reluctant to go out with him on his yacht. I certainly was, and add that in this respect Malcolm was much better than I, going out much more frequently and willingly.

Actually, it is one of the regrets of my life that I did not like my father's yacht. Apart from foregoing the chance to spend time with him and get to know him better, I believe that most people would relish the opportunity to go out on a good yacht with a good yachtsman. I now see only sheer folly in repeatedly turning down such invitations or accepting them ungraciously. I do recall getting seriously sunburned on one occasion and that probably affected my attitude, but there are effective ways of overcoming and preventing sunburn, and I should have adopted them.

WHERE WE LIVED

The house where I was born and brought up was built during the Depression, at a time when building was cheap. My parents called it Harpenden after a very pretty English village in then rural Hertfordshire which struck them by its beauty. Harpenden is now a big, but upper-class suburb in outer north London which is so significant that there is a House of Commons constituency of Hitchin and Harpenden – a safe Conservative seat. The house was double-storied and beautiful, with a substantial ground that included a line of poplar trees along a sloping driveway and a large paddock at the back.

My sister Elizabeth had a pony called Tim, which was very quiet and tame. I was taught riding at a special school nearby and I enjoyed riding round in particular parts of the neighbourhood. I still think it was very good to learn to ride. I must admit that Elizabeth later acquired a friskier pony called Pepper, which threw me off, and I have not ridden a horse much since then.

Our family had a cow during most of my childhood and we produced much of our own milk. We also had space for a vegetable garden and chickens, which meant we were at least in part self-sufficient in terms of fresh food. My mother was very much against forcing children to eat what they did not like. On the other hand, I think she gave us good fresh food and we all grew up pretty healthy.

I was very early inoculated against many of the standard diseases, such as measles, mumps, and chicken pox. I was sent to hospital due to scarlet fever, but do not recall much sickness as a child. I was definitely not encouraged to think of illness as a valid excuse for getting out of work and quickly came to think of it as shameful to miss days at school due to sickness.

I enjoyed a rather free childhood. One illustrative example springs to mind. There was a very tall pine tree opposite Harpenden. Together with a friend and Malcolm, I used to climb to the top of this tree and sit there for extended periods. Looking back, I realize that this was certainly dangerous and a fall could easily have been fatal. My mother knew of this and made no attempt to stop me.

We all roamed fairly freely by bicycle, horse and train. I recall making a very long bike ride one day without my mother's knowledge, and returning exhausted in the evening. She was not annoyed or put out. My siblings and I made suburban train journeys quite frequently, just to take a look around.

Alastair and, to a lesser extent, Neil were real train buffs, and passed on their enthusiasm to me. Alastair knew the country time-tables by heart and all the different types of locomotive (all steam in those days, of course). He also learned the names of the railway stations by heart on some of the country lines, and I learned the main ones too, notably all those from Sydney to Bourke in the far north-west of New South Wales.

In those days, things were much safer than at present. It simply never occurred to anybody that sexual predators or similar people would try to harm us. There was a certain innocence about life in Sydney in those days that has disappeared now.

At that time, Turramurra was to some extent semi-rural. There was a suburban train, with Turramurra railway station about ten minutes' walk from Harpenden. From the earliest times I can remember, my mother had her own car, and a bit later my father bought one too.

In addition to Harpenden, our family had access to another, much smaller property. My father owned a cottage at Leura in the Blue Mountains to the west of Sydney, which was called Ashmead. Though we never lived there, we sometimes went there for a holiday. Over a single day we could do one of the long walks in the mountains. One particularly beautiful one was the Federal Pass, which ended in the spectacular Scenic Railway. This was a small open train pulled up the steep cliff and ending near the Three Sisters, three enormous and beautiful natural rocks that stick up out of the landscape.

FAMILY LIFE

My mother's conversion to Catholicism framed her world-view as well as her interest in history and the arts. As a child many of my own views were, at least temporarily, formed by the conversations our family held over dinner. My own recollections conform so precisely to the following statement by my elder brother Alastair that I feel justified in quoting it extensively.

My mother was a woman of very strong personality and she dominated nearly any gathering of which she was a member. She certainly dominated our rather noisy household. She presided over the dinner table while conversation ranged over intellectual topics such as history, music, literature, philosophy and religion, on all of which she had definite and often controversial, certainly unconventional, views. Current affairs were also discussed but not as much as those other things. Such subjects as sport, which she regarded as trivial, were never mentioned.[6]

I add that, though sport is clearly very important in Australian and world society, it has never interested me, and I think I got this attitude from my mother. Although in later life, I have got very interested in physical fitness, I always hated sport at school, and exercise for me means walking and going to the gymnasium, not competitive sport.

The other point I'd like to add to Alastair's comment is that the history, music, etc. almost always meant European. None of my siblings was interested in Asia, when I was a child. Our mother was not especially interested in the United States, despite having lived there for three years, and was rather anti-American. Although her family had contributed greatly to Australian history, and she was very proud of that, my memory is that she tended to look down on Australian culture, regarding things in Australia as very inferior to British and European. My father, by contrast, was rather pro-American and very patriotic, although in a quiet and non-jingoistic way. He was very pro-British, mother less so. They both spoke with educated Australian accents but mother was the more anglicised in her speech.

We were always encouraged to share the household chores. For instance, although mother cooked the meals, Malcolm and I had to help with the washing up. I usually dried the dishes, even though I recall preferring the washing part. Later, my mother bought a washing-up machine, which was quite rare in those days.

Our father did not help with the household chores, a fact my mother came to resent. On the other hand, he was a very good handyman and, for example, made the gramophone that played such an important part in my early years. One of his passions was astronomy and he made his own telescope. I recall his showing the family his favourite stars and planets. One of these was the red and main star in the constellation Scorpius, named Antares, after which he called one of his yachts.

One of my clearest memories of my childhood in a large family was the lack of quarrelling. I do recall some odd moments of tension with my twin Malcolm. But I have no recollection at all of any bullying by elder siblings against younger, or even minor quarrelling. I suppose I can't overlook the possibility of selective memory and some people to whom I've mentioned this find it simply unbelievable.

In this connection I'm struck by similar recollections among my siblings and others. Alastair has written of our family: "We were all good friends. Indeed I can never remember a family quarrel".[7] The late Joan Priest wrote an account of the Mackerras family and raised this issue. She accepts this lack of quarrelling and attributes it to my mother's influence. Referring to a period before I was even born, she writes that Catherine one day found my three eldest brothers (Charles, Alastair and Neil) fighting.

"Don't tell me whose fault it is, it's everybody's fault", she told them. "There is one rule in this family, *you must not quarrel*, and believe me, when you're older you'll find that your own flesh and blood will stick to you when nobody else will." All three vouch for the fact that thereafter they obeyed this rule as did the younger ones as they grew up.[8]

Considering that my parents did not get on with each other, I find it noteworthy that their children on the whole should enjoy relatively harmonious relations with each other. Apart from the story about my mother's opposition to quarrelling, I think it worth adding that both were very much against fighting and it is one of the few things they really agreed about. I've already commented above about my father's rather pacifist personality and I think in this respect he taught by example. Looking back from the vantage point of old age, I believe I undervalued my father. I remember in youth finding his passivity irritating, but the years have taught me otherwise.

EDUCATION

As a very small boy, I went to the convent, Mt Saint Bernard's, which was run by nuns. It was a girls' school and only very small boys were allowed in.

Although the physical environment was beautiful, I do not have pleasant memories of schooling at the place, as the nuns seemed to me rather bad-tempered. I recall being beaten with a ruler on the knuckles if I made a mistake or did something that displeased them.

For four years of primary school, from 1947 to 1950, aged 8 to 11, I went to Saint Aloysius College, Milson's Point, run by priests of the Society of Jesus, or Jesuits, and then from 1951 to 1956, to Sydney Grammar School. My parents had reached an arrangement that the boys would go to the Catholic school for primary school education. Our father had been educated at Sydney Grammar School, with which the family had long-standing links.[9] And these links were to be strengthened.

Saint Aloysius College

Jesuit schools have come in for some criticism in Australia recently, especially by people on the left. They are considered to produce graduates who are too conservative in their political and social attitudes. However, I believe I got a good education at Saint Aloysius. I certainly gained a respect for the Jesuits, which I retain to this day, even though I no longer subscribe to the Catholic faith. I made some very good friends at Saint Aloysius, the most important being John Sheldon. I admire the discipline, respect for people and knowledge, as well as dedication to their particular version of morality that the Jesuits hold and try to impart.

I recall occasionally being bullied by other boys at Saint Aloysius, which the staff tried at all times to prevent. I also recall that they used a leather strap on the boys as punishment. I was occasionally on the wrong end of these straps. However, that was taken for granted in those days. I certainly do not look back on the Jesuits as cruel or even slightly abusive. In the light of conditions and thinking at the time, I think their approach to discipline was effective and defensible.

One of the things I recall very vividly about my education at Saint Aloysius College was the annual Gilbert & Sullivan operas, produced by a Father Comerford, whom I remember as a kind, knowledgeable and dedicated individual. What an enormous amount of work went into those productions! They may not have been so unusual then in the Anglophone world, but I think the benefit they conferred was immeasurable. Unlike my elder brothers, I was unfortunately never selected to be a principal, but was always just in the chorus. I was a "school girl eighteen and under" in *The Mikado*, a "heavy dragoon" in *Patience*, a fairy in *Iolanthe* and a *contadina* in *The Gondoliers*.

I want to add two points here. One is that *The Mikado* was just about my first taste of anything Asian that was even mildly positive. Of course, we all know that both Gilbert and Sullivan, and especially the former, really had England in mind not Japan, when they mocked society and the emperor's "daughter-in-law elect". As an image of Japan it is pretty skewed.[10] But it was a very early image of Japan for me, even though we had just come out of a long and painful war with that country. As a child, I thought the opera funny and light-hearted and I just loved it. (Actually, I still do). It made me think of Japan as a place where it was possible for things to turn out right and for people to be happy, rather than just a place of grim suffering and crass stupidity, of unjustified aggression against other countries and people and the inevitable resultant humiliation. And curiously enough, there was a spin-off in a mildly positive image of other Asian countries as well. Of course, everybody knows that the Chinese have bitter memories of the Japanese occupation and it remains a live and negative factor to this day. But I knew nothing of China and thought of it just as a nasty place "over there".

The other point about taking part in Gilbert & Sullivan operas is also very important for me. I learned several of these operas more or less by heart. It was part of life in our family that we quoted Gilbert & Sullivan to each other. I look back on this as wholly pleasant and desirable. I think it is good to learn things by heart. It also got me into the habit of really getting to know thoroughly something one really loves.

Sydney Grammar School

During most of my time at Sydney Grammar School I was entering or had entered adolescence, and so it lies beyond the scope of this article. However, a few brief points may be permissible. I was generally very happy at the School. I started learning foreign languages, especially French and German, and have treasured this knowledge all my life. Although I was never very good at the sport that was so important at the School, I made up for that in other ways.

My brother Alastair had been in Britain several years, but returned to Australia and took up a job at Grammar when I was there as a student. The profound influence he had exerted on me as a child persisted at Grammar. He founded a chess club of which I became an enthusiastic member and taught me mathematics, at which I was pretty good. He influenced my views on life and society, especially religion and ideas. He was Headmaster of Sydney Grammar School from 1969 to 1989, but had already been teaching there for many years before.

Alastair had a coherent educational theory based on respect for the student, high intellectual attainment and appreciation for culture and beauty. He wanted to change the emphasis away from sport achievements and towards cultural. He believed Australia was too anti-intellectual, even "philistine" and wanted to change that. He was also very conservative in social and educational matters and opposed the sorts of innovations that he regarded as downplaying quality at the expense of equality.[11] In the big picture, I think

Alastair had a very positive impact on the Grammar School and on education at secondary level in Australia. In particular, his insistence on the importance and value of music in education, which is reflected in the Alastair Mackerras Chamber Orchestra at the Grammar School, not to mention many other musical activities there, was well placed and of great assistance in overcoming the "philistinism" he rejected so strongly.

One other general point is that both schools I attended were for boys only. Despite his conservatism, Alastair as headmaster made a proposal to make the Grammar School coeducational.[12] In Australia, the trend towards coeducation in formerly boys-only schools has gathered momentum, though girls-only schools are still acceptable. I don't wish to enter the debate here, but feel entitled to comment that I have no regrets at all about being educated at boys-only schools.

MUSIC IN MY CHILDHOOD

Of all things that bound our family together, perhaps the most important was love of European classical music. Although there was unequal intensity in this love, both parents and all siblings were music-lovers. Charles was the outstanding one and became famous more or less world-wide for his conducting and the numerous recordings he made.[13] But Joan remains a long-term professional violinist, pianist and music-teacher. Alastair and Neil both knew a great deal about music, especially Alastair, as does Elizabeth.

I learnt to play the piano from early childhood. By far the main teacher I had was Dorothy White, a distinguished Sydney musician whose passion affected not only me but my sister Joan. She lived not very far from Harpenden and I often used to ride a horse to lessons. She taught me not only piano but a great deal about musical appreciation and the rules of harmony. She had annual concerts in her own drawing room with pieces performed by her own students, and I played regularly at these. She also had a swimming pool, in which I enjoyed swimming and she would pay me to clean it out from time to time.

My parents and brothers had an extensive collection of records. We also had a gramophone which, though far from the quality available today, was pretty good by the standards of its time. The records were all the very old 78 rpm discs. Of course these had serious failings and needed to be changed all the time with interruptions to the music. In those days, we had no television. We did have radio, but only the Australian Broadcasting Commission (as it was called then) broadcast classical music frequently.

From the time I was a very small child, my mother and elder brothers would hold musical parties, inviting many friends in to listen to J.S. Bach's *St Matthew Passion* at Easter time and George Frederick Handel's *The Mes-*

siah at Christmas. I recall these parties had a big effect on me. At first I was too small to appreciate them very well, but I recollect very strongly that I got to love the music and was able to sing much of it by heart.

I have vivid recollections of going to sleep while my elders played music on the gramophone in the living room downstairs. Such works as W.A. Mozart's last symphonies and *Concertante Sinfonia* in E-flat major for violin and viola, Franz Schubert's Symphonies no. 5 and 8 (the "Unfinished") and Johannes Brahms's violin concerto are so deep in my consciousness that I really cannot remember the time they were not familiar to me as beloved great music.

Performing in Gilbert & Sullivan operas at Saint Aloysius College had taught me the importance and joy of learning operas (or at least parts of them) by heart. It was not long before my interests grew beyond these operas. The biggest influence on my tastes as a child was Alastair whose knowledge of and passion for music among amateurs at that time in Australia was unsurpassed. He performed as an amateur in the priests' chorus in a performance of Giuseppe Verdi's *Aida* by an Italian company that visited Australia in the early post-war period. He was a great admirer of Giacomo Puccini's operas, but loved Verdi even more. His greatest loves, however, were the operas of Mozart and Wagner, and his passion had a very deep influence on me, which survives to this day.

One of the things he did was to buy second-hand gramophone records of great singers of the past. Of course, the standard of recording cannot compete with the present technical level. But the performances of people like the Wagnerian tenor Lauritz Melchior, sopranos Frida Leider and Kirsten Flagstad, and baritone Friedrich Schorr remain legend. I was very fortunate to get to know the great Wagner operas through recordings Alastair bought of these great artists.

In the 1950s, when the long-playing records became available, they rendered the old 78s obsolete. Alastair bought a recording of the 1951 Bayreuth production of Wagner's last opera *Parsifal*. I simply fell in love with this music and played the opera repeatedly.

At the time, I renewed my friendship with John Sheldon, a highly educated and learned music-lover, whom I had known at Saint Aloysius College, and we shared our passion for Wagner and other music. Later both John and I, largely under Alastair's influence, got to know the other great Wagner operas thoroughly. John and I developed a life-long and close friendship, as well as a shared love for opera and music.

CONCLUSION

What I've included in this account of my childhood tries to emphasise what I believe affected me most at the time. Of course, I can't avoid some hindsight, but have tried to keep that to a minimum. For a historian it is always a challenge to distinguish between how things look at the time of writing and at the time they actually happened. As the reader will have noticed, I have drawn not only on memory but on written records written by other people.

There are inevitably silences here. For example, in my childhood, my family was not concerned with Aboriginal issues at all. Later on, my brother Neil grew extremely passionate about them, even to the extent of assisting actively in an Aboriginal legal service. But that was after the period of concern here.

As for politics, our whole family was conservative in sympathy. In 1956, after the highly conservative Democratic Labor Party was formed, Neil resigned from the Liberal Party of which he had been a member to join it and became very active in its affairs. I do recall that Malcolm and Neil shared a passion for politics from an early age and discussed it endlessly, and Malcolm has achieved great distinction in the academic fields of politics and psephology. But in childhood, politics was not a major interest for me, and I did not question that Robert Gordon Menzies (prime minister of Australia from 1949 to 1966) was doing a good job and should continue in his position. I changed my opinion drastically due to my interest in China and to living there from 1964 to 1966. But by that time I was no longer a child.

What I recall is a happy childhood in a large family in which the siblings got on pretty well with one another. Most of the friction that existed in our family was between our parents. It was largely for the children's sake that they continued to live together. Actually, I don't think either ever considered divorce seriously. It just was not done in those days. I think staying together caused both some pain. But a split would have caused much more suffering for far more people. I personally think they did the right thing and am convinced that I benefited from their decision to maintain family unity.

Apart from my school-work, in which I scored very high marks, my greatest interest was classical music and especially opera. It is something that has stayed with me my whole life so far. It seems to me to have enriched my life and I know it has brought me great happiness.

As I child I was not at all interested in Asia. It is a great irony for me that it was my mother who was mainly responsible for getting me interested, the same person who herself had no interest in Asia. She saw an advertisement for scholarships in Asian studies, and suggested I apply. My father agreed, one of those rare occasions when my parents were of one mind! I did apply, successfully, and that transformed my life. My mother's dislike of Asia and especially China did not prevent her thinking that the region would be very important for Australia's future. I never cease to thank my parents for their prescience, but especially my mother for noticing that advertisement.

NOTES

1. He died in 1973, she in 1977.

2. Catherine Mackerras, *The Hebrew Melodist, A Life of Isaac Nathan*, Sydney: Currawong Publishing, 1963.

3. Catherine Mackerras, "Nathan, Isaac (1790-1864)", in *Australian Dictionary of Biography*, Vol. 2, Melbourne University Press, 1967, web version http://adb.anu.edu.au/biography/nathan-isaac-2502.

4. Mackerras, *The Hebrew Melodist*, p. 96. For a very fair and insightful account of this opera see Nicholas Tarling, *With Respect to Opera*, Auckland: Dunmore Publishing, 2014, pp. 75-85.

5. See Lesley Williams, "Mackerras, Ian Murray (1898-1980)", in *Australian Dictionary of Biography*, Vol. 15, Melbourne University Press, 2000, web version http://adb.anu.edu.au/biography/mackerras-ian-murray-10992, and Lesley Williams, "Mackerras, Mabel Josephine (Jo) (1896-1971)", in *Australian Dictionary of Biography*, Vol. 15, Melbourne University Press, 2000, web version http://adb.anu.edu.au/biography/mackerras-mabel-josephine-jo-11411, accessed 25 January 2016. Actually, this is a joint biography.

6. Alastair M. Mackerras, "Foreword", in *Divided Heart, The Memoirs of Catherine B. Mackerras*, Sydney: Little Hills Press, 1991, p. 5.

7. Mackerras, "Foreword", p. 8.

8. Joan Priest, *Scholars and Gentlemen, A Biography of the Mackerras Family*, Brisbane: Boolarong Publications, 1986, p. 55.

9. Clifford Turney, *Grammar, A History of Sydney Grammar School 1819-1988*, Sydney: Allen & Unwin, 1989, pp. 303-4.

10. For comments on *The Mikado* in the context of orientalism, see Nicholas Tarling, *Orientalism and the Operatic World*, Lanham: Rowman and Littlefield, 2015, pp. 267-9.

11. See "the Mackerras philosophy" of education explained at some length in Turney, *Grammar*, pp. 304-7.

12. Turney, *Grammar*, pp. 324-5.

13. See, among other works, Nigel Simeone and John Tyrrell, eds, *Charles Mackerras*, Woodbridge: The Boydell Press, 2015.

Memories of Childhood

Ruth Malcolm

At 10:46 am 3rd February 1931 in two and a half minutes my hometown, Napier, New Zealand, was shaken to pieces by a violent earthquake. I remember Napier as a town of demolition and rebuilding. I saw Art Deco buildings replace the rubble. I listened to stories about the 'Quake. The end of my bed was splintered where the wardrobe had fallen across it. I was used to the hundreds of aftershocks that persisted over the years. I assumed that the world was like that.

When the 'Quake happened Edmée (or Ed), my mother, heavy with her first child, was standing on the step shaking floor mats, when the ground growled and cracked towards her. She had the impression of telegraph poles swaying wildly by the fence, and found herself sitting on the path as the brick chimney fell with a crash right beside her.

My father, Tom, hurried towards home through the destroyed town centre. The destruction was total. With a bucket of water he could have put out the beginnings of what became a major fire, but there was no water to be found and beating out flames proved impossible.

As soon as my Auntie V heard the news of the Napier earthquake (7.9 on the Richter scale, the radio said) she took a train as far as it went and then begged rides to Napier. Near the town the roads were impassable. She was dropped off and walked the remaining miles.

She had only two things to say about the fear and chaos of that time: there was never a more beautiful sight than to see Tom walking along the street towards her, AND she had ruined a perfectly good pair of shoes.

V and Tom and Ed sat round the dining room table and ate and talked, taking it in turns to catch the kerosene lamp as aftershocks tipped it over. Roads were badly damaged and no buses or trains were running, but they agreed that V should take Ed back with her to the safety of Palmerston North,

79

and Tom would stay and help with demolition work in the town. - Apart from electricity, gas and water, the most urgent need was for able-bodied men first to make damaged buildings safe, and then to demolish most of the central business buildings. V packed up and cared for Ed on the long, difficult journey to Palmerston North where my sister was born six weeks later.

In 1932 - 33 Tom built the house I spent my childhood in - a three bedroom bungalow. The timbers are heart rimu throughout, the roof corrugated iron. It's a very cosy feeling to go to sleep with rain beating on the iron roof and the waves breaking rhythmically on the shingle of the beach nearby. Tom's shed and yard from which he ran his contracting business were behind the house. Ed kept a beautiful flower and vege garden.

Then in 1934 I was born. I was their third child in three and a half years. I screamed for ten days.

"We'll call her Ethel (my Grandmother's name)."

"Can I name her instead?" asked Ethel. So the baby was named Ruth. Edmée Ruth they decided at last.

"Do we have to take her home?" grinned Tom listening to the unremitting screams.

Three months old and a visit to Palmerston North. Ethel leaned over the bassinet looking carefully at baby Ruth. Finally she suggested a visit to old Scottish Dr Godfrey.

"Milk," was his judgement. "You'll have to take her off milk." Ed looked shocked. What else do you feed babies on? But Dr Godfrey showed her how to make oatmeal gruel, how to strain it and feed the liquid to the baby.

"As she grows older we'll leave more oatmeal in, but just now, the liquid is enough for her."

Wonder of wonders, I took the gruel and began to thrive at last.

I've never known a time I couldn't read. When I was three and the world was sliding nervously towards the Second World War, I marched into the kitchen dragging the newspaper by one corner loudly demanding to know,

"What does ath-ath-in-a-ted mean?"

Ed looked hastily at the paper. Bold headlines ran across the top: "assassinated". The newspaper was banished to the top of the sideboard.

One of my earliest memories is going to town on the bus with my mother.

"Mummy, what does Co Ltd mean? What does Co Ltd mean? What does Co Ltd mean?"

How could you ignore it? A lady at the front of the bus queue turned and stared at us, and my Mother snapped through tight lips, "Company Limited."

From the tone of voice I knew better than to persist. Climbing on the bus I looked around. On the way to town I counted seven passengers. Then I counted the seats. There were twenty-three. Why did the silly driver limit the company to seven, when there were so many empty seats?

At the Bank of New Zealand corner there was always a street photographer. I watched him wondering how his camera worked. He gave my Mother a white card and now I have for all time, a record of a small child, Shirley Temple curls, hand-embroidered frock, out for a day in town.

In the Department store I perched on the little impossibly high chair by the counter. The shop lady stuffed my Mother's money and a piece of white paper into a capsule, opened a lid and with a whoosh it was sucked into a pipe. We waited until it was just as violently spat out into a basket, and there was the paper and some change. Everyone smiled and said thankyou and we were out on the footpath with our brown paper parcel tied up with string carried safely in her shopping bag.

I tried not to look at the Government Buildings. It was there my Mother had taken me, unwilling, for my diphtheria injection. I'd heard all about the dreaded needle and as soon as the nurse in starched white came towards me I buckled over and bawled, yelled, screamed and stamped. She paused, uncertain, but my Mother seized me and the injection was plunged into my arm. Then she bought me an ice-cream. I wondered why, when I'd been so naughty, I got the rare treat of an ice-cream in a cone. I didn't think I'd ever understand grownups, so I just sobbed and ate it.

Recently I've revisited Bowman's Building, built in 1933. In 1942 I thought it was very grand. The lino in the foyer looked like the original green I remembered, and I ran my hand up the wooden banister I had slid down so often after my elocution lessons. My teacher, Miss Mac's, door was the same wood panelling, but the voice that responded with a loud and cheerful, "Come in!" has gone. The shy, lisping child is in my past too. So are the pantomimes we were in at the Municipal Theatre. I peeped into Constance MacDonald's dancing classroom. Do children's presence and the fun and action leave a whisper in the corners? I swear I caught it.

I learnt singing too and now the airwaves ripple on forever with the sound of Helen Dykes' 'Stars of Tomorrow' as we broadcast children's sessions from Radio Station 2YH - 'Somewhere Over the Rainbow', 'On My Little Toboggan in Switzerland', and 'There'll Always be an England'. Where are those Stars today?

When I started school I was very useful. "Sit here and hold Eric's hand." The Primer Three teacher showed me what she wanted me to do. Reluctantly I put my hand over Eric's. It was small and thin and rough with warts. "Lack of calcium," the School Nurse had said as everyone nervously lined up for their regular health checks. Eric's mother looked even more depressed and anxious than usual. It was apparently her fault that Eric had warts through 'lack of calcium'.

From my chair in the queue beside my Mother, I watched carefully. My mother had told a neighbour that Eric's mother had eight children and she didn't know how she was to sew them all pants.

"What does Ruth eat for breakfast," asked the School Nurse. "Weetbix." "Useless! Give her cornflakes. Pressing them together like that destroys all the food value." And we escaped.

When Eric stood in front of the whole class in his sad clothes, barefoot even in a Hawkes Bay frosty winter, and took his turn to talk I fixed my eyes on him and willed him to come out with his first word. Eric stood there in the centre of the wide floor, painfully embarrassed and struggled with his hopeless stutter. When at last he'd mouthed a few words the teacher motioned him to sit down and she marked something in her big book, probably saying that he was no good. Eric gratefully retreated to his seat near the bottom of D Row.

I guided Eric's hand through endless lines of writing shapes - circles, ovals, rectangles, squares and triangles. Over and over again I sat beside him in the writing lesson. I never knew if he managed to write for himself.

When we got home from school we would usually play outside. My friend and I would climb her Granny Smith apple tree and pick an apple. Then we would go the front fence and sit in her pepper tree, eating our apples and watching people walk past along the footpath. We found plenty to talk about.

We didn't have many indoor games. I loved to play with my family of dolls. My brother built Meccano and he had a clockwork train and my little brother had some lead cars. In the evenings we listened to children's serial stories on the radio and read our books. I had my own bookshelf and I always asked for a book for my birthday. We played card games that often ended in an argument. I had one jigsaw puzzle. I did it so often I used to turn the picture facedown and do the puzzle with the blank side up. I had a scrapbook and cut out pictures to stick in with flour and water glue. We had plasticine and chalk and marbles and I had a little china tea-set.

My father dumped a whole truckload of white sand in a corner of our backyard and we spent hours digging in it. One year we decided to dig to Spain. We recruited sixteen children to help us and we dug every afternoon after school. Our hole got wider and wider and we never got to Spain!

We all went to summer concerts at the Soundshell beside the immaculate council gardens covering demolition rubble that had been dumped along the seafront. We learnt to skate on the old skating rink there, uneven from subsidence of rubble beneath.

Sometimes when the weather was very fine we paddled cautiously in the sea. The undertow dragged the sand and shingle from under my feet. People drowned in that sea off Napier Beach! Occasionally we picnicked and swam at the safe beach at Westshore nearly 5 kilometres away by bus along an embankment road raised above what had been tidal flats. In the 'Quake the embankment road had collapsed and the whole bus had fallen into a large hole.

I knew all about drowning. When I was four years old our family went to a school picnic at Blackbridge. My mother took a vast array of home-cooked picnic food - bacon and egg pie, sausage rolls, sandwiches and scones and cake tins full of home-baked cakes and biscuits which she shared all round. (We never ate bought cakes or biscuits so of course regarded them as special treats.) All the children swam. I watched my big brother walk across the river to the other side. The water came right up to his chin. I followed him across the river to the other side. I hadn't realised that he was a head taller than me and so the deep part in the centre was right over my head. I walked into a hole. All sound of children shouting and laughing faded. The world was eerily silent and I was quite alone. At first I thought I would kick off from the bottom but when I floated down I just rose upward again. Then I thought I would put my head out when I got to the surface, but I just began to go down again. I realised I was not going to be able to do anything. Then a pair of strong legs strode towards me. A hairy chest and two strong arms lifted me out and carried me over to the riverbank where both of my parents were looking the most distressed I have ever seen them. It was the school head-master - and I was not even yet going to school. What a way to meet your future headmaster!

I never learnt to swim. For six years I walked backwards and forwards across the School swimming pool and never once put my head under the water. To this day I wear a lifejacket when boating!

School holidays were special because then we visited Grandpa and Nana in Palmerston North. Washing was fun to watch at Nana and Grandpa's. Nana still had her copper and two wooden tubs and a hand mangle to wring the water out of the washing, and she had a washerwoman, Mrs Wild, who came in once a week.

Early on washing morning Grandpa filled the copper with water and then lit the fire under it till the soapy water boiled and frothed. We watched as Mrs Wild fished the boiling linen out of the copper with a big copper stick and dropped it into the first tub of cold rinsing water. She turned the mangle to wring the washing and put it into the second tub of water with Reckitts Blue in it. Then she mangled it all again to squeeze the water out and dropped it into the laundry basket, turning the mangle with one hand and expertly twisting clean sheets and tablecloths round her other hand.

"Can't catch us!" we shouted.

"Wild by name and Wild by nature!" shouted back Mrs Wild waving the copper stick at us, but she was all smiles as she sat at the kitchen table having a cuppa tea with Nana, her hands all soft and red from washing water, and the lines outside billowing with snowy sheets.

One holiday: "Grandpa, Can you write in my autograph book?" Grandpa took out his big flat carpenter's pencil and sat down. Slowly and carefully he wrote in the book and handed it back.

'Men and dogs
Were made to roam.
Cats and women
Stay at home.'
Signed: J H Willson
And Nana got cross with him!

It was 1940. We usually had Christmas at Nana's and Grandpa's. My father drove us there in the Chevrolet. "I was carsick five times," I boasted. "I was sick seven times," chimed in Beverley, "and David wasn't sick at all."

Nana laughed and hugged us all. "It's the Manawatu Gorge," she said. "Did you sit up and look out the front?"

"It's the Chev," we told her.

"It's stuffy."

"Dinner's ready." And the sickness was forgotten.

After Christmas dinner everyone gathered in the sitting room, adults squashed onto the chesterfield suite and the dining room chairs, the children sitting on the carpet. All eyes were expectantly on the door. Father Christmas was coming any minute.

Father Christmas had been a big problem that year. "No," said Grandpa loudly and that was the end of it for him. "I'm their father," said Tom. "They'll recognise me." Uncle Jim and Uncle Bill were in army and airforce camp and Uncle John was already overseas with the New Zealand army.

But right on time, very quietly, and looking rather thin, Father Christmas arrived. The only puzzle was that when the presents were given out Father Christmas insisted that all the children say, "Thank you, Auntie Christmas."

And there above the big white beard twinkled Auntie V's brown eyes. But the presents were real.

Back in Napier, American soldiers were camping at McLean Park. They smiled at the children and gave them Granny Smith apples and American chewing gum, the only sweets we saw in those days of sugar rationing. One afternoon David came home. "Can I ask a soldier for dinner?" he asked.

"Of course." So the soldier came and sat at the dining room table like a real visitor and we ate a good dinner (even top-o'-the-milk Ed had skimmed off for pouring over the golden syrup pudding - cream and sugar were rationed) and he talked to Ed and Tom.

After he had gone Ed remarked sadly to Tom, "He's just a homesick boy." And the soldier became another of Ed's 'Boys Overseas' - Though how you can be a 'boy overseas' when you're safe in Napier took some thinking about.

Now when we went to the beach to play there were barbed wire entanglements to explore and find the secret entrances in, and 'pill boxes' (gun emplacements) to hide in, and an EPS (Emergency Precaution Scheme) man in a shiny tin hat to watch us. Our father was too old to go to camp, and he joined the EPS. Japanese reconnaissance had been sighted off Hawke Bay and the EPS were going to protect the beach all the way south from Bluff Hill to Awatoto 5 kilometres away. Like all the fathers he dug an air raid shelter in our back yard. "It's not as good as Grandpa's. He's got sandbags on the top and a big water jar for Nana to drink out of," we children told him.

He took us to an EPS film ("Going to the flicks," David called it) and we learnt how to put out incendiary bombs. As the film flickered, before our horrified gaze a hand appeared through a kitchen window and a thing like a fire cracker was dropped on to the bench. A mother rushed into the kitchen and put the fire out."Why," I wanted to know as we walked home through the blackout, "Why did they want to do that for?"

At nine o'clock every evening the radio announced 'a moment of silent prayer during the chiming of Big Ben'. And the silence was immediately shattered by

BING BONG BONG CRASH
BING BONG BONG CRASH
BING BONG BONG CRASH
BING BONG BONG CRASH
DONG DONG DONG DONG DONG DONG DONG DONG DONG

Then we children had to be very quiet while Tom and Ed sipped their tea and listened with growing concern and fear to the BBC news, by a modern miracle broadcast from London 12,000 miles away into 21 McGrath Street, Napier, New Zealand. "This is London calling . . . .." Why over the radio did everyone in England sound as if they had sore throats?

It was 1942 when David came home from school with whooping cough. They called it 'whooping laugh' because every time he whooped he finished with a laugh, and he quickly got better. Not so I, who caught it from him. The cough rapidly turned to bronchitis, and the bronchitis to pneumonia. "Fresh orange juice and glucose barley sugar," advised Dr Barnett, who by this time was calling in every time he passed the house. He smiled at me and prodded me gently in the ribs.

"When I started to come you were quite tubby, but now I can count all your ribs," he scolded.

I smiled up at him. I liked him. He always warmed his hands at the fire before he listened to my chest and he was always fun.

Outside the closed door there was no fun. He gave what advice he could and Ed followed it to the letter. Both of them knew that nothing was changing the course of the illness. Then one day Dr Barnett called in with a letter. It had just arrived and it contained a sample of a new drug called penicillin. Would Ed and Tom be willing to allow him to try it for me? He had no idea whether what the letter claimed for the drug would work for her. He looked hopefully at Ed. Both of them knew it was a chance, and no more. Would they be any worse off for trying it? What risks were there? They didn't know.

Tom and Ed gave their permission. What else could they do? And the next day Dr Barnett drove around every Doctor's surgery in Napier. Could he please have their sample of penicillin that had come in the mail? He gathered up a whole course of the medicine and began the first dose.

After an agonising week of waiting and watching, he paused in his daily check of my chest and looked up at Ed. A delighted smile told me all I wanted to know. The penicillin was working!

All the children in our neighbourhood went to the little church on the corner for Sunday school. We learnt about the Christian faith and behaving well. I started at Sunday school when I was three years old. I wore a new blue coat and my hair was curled just like Shirley Temple's. (She was a famous child film star and all the mothers wanted their girls to look like her.) In my blue purse I carried a penny. All went well till the children began to sing a song. I didn't know the song. I didn't know any of the children. I didn't know the teachers. To my surprise we took our pennies out of our purses, lined up and gave our pennies to the teacher. Our pennies were all dropped into a basket to be given to Jesus. I wept loudly. The teacher decided I must be missing my Mummy, which I wasn't, and took me into my big sister's class. My sister clearly didn't want me embarrassing her in front of her friends so I just sat there, penniless, and sniffed loudly and pathetically.

I gradually got used to the Sunday school ideas and some of them turned out to be part of the grown-up world - as when my mother tiptoed into my bedroom and stood for a moment by my bed.

"Are you asleep?"

"No."

"Would you pray every night for our boys overseas? God might hear the prayers of a child." And she was gone as quietly as she had come.

What boys? Where was overseas? Never mind…. I said my prayers:

"Gentle Jesus, meek and mild

Look upon a little child.

Pity my simplicity

Suffer me to come to Thee."

I wasn't sure what sim - pli - ci - ty meant.

"- and pray for the boys overseas."

Years later I learned that Uncle John was missing in action in Egypt.

Mr McCutcheon, our bus driver, was overseas along with all the other young men – conscripted, it was called, so we had a new bus driver. I think it was her war effort. A little, thin woman, hair cut short-short, she wore a khaki shirt and trousers and a military cap and she was ferocious. She strode around, slinging heavy split-cane prams up on to the bus hooks and punching tickets. Not even babies yelled on her bus. Even if we weren't on the bus it was bad enough to see her drive past. We were all scared of her.

Every morning before school it was my job to ride on my bike to the dairy to buy a quart of milk. Boring! I was getting good at riding no hands, carrying the billy of milk. Then I experimented as I rode, swinging the billy faster and faster round and round above my head – the milk stayed in it, even when I'd forgotten to bring the lid. Try it sometime! It's called centrifugal force.

One morning I hit a bump and crashed, milk everywhere, and bike, billy and I spread out over the road, pouring blood from both of my grazed knees. To my horror I looked up into the concerned face of the lady bus driver who'd sprinted out of her house opposite.

Next, I was in her living room and she produced the biggest First Aid kit I'd ever seen. She was fighting the War from her own bathroom. Expertly she cleaned my knees with Dettol, spread germ-killing ointment all over them and tied them up with gleaming white bandages.

Then I was set on the footpath to limp home, dented billy hanging shamefully off the handlebar. But when my Mother took me to visit her the next day with a large bunch of sweet-smelling lilac from our garden she was covered in smiles, arranging them in a pretty vase as they chatted away like old friends.

Everything was different after the war - no more blackout, no more rationing and the Boys Overseas in their hundreds came home on troop ships - and we were having another holiday in Palmerston North with Nana and Grandpa and Auntie V.

"After work on Friday, I'll take you to town" promised Auntie, so we three children walked into town along Main Street and at five o'clock were waiting for Auntie outside the Social Welfare office. (Auntie always teased Ed to name one of her girls Martha Mary Violet Pansy May after a baby on her files, but luckily Ed didn't. She also knew a baby that could say 'pretty flower' and wanted her nieces to say ''magnificent blossom' by the time they were one, but they didn't do that either.)

First we went to a little restaurant in Melody Lane for tea. Then unbelievably Auntie V produced sixty pennies each - a fortune, adding up to five shillings each! - and we walked round to the Arcade and spent them all playing games on the slot machines.

One of Auntie's horrified friends met us as we came out, clutching popcorn and cheap prizes, and said, "I can't believe I'm seeing you coming out of THAT place!" But Auntie just laughed.

Now it was after dark and the town was in party mood - bustling busy, and lights shining everywhere as we headed for the big crossing on Broadway. Halfway across the road was a safety island made of a round concrete hump painted bright yellow, surrounded by a wide white circle. We children called it the 'fried egg'. We waited with Auntie V till the 'Cross Now' lights turned orange, and then, holding hands and squealing with laughter all four rushed as far as the fried egg, to be trapped there when the light turned red. Cars whizzed all round as we clung together on the yellow 'yolk'. "Do it again, Auntie! Do it again!" we clamoured from the safety of the footpath.

Round the Square to Rossco's enormous three-storied Department Store and up and down in the lift several times. Back across the fried egg, and on to PDC where there were more lifts. Up to the very top, down to the second floor, back up to the third and a last ride down to the ground floor - and then the long walk home.

Chattering turned to star-watching, and star-watching turned to plodding along holding Auntie's hand, and three tired children were glad to be home and tucked up in bed with a stone hot water bottle wrapped in one of Grandpa's thick woollen working socks.

I brushed my hair a hundred times as Auntie V had told me. I was getting ready to go out for a special afternoon tea with Auntie Sylvia at Rossco's. "Nice manners." warned Nana.

At Rossco's Auntie Sylvia and I took the lift to the third floor. The restaurant was enormous, with soft lights and polished wood pillars and a lady who played the piano, and sparrows flying round hoping to find crumbs. We took a table by the window.

Soon a three tiered silver plate holder was set before us. On the bottom were tiny sandwiches. The middle tier held a middle-sized plate of savouries, and the very top held the smallest plate filled with bought cakes.

Auntie Sylvia took a little sandwich and ate it between sips of tea. I took a little sandwich and carefully sipped my fizzy drink between bites. Auntie Sylvia took a savoury and ate it. I took a savoury and ate it.

Then Auntie Sylvia poured herself a second cup of tea and, reaching out to the top plate, took a butterfly cake. I helped myself to a cream horn, which I had been secretly eyeing all the time the sandwiches and savouries were happening.

Auntie Sylvia picked up the silver cake fork lying on the starched white cloth beside her plate. She delicately used the side of the cake fork to cut a little piece of the sponge butterfly cake and put it in her mouth.

I picked up my cake fork and tried to cut a piece off my cream horn. Cream horns are made of very hard, flaky pastry, and the side of the little cake fork wouldn't cut it. Twice I tried, and then, lifting the cake fork I brought it down with a sharp thump on the cream horn.

Bits of pastry flew everywhere! Cream and raspberry jam spread over the plate and glued some of the bits together, but the rest exploded onto the spotless white tablecloth.

With a twinkle in her eye, Auntie Sylvia leant across the table and said gently, "I think perhaps you can use your fingers."

And then it was winter - time to light the fire, to read, to knit, to listen to the radio, to go to sleep over the newspaper, to write endless homework, to play on the warm floor, to set the chimney on fire, to make Tom leap up and rush outside in his socks for the ladder and a bucket of water . . . . "I'm going to teach Ruth how to tatt," announced Ethel. "She'll never learn to knit. I've tried and tried. She can't seem to learn even to sew chain stitch."

Ed sighed. She hadn't told Ethel about the school sewing lessons. She had finally told me to sew in class with no cotton in my needle. It took forever to unpick the tightly pulled mess the work came home in. I had even threaded two pieces of elastic into one leg of the bloomers I was sewing, and spent the rest of the lesson fruitlessly searching for the elastic to thread into the second leg. How was Ethel to teach me to tatt?

I sat beside my Nana and watched her carefully. Nana had bought a tortoiseshell tatting shuttle for me, and for the next two years, every time she came to stay the two of us sat on the back porch and Nana demonstrated the basic tatting knot over and over again. Ed, watching, thought her mother looked happy, and hoped she wouldn't be too disappointed at the inevitable outcome. But, surprise, I suddenly mastered the knot and produced a hand-kerchief edged with lace as a gift to Auntie V, who wore the lace hanky with pride, folded into the front pocket of her suit, for her wedding day. Years later I made intricate lace like Nana's for our daughters' wedding days.

It was February 1948 and there was a major polio epidemic. All the schools were closed and we lived in isolation out on the Pakowhai Riverbed in our caravan. It was my first year at secondary school. Napier Girls' High School began in February with correspondence lessons – very disappointing when a new uniform was hanging in the wardrobe. However, after five years of cycling in Napier's February heat in my uniform, topped by a navy serge tunic, holding my panama hat on with one hand and carrying my schoolbag full of books, and then running up 184 steps to the school at the top of Bluff Hill, I felt correspondence lessons had some advantages. And no: I would NOT wear black hat elastic under my chin!

In winter the panama was replaced by my navy felt hat, steadily growing more and more shapeless in Napier's rain and winds, black woollen stock-ings and a navy winceyette shirt and tie under the not so new serge tunic. Impossible to ride a bike, hold the hat on and carry my bag without 'gaps' showing. (Suspender belts hooked onto the tops of our stockings left a 'gap' of legs visible between black Italian cloth bloomers and stocking tops.) 1948 was only three years after the end of World War 2. Shortages were with us still and our economical school decreed that Italian cloth, stocked in vast quantities for blackout curtains and now not required, was ideal for bloomers which doubled as P.E. (Physical Education) rompers. It wasn't. It ripped. The pattern was awful. How could our mothers have let us look like that??

Of course when it rained I got wet, and then my shoe bag was raided for a change of stockings and sandals, permissible inside only. Black lace-ups were obligatory streetwear. And how did we cope with holes in our black stockings? The cork of the fountain-pen ink bottle of course, painting white legs blue-black.

Our moment of uniformed glory came, however, at the end of the year when white piqué uniforms were worn for the carol service and breakup evening at the Municipal Theatre. As they were starched so stiffly that we could stand them up on the floor, worn with a white shirt and school tie and 'flesh-coloured' nylon stockings, we were reluctant to sit down, or even move. I devised a way of biking without sitting on my pleats. Gaps were an even bigger problem. But we felt good.

Did we learn better for all this sartorial elegance, in which we were forbidden to eat in the street, linger on street corners or talk to BOYS? We certainly had a feeling of belonging!

And then as all children do, I grew up. The Soundshell resounded to our class of Girls' High School leavers, wearing our stiffly starched white pique gymns, doing the Hokey Tokey after our final prize-giving ceremony in the Municipal Theatre. A young constable appeared on the steps. We were not allowed to dance and sing in the soundshell. He encouraged us to move down to the beach, but it's not possible to dance on a shingle bank, and the group soon broke up and for the last time from school I went home.

Growing Up in Penang in the '60s and '70s

Shakila Abdul Manan

THE CITY CENTRE

I grew up in the heartland of George Town,[1] Penang, in the '60s and '70s, a stone's throw from busy Penang Road (Jalan Penang), then the city's main commercial hub. It was a vibrant city centre as it drew crowds of people who thronged the eateries serving all kinds of delectable dishes in the vicinity. These included Craven 'A' Café, Kassim Nasi Kandar, Ghani Biryani, Kek Seng restaurant as well as small hawker stalls, all renowned for their signature dishes. The aromatic smell of Indian, Malay and Chinese foods that wafted from restaurants, cafes and sidewalk tables was enough to titillate your palate and make you salivate. Penang was also a shopper's paradise as there were a variety of shops selling all kinds of household items, ranging from textiles to watches and jewellery. For bargains, my family and I shopped at the Penang Bazaar or *jual murah* (cheap sale) which sold textiles, shirts, pants, handbags, and shoes at affordable prices. It was a must for visitors to drop by the bazaar as they could bargain or negotiate the price of goods with the shopkeepers. Pitchay Gunny was a famous shop that sold jeans while Abbas and Sons sold little porcelain figurines, decorative items and gift sets. Open or vacant lots were occupied by medicine men who used loudspeakers to convince shoppers to buy their potent ointment and products. In such spaces, one could also find magicians and snake charmers who performed all kinds of tricks and stunts with venomous snakes such as cobras and pythons. For a small fee, one could touch or caress one of those slithery creatures: definitely not for the faint-hearted. Covered in old bite marks and scars, the snake charmers charmed not only just the snakes but also the crowd of curious onlookers with their hypnotic music. These snake charmers, migrants from Bangladesh, are a dying breed. Currently they no longer perform in the city centre but at snake shows for tourists at popular beach resorts along Batu Feringhi on the northwest of the island.

CITY ENTERTAINMENT AND SHOPPING

For night time entertainment, some of the locals frequented an amusement arcade, the Great World Park or *Tua Se Kai*, or watched movies at the Royal, Paramount, Cathay and Odeon cinemas. The Royal and Paramount cinemas screened the latest Hindi and Tamil movies while Cathay and Odeon featured Hollywood and Chinese films. Sadly the Royal and Paramount cinemas were demolished in the '70s to make way for the state's urban re-development project. Now Prangin Mall, a mega shopping complex stands in the place where Great World Park once was. Before it was torn down, my late father used to ferry the whole family to the entertainment park allowing us to enjoy the merry-go-round and Ferris wheel rides. The park was transformed into a magical land at night as it was brightly lit with all kinds of lighting and decorative bulbs. To add to its festive cheer, melodious music and songs from latest Hollywood and Chinese movies entertained the crowd. Watching the latest Hindi movies at the Royal or Paramount cinemas was a rare treat for us as it was an expensive affair. I lived with my extended family which included my parents, siblings, uncles, aunts and cousins. A trip to the cinema would mean buying tickets for sixteen family members at any one time. It was fun, however, as we had the whole row of seats to ourselves. Before the show commenced, we bought all kinds of edible snacks such as roasted and salted peanuts from an Indian vendor who sold them wrapped in paper cones. Snacking during movies was certainly a fun thing to do. Besides the Great World Park, we made frequent trips to Wembley Park, another shopping outlet especially for those living in the vicinity of George Town's seven-street precinct in the '60s and '70s. Sandwiched between Noordin Street (Lebuh Noordin), or as the locals call it, *Jee Teow Lor* (2nd Street), and Magazine Road (Jalan Magazine), *Thau Teow Lor* (1st Street), the recreation park housed small retail shops selling foodstuffs, toys, stationery, clothes, shoes, Chinese praying paraphernalia, and local hawker food. We bought our toys and stationery from the retail shops while school uniforms were bought from Kim Novak, a shop known for selling school uniforms that remains in business.

ROADSIDE CHATS AND MALLS

In those times when television and smartphones were non-existentant, chatting was a favourite pastime of the local residents. It was a common sight to see locals sitting on low stools, engaging in small talk by the roadside pavements or inside the grassy area of Magazine Circus, a six-pointed roundabout, which Malays named *Simpang Enam* and Hokkiens, *Goh Pak Theng,* meaning Five Lanterns. These lanterns referred to the five lamps that were hung on the five lamp posts at the roundabout. The roundabout functioned as a centre point linking six different roads, namely, Penang Road, Brick Kiln Road (now Jalan Gurdwara), Magazine Road, Macalister Road, Gladstone Road (now demolished) and Dato Kramat Road. I can vividly recall the linguistically rich nightly chatter at the roadside pavements and roundabout as the locals spoke in Hokkien, Malay or Tamil. In terms of ethnicity, they consisted of Hokkien-speaking Chinese, Malays and Indians. But this did not deter them from freely mingling with one another, sharing personal narratives, anecdotes, experiences and the various struggles they faced at work or at home as working class people. Their children played catch, hopscotch and hide and seek with one another. Unlike children nowadays who spend more time in the virtual world, children in those decades spent their time with real people, playing games and interacting with one another in open multicultural spaces.

However, in the early '70s, this kind of interaction became a memory of a distant past when KOMTAR (acronym for Kompleks Tun Abdul Razak), a colossal 65-storey high rise tower, looming above rows of pre-Pacific war double storey shop-houses in the city centre, was erected. This was part of the government's ambitious urban renewal plan that resulted in the disappearance of the Magazine Circus roundabout and Gladstone Road. The roundabout had to be demolished as the volume of traffic increased when KOMTAR became a tourist attraction. KOMTAR was a prominent landmark of Penang and its 58th floor offered a panoramic view of George Town and Butterworth on the mainland. In the '70s, it was a rare sight to see locals sitting on low stools, chatting and revelling in the fresh night air. Instead they began patronising the shopping malls and departmental stores that sprouted in the city centre. Malls are generally impersonal although they help in merging all kinds of shops for the convenience of the consumer. However, they deprive the consumer of the opportunity to have human interaction with shopkeepers and with fellow consumers as you would have in the old days with smaller sundry and retail shops. I remember being able to walk down the street from one end to another to greet and to have a casual exchange in Hokkien or in *Bahasa Tanjung* (bazaar Malay) with the shopkeepers in the area where I lived. The shopkeepers were much more relaxed and as such they were happy to chit-chat with their customers. They had lived in that area for some time and the sundry shops that they operated were family busi-nesses that they had inherited from their forefathers, migrants from China. When GAMA supermarket and departmental store opened for business in the '80s, it devoured all the sundry shops in the vicinity and gradually drove them out of business. In its place, an open car park was built for GAMA shoppers. The destruction of the shops eclipses the street's history, tradition, community as well as humanity.

MY PAKISTANI FAMILY

I lived in a pre-war wooden bungalow in town which was bought by my maternal grandfather who migrated from Dhodial, a small peasant village situated north of the city of Islamabad in Pakistan. Like other migrants in the neighbourhood, he was forced to flee his homeland and to seek his fortune in Malaya for socio-economic reasons. However, he also had another compel-ling reason. He was determined to make his fortune in a foreign land as he had to save enough money to marry a local village beauty in Dhodial, one that he was besotted with for some time. So, with nothing but clothes on his back, he journeyed to Penang, worked as a contractor in the construction site and then as a trader or small town businessman, dabbling in real estate and then amassing a small fortune for himself. He eventually married the village beauty and set up home in Penang. However, life dealt him a cruel blow as his wife died in her early 30s, leaving behind an only daughter. My grand-father remarried another Pakistani woman who later bore him ten children. She was my beloved grandmother but I never had a chance to meet or know her as she died when I was a knee-high toddler. Sadly, I never met my grandfather either as he died in his early 60s but I was told that he was a towering figure, stern but well-liked and highly respected by the local resi-dents and this included the Japanese soldiers during the Japanese Occupation (1941-1945). Perhaps this helped to explain how he managed to save a young Chinese girl from the clutches of an amorous Japanese soldier, a story that my mother recounted several times to us with pride in her voice.

My mother was married at sixteen and gave birth to me a year or two later. It was my grandfather who arranged my mother's marriage to my father, a distant relative's son. Elders jealously guarded the sanctity of this diasporic community and that was why an arranged marriage was a common practice in those days. My father was a poor immigrant who came to Penang for the sole purpose of fulfilling my grandfather's wish: to marry his eldest daughter and to eke out a better living in this land of opportunity. He worked as a delivery man at the Cold Storage Creameries after tying the knot. The Cold Storage was a posh place renowned for its milkshakes, sundaes, cakes and freshly-baked bread. It was patronised only by the European expatriate community and rich Chinese families. Although we were not privileged enough to savour the cakes and ice cream at the Cold Storage parlour, my father bought ice cream cakes at a discounted price to celebrate our birthdays. The ice cream cakes were super-delicious and would be cherished forever as each ice cream cake was personalised because on it was written the name of the one celebrating the birthday. I guess this was how my father expressed his love for his children. As with other immigrants, life was initially a struggle for my father as he had to feed a young family of five on his meagre income. My mother, a home-maker, augmented the family's income by selling *batik*, bedspreads, carpets and other items to friends and relatives who lived in nearby workers' quarters and houses. It was tough for her as she had to look after the family in the day time and work in the evenings and on weekends. That is the story of many women immigrants: their fortitude and resilience in the face of life's adversity. Although she was illiterate, she was able to remember who bought her stuff and how much they had paid or still owed her. With her children's help, she would document her sales in a little book when she got home. Later on, my parents ventured into the food business by setting up a restaurant in the suburbs that saw us through school. They encouraged us to excel in school as they knew that education was the key to a successful life. Indeed, they were good role models as they taught us the value of diligence, thrift and of taking responsibility of our lives.

MY HOME AND NEIGHBOURHOOD

My extended family and I lived in the old double-storey bungalow that belonged to my grandfather. It was a unique house as it had its own distinctive design, unlike other pre-war shop-houses in the vicinity. In some ways, it represented an interesting fusion of the East and West. It had a *serambi* (porch) like other Malay houses but it had French-style louvered shutters that kept out the warm sun in the day and allowed the cool breezy air in at night. There were two staircases leading to the upper floor, one outside where the *serambi* was and the other in the dining room. The former was used by male relatives who were visiting, the latter by the females. Family members, male or female, used the staircase in the dining room. It was an interesting design, one that aimed to maintain decorum in this conservative society by separating male and female visitors. However, such a separation of men and women into two separate realms of living, the private and public spheres, is revealing as it tells us something about gender roles and gender relations in that society. The huge house had eight bedrooms, three upstairs and five downstairs. We lived upstairs while rooms on the ground floor were sublet to Malay, Indian and *Jawi-Pekan* (people of mixed parentage such as Arab-Malay or Indian-Malay) families working in the nearby tin smelting plant known in the

late twentieth century as the Eastern Smelting Company, later renamed Datuk Keramat Smelting Sdn Bhd.

This plant, built at the turn of the century, provided employment to many
local residents living in the nearby Kampung Jawa Lama and Kampung Jawa
Baru areas. Some lived in quarters which were built within the compound of
the plant while others rented rooms on nearby streets. The plant smelted tin
that was mined in the northern part of the Peninsula. Noxious fumes emanating from the plant made life quite unbearable especially for those with respir-
atory problems who lived nearby. Shortage of tin ore in the late '90s caused
the plant to close down. In its place, Penang Times Square, part of the
massive urban development project, was built. The juxtaposition of the old
and new is bizarre: surrounding this huge modern complex are some old
kampung houses, double-storey pre-war shop-houses and dilapidated huts.
Birch House, the Datuk Keramat Smelting's main administrative centre, still
stands strong after being given a face lift in the early 1990s.

CHINESE NEIGHBOURS AND SHOP-HOUSES

Opposite my grandfather's house was a row of identical Chinese shop-houses
which were mostly owned by rich Chinese *taukehs*[2] or businessmen. They
lived elsewhere but they rented out these shop-houses to poor or working
class Chinese families. Their tenants were employed as labourers in the
construction site or as shopkeepers, fishmongers, foundry workers, mechan-
ics, and lorry drivers. Some of these houses were turned into sundry shops,
selling groceries and other household items while one or two operated a
foundry, a smallish factory for welding and casting metal. There was also a
neighbour who managed a highly successful *nyonya kuih* shop as she supplied such snacks to the many hotels and restaurants in Penang. *Nyonya kuih*
refers to snacks and desserts that were made by the *Peranakan*[3] community,
one who is an ethnic Chinese but has adopted local customs and practices.
Cars and vans queued up to collect the *nyonya kuih* causing bottlenecks at the
road junction. Adding to this hustle and bustle, Indian vendors carried these
snacks in covered baskets on their bicycles along the same road. The snacks
were then sold to residents living in the nearby inner city areas.

In these houses, the tenants lived upstairs while the ground floor was used
as a commercial or business site. The shop-houses were quite long and narrow; they had a courtyard in the centre which separated the living room from
the kitchen, a back lane and a squarish five-foot walkway that joined one
house to another. Children used this walkway to play badminton, catch and
other games in the evenings while women relaxed on stools, lazy chairs or
the swing and chit-chatted with one another after a hard day's work. Once in
a while, we played with the neighbourhood children and that was how we

picked up Hokkien. There was great camaraderie among neighbours as we celebrated birthdays and festive days together. During *Eid* (Muslim New Year) celebrations, my mother would present a gift of cookies and cakes to our immediate neighbours and they reciprocated with an *ang pow* (a red packet) that contained a sum of money.

On the flip side, the city centre was also notorious for its criminal activities. Drug trafficking, illegal gambling, betting, gang clashes, and prostitution were quite rife. Grinding poverty and unemployment were two factors that may have encouraged a small number of the locals to be involved in a life of crime. It was rumoured that the flesh trade was a tradition that was passed from one generation to another for two families living on that street. Daughters of these families became sex workers with consent from their families. I remember how they had to drop out of school and were whisked off to another town and only to be seen with a child or two after a few years. The children were left in the care of their grandmothers and then they would take off again for an indefinite number of years. There were frequent gang fights, normally over drugs, women and profits accrued from illegal gambling money. The streets were rather quiet in the mid-'70s as many of the gang members had either moved out of the area or were serving a long jail sentence for drug trafficking or for carrying dangerous weapons or other serious crimes.

THE CHINESE OPERA

Given my closeness to my Chinese neighbours and my interest in Hokkien, it is hardly surprising that Chinese operas fascinated me: I was drawn to their stories, dramatic costumes, thick makeup and highly stylised acting. These opera shows were staged during the month-long Feast of the Hungry Ghosts. We knew when the opera was in town as the troupe and community members would be busy preparing a temporary wooden stage on stilts at the corner of the street. Before the start of the opera, actors would nap or rest on hammocks slung between the wooden stilts. Others would be busy trying on their make-up or costumes backstage. The shows usually went on till midnight. Once the stage was ready, stools were placed in front for the audience, but we were reminded not to occupy the two front rows as they were meant for the ghosts. The audience included Chinese families living in the neighbourhood. People from other ethnic groups came to watch the opera as well but they were fewer in number. It was usual for the shows to be played to a packed audience, but the numbers started dwindling in the early '70s. This was mainly sparked by the urban development project which resulted in a spike in the rentals of pre-war landed properties and shop-houses once protected by legislation.[4] Many city dwellers opted to move to the suburbs such as Bayan Baru to rent or buy cheaper flats which were being built by the state government. Bereft of people, the city centre soon lost its old charm and significance.

MY SCHOOLING

Like many other things in my childhood life, schooling was urban-centred. I spent my primary schooldays at the Convent Penang Road in the upper part of Penang Road. It was a smaller convent compared to the other convents such as Convent Light Street, Convent Green Lane and Convent Pulau Tikus. Located within the same compound of the St Joseph's Orphanage and the Church of Francis Xavier, the convent was an all girls' school, run by a Catholic nun, and helped by other nuns and teachers from diverse ethnic and religious backgrounds. The nuns were very strict and they taught us etiquette, politeness, morals, and positive values apart from the prescribed curriculum. They stressed the importance of mastering the English language. As a result, we were expected to read all kinds of story books and to write summaries of these stories every week. Failure to do so would result in punitive measures such as smacking the knuckles with a ruler. Eventually, we cultivated a voracious appetite for reading, and as many of us who could not afford to buy books, we would rent them for a small fee from second-hand book vendors operating in their kiosks on Macalister Road. In this sense, we are very appreciative of the nuns' efforts as it had helped to hone our English language skills. During assembly, prayers were recited and Christian hymns sung. Over time, I learnt those prayers and hymns and could recite or sing them effortlessly. Every Friday morning, in single file, we were shepherded to the church to join the congregation. The Catholic students sat in the front pews while those who were of other faiths occupied the back ones. To be sure, this experience did not dilute or alter my Muslim faith in any way or made me a lesser Muslim. What it did was to strengthen even further my belief in God.

CLOSING REMARKS

Despite the frequent street brawls in town, going to school by bus, which was one of the cheaper modes of public transportation at the time, was relatively safe for a young child like me. In fact, I also used to take a bus to my tuition class which was located on China Street, quite a distance away. Of course, one would not dream of doing such a thing these days when crimes such as child kidnapping are rampant. Such trips on my own taught me how to be independent and self-reliant. Living in the city centre and with an extended family had its ups and downs. The air and noise pollution, occasional street fights, poverty and the crowded house that was filled with conflicts eventually turned out to be valuable life's lessons. In many ways, they have helped me to be understanding, compassionate, tolerant and appreciative of life's diversity.

NOTES

1. George Town that occupies the northeast portion of the turtle-shaped island of Penang was and still is the administrative and commercial centre of Penang. The state of Penang, one of the thirteen states of the Federation of Malaysia, comprises Penang Island and Province Wellesley or Seberang Prai.

2. The term *taukeh* (*towkay*) denotes a Chinese of standing usually to an entrepreneur, a proprietor of business concern, a communal leader, owners of tin mines or rubber plantations. Basically it refers to an individual of means and respectability. This term is often used as a prefix, Taukeh Khoo as a mark of honour and respect.

3. *Peranakan* literally means "of local born", to differentiate those who were born in China. In George Town, the union of Chinese men with local women of Malay stock produced the Baba Nyonya peranakan that generally retained Chinese traditions in terms of beliefs, language (dialect), and cultural traits but adopted and adapted local (Malay) sociocultural practices such as attire (particularly for females) and cuisine. The Hokkien spoken is heavily juxtoposed with English and Malay terms and phrases.

4. The Rent Control Act 1966 that incorporates earlier ordinances viz. Rent Control Ordinance of 1948 and 1956 was designed to overcome the post-war acute shortage of housing that led to squatting and high rentals. In essence, the Rent Control Act of 1966 basically controls the amount of rent to be collected from tenants as well as protecting them from eviction by property owners.

Childhood Memories

Ooi Keat Gin

WAVING AT THE CRIB

Unlikely that I had done such a thing considering that I was merely one or two days' old, but my imagination fuelled the following scenario:

Saw Lian and Saw Ean, elder and second sister respectively, came to visit Mamak (my mother), and newly-born me. "Silly girls were responding to another crib, and not mine", thought I. In desperation I had had to do something for after all they were my first visitors. Hence I started waving and shouting "Over here!", "Over here!" frantically and in the loudest sound that I could possibly muster until I finally got their attention. Phew! Sisters!

I was born on 3 October 1959 in George Town, Penang, Malaysia so I was told and it is evident from all legal documents, namely my birth certificate, identification card (IC), driving license and all other official paperwork. According to Mamak, the premises that I was born on Transfer Road (Jalan Transfer) remained intact to the present (2010s) unlike the buildings where Lian's and Ean's birthplace had since been demolished. This fact appears to be 'important' to Mamak. Perhaps it was that I was the only male offspring, and the third and last child. From my mother's account, I was delivered in a private house attended by a midwife and a doctor. Thankfully there were no complications when I came into the world apparently without much fuss or drama as I was told.

My birthdate of '3 October' is an auspicious date it seems to my mother who proudly claimed that my birth coincided with the Vegetarian Festival of the Nine Emperor Gods that span over nine days in honour of the nine brother deities much revered by the Hokkien community.

I was told by my mother and sisters that I was a skinny boy, and snapshots when I was three or four-year old testified to this slim image. But it

appears to be a contradictions of sorts as I was also told that I had a vocifer-
ous appetite. I suppose I gradually added bulk over the years as when I first
stepped into 'real' school, that is primary school, I was quite a chubby lad
vis-à-vis my classmates. Being described as "skinny" during pre-school days
appeared to be a 'commendable' attribute, for since then the skinny label has
never stood a chance.

MR POH'S KINDERGARTEN

A year prior to "real" school, I attended 'Mr Poh's kindergarten' at Seang
Teik Road (Jalan Seang Teik). My childhood recollection depicts a spacious
building with an equally expansive compound for play. There was the canteen that served one of the best bak moey (minced pork broth). Mamak was
pretty proud of me as I easily finished two bowls whilst the other kids were
struggling with theirs. Other mothers commended of my appetite much to
Mamak's delight. Apparently a good appetite is a highly commendable trait
in Chinese culture.

I remember accompanying my mother to the kindergarten when Ean was
a pupil. There was a small toy shop just next door. After having purchased a
toy, I would trouble my mother to go home as I was anxious to play with it.
All the mothers including Mamak would share 'notes' of domestic issues;
nothing that interested a four-year old boy clutching his new toy still in its
packaging. (Mamak would not allow me to open the box or packaging until
we get home.) I do not really recall what I did then, probably distracted
myself by watching my sister and her classmates playing or performing some
exercise on the compound. My mother had no recollection of my ever sulk-
ing.

12 CLOVE HALL ROAD

Chiah Chooi Tau Teow Am Lor, literally 'First Dark Road off Water Carrier
Road', denotes Clove Hall Road (Jalan Clove Hall), the first road (from
downtown George Town) on the right off Burmah Road (Jalan Burma). The
latter thoroughfare in the pre-war days witnessed oxen-drawn carriages that
transported water from Waterfall (in the interior of the island; present-day
Penang Botanic Gardens) to the waterfront at Weld Quay, hence Water Carrier Road. That phrase - *Chiah Chooi Tau Teow Am Lor* – I recall often
hearing it uttered by Mamak to the *lang chieh lang* (trishaw rider) after
shopping in downtown and going home. Memories on the *lang chieh* is of
sitting on Mamak's ample lap, a pleasant and comfortable position affording
a full view of the road and traffic ahead.

12 Clove Hall Road prompts memories of a large garden in the front, a porch where a car is often parked, a spacious front hall with a left and right wing, a second hall which is comparatively smaller, a third hall which is long, wide and large leading to a vast kitchen. The second and third halls always seem to be in twilight but surprisingly emitted a warm ambience. Notwithstanding the 'darkness', I do not recall being afraid, but the upper floor somehow frightened me during the night with its single light bulb. I remember the downstairs with its many halls to be somehow (unspoken) off limits to me and my two elder sisters. Our domain was upstairs where we had total access to every nook and corner. Only two main rooms, directly facing one another were forbidden without prior permission, namely the rooms of my mother's cousins, Tua Ee (Big Aunt) and Kin Ee (Aunt Kin).

Our family – my parents, two sisters and I – occupied a makeshift 'room' on the upper right wing with two large open windows on the front and the side. Often opened was the small window on the front whilst the rest with louvre-shutters were closed. Although rather congested, it was 'Home-Sweet-Home'.

A household containing my maternal relatives of aunts but no cousins, 12 Clove Hall Road was a female domain of my mother's family. Mamak was the only child of Ah Mah (maternal grandmother) and Ah Kong (maternal grandfather): the former I never knew as she passed away before I was born, and the latter was the only grandfather whom I knew. (My paternal grandfather died when my father was 16 years old.) Ah Mah was the eldest female in her family of five daughters and two sons. Tua Ee, Keat Ee, Kin Ee, and Nee Ee were the spinster daughters of Sar Ee Poh (Third Grand Aunt), the third sister of Ah Mah. The two grand uncles I have only heard of as they had passed away prior to my birth: one grand uncle was a medical doctor, a contemporary of Dr Lim Chwee Leong, the father of Dr Lim Chong Ewe (chief minister of Penang, 1969-1991), and the other served as a clerk at the Chinese Chamber of Commerce. Apparently I was told of another grand uncle who graduated as an engineer from the prestigious Hong Kong University. Both the doctor and engineer grand uncles died in their early thirties. The doctor was taken ill, and after recovering he spent a period of convalescence in Brastagi, North Sumatra. Shortly thereafter he passed away and was buried there. All this I heard as a child from Mamak.

Then there is Ee Poh and her husband, Tiau Kong. Ee Poh is the youngest sister of Ah Mah and had a daughter, my Eng Ee, and a son, my Ah Koo. Goh Ee Poh (Fifth Grand Aunt) is the adopted daughter and half-sister of Ah Mah. This rather well-padded grand aunt, a specialist *kueh*-maker, spent her twilight years at Clove Hall Road where she had resided prior to her marriage.

12 Clove Hall Road housed three families: Sar Ee Poh's family, Ee Poh's family, and our family. At any one time when I was a child there were at least

12 or 13 individuals in the house. My Ah Kong and Ah Pa, who both worked on a rubber estate in neighbouring Kedah, took turns to be home with us on a monthly basis; it has always.

Undoubtedly there are altercations amongst members of this large household but as a child I was completely oblivious to any as I happily played with my toys of plastic soldiers and looked forward to every meal.

WHO'S WHO

I remember Ean to be rotund like Mamak, the latter naturally much taller, and Lian being tall as Ah Kong who is much taller and slimmer. I always seem to recall Lian in her white school uniform. Ah Chee[1], my eldest half-sister, on the other hand reflects on my memory bank as a slim, petite woman in loose black pants. Funnily I don't really recall what type of blouse she wore. Another indelible memory of Ah Chee is of her habitually eating a pinch or two of rice prior to commencing the meal proper that is rice with other dishes. She alone ate with her fingers. Ah Pa was also fond of using his hands at meal times, but never with Ah Kong. We children occasionally used our fingers Indian-style to savour *nasi kandar*.[2] Even from my boy's viewpoint, Ah Pa was short, at slightly less than five feet (1.5 metres). Ah Kong appears to be the tallest individual I knew then.

Tiau Kong in my memory presents a portrait of an old man with hands that tremble noticeably in tying strings into knots on my kite. He, like Ah Pa, emits post-smoking odours making me wonder if I need to smell similarly when I grow up as a man. I don't recall Ah Koo reeking of cigarette smell; in fact, an image of him wrapped in a towel after a shower exposing his fairness is the most vivid. He often smells good with some kind of manly perfume that lingers on even after he had descended the stairs. Unlike Mamak, Tua Ee appears to be 'distant'. Kin Ee and Eng Ee are both approachable. Ee Poh tends to talk a lot to herself most of the time and seems to be in a hurry going somewhere or meeting up with someone or other. In my boy's mind, Ee Poh leads a hectic type of lifestyle and I hope that I do not have to follow in her footsteps. Eng Ee is notoriously late for everything it seems. Lian on the other hand always appears to be studying, Mamak telling me that I should not disturb her. Kin Ee drives a Ford car and works in some government place. Once Ean and I visited her office where we got pretty busy with rubber stamps. Kin Ee seems to bring us children –Lian, Ean and I – to visit restrooms of newly opened hotels. I doubt I ever peed in those good-looking toilets.

I vaguely remember the other members of our household notably those that resided downstairs. I think there was an overweight dog, Blackie, which had difficulty even in walking. I recall Ee Poh feeding her obese dog rice with *tau eiw bak*. I rarely went or was allowed to venture downstairs in my pre-school years.

FOOD GALORE

'Don't bother about their food intake; they will know when to stop when they are full' is the principle my father pronounced to my mother relating to our – meaning my two sisters and I – eating habits. On hindsight, Ah Kong was to be 'blamed' for offering lavish breakfasts, lunches, and dinners, not forgetting feasts at restaurants on auspicious occasions or simply a night out for a meal. A rainbow spread of foods was laid out on the dining table for us grandchildren and my parents to feast. Dim sum (an assortment of small morsels of steamed pork, prawns, and chicken), *chee cheong chook* (pork entrails porridge), *jiu char kueh* (Chinese crullers, *yau char kwai*), *ban teng kueh* (sweetened pancakes with crushed peanuts), *siew bak* (roasted pork), *char siew* (barbequed pork), *nyonya kueh* (a variety Nyonya[3] cakes), and others. The aforesaid list was simply Ah Kong's breakfast to kick start our mornings. By the time Ah Kong returned from marketing with all the breakfast goodies, often about quarter to eight or so, I was the first at the table to sample the inviting foods whilst my sisters, especially Ean who was averse to waking up early, were struggling out of bed, toiletries, and morning prayers. When both Lian and Ean joined in for breakfast, usually half past eight, Ah Kong and I sat back and relaxed after savouring the delicacies. Ah Kong ate moderately, a bit of this and a bit of that: he loved nothing more than to see us, particularly his grandchildren, tucking in.

Home-cooked lunches during Ah Kong's sojourns were generally pork-based. Entrees included *tau eiw bak* (pork belly in dark soy sauce), *kuah ah-sum* (stewed pork trotters with vegetables and lemongrass), *too kar kiam chye th'ng* (pork leg soup with salted vegetables), stir-fried vegetables (whatever leafy green vegetables accessorized with slices of pork and shrimps), and many more appetizing dishes that go well with steamed rice. Chinese-style lunches often have at least two or three entrees, a soup, and some side dishes. Spicy hot *sambal belacan* is a common side dish as an accompaniment: basically red chillies pounded with *belacan* (shrimp paste), *hair bee* (dried shrimp), a dash of *sui kam* (calamansi) juice. Ah Kong was insistent that everything on the table needed to be piping hot, a typical Chinese trait. Oftentimes dinners outside were at the all-time family favourite of Loke Thye Kee, reputedly the foremost Hainanese[4] restaurant of the 1950s until the mid-1970s. Its menu comprised favourite family staples such as *gulai tumi* (curry fish), *lor bak* (pork sausage-like rolls), *jiu hoo char* (fried *meng-kuang*, cabbages, carrots with belly pork, dried black mushrooms, dried cuttlefish stripes, all thinly sliced), *cheem baked* (baked crabmeat), *bean chee bak* (stir-fried potatoes, carrots, lean pork, onions topped with a deep fried-bread cut in cubes), pork or chicken chop a la Hainanese, *choon pieh* (a richer version of spring roll with pork and crabmeat fillings besides).

Ah Pa, on the other hand, adhered to a non-pork diet. He was a connoisseur of sea foods: fishes, prawns, crabs, mussels, cockles. At the same time, he delighted in beef and mutton dishes prepared by Malay Muslims and Indian Muslims served with *biryani* (spiced rice). Breakfasts for Ah Pa was *roti canai* (kneaded flour dough and pan-fried), Nyonya-style *nasi lemak*,[5] *nasi kandar*,[6] and the occasional *oh-kuah moey* (dried oyster porridge). *Hoo tau gulai tumi* (fish head curry) and *sambal udang* (shrimp curry) were the all-time favourites of my father. Ah Chee had to be prepared for these dishes when it was my father's homecoming. As Mamak, Ah Chee and Ean did not consume beef, no beef was cooked at home and we – Ah Pa, Lian, and I – ate beef outside at restaurants. Home-cooked mutton soup was another of Ah Pa's favourites: according to him, it eased his legs' cramps and aches.

One of the most memorable recollections of Ah Pa was his coming home from marketing with *nasi kandar* wrapped in banana leaf for breakfast. Mine was usually *daging* (*daging rendang*, beef pieces in thick curry), one hard-boiled egg sliced into two and rice with a generous cover of a combination of several curries. Ean would have fish curry, okra (or ladies fingers as we were taught in school), and Lian, sometimes *daging* but mostly fish curry. At other times breakfast came to our doorstep, literally: a Tamil man would carry (later on a bicycle) a big covered tray with a delightful array of Nyonya *kueh* (cakes) and Nyonya-style *nasi lemak*. Ah Pa's favourite was *kueh talam* (white-on-green cake) likewise mine too. The whole family would breakfast on *nasi lemak* wrapped in banana leaf into a pyramidal packet. On reflection it was a piece of dainty art in itself. The *sambal belacan* was given on a separate banana leaf as well as the cucumber slices.

Lunch when Ah Pa was home often comprised seafood dishes such as *hoo tau gulai tumi*, *sambal udang*, *kiam hoo belanda* (salted fish in tamarind sauce), *sotong rempah* (squid in thick spicy sauce), *haam* (boiled cockles), stir-fried with garlic *lala*, *siput*, *kappa* (various types of mussels), *gulai kay* (curry chicken with potatoes). Eat-out for lunch was usually at favourite Indian Muslim restaurants patronized by my father, namely Dawood, Meerah, and later, Hammeediyah. *Murtabak* (Indian-style pancake with minced mutton filling), Indian-style fried *mee* (fried yellow noodles), or plain white rice or *biryani* or *nasi minyak* (oiled rice) with a variety of curries, viz. *oar-chieh hoo* (black pomfret), *kambing kurma* (mutton *korma*), *ayam rost* (roasted chicken in spicy paste), *sotong rempah* (pan-fried squid in curry paste), *udang rempah* (pan-fried shrimp sautéed in spicy paste). If my father buys back supper, it was either *murtabak* or Hokkien *char* (fried yellow noodles), the latter with shrimps lest pork. Occasionally Ah Pa would get supper of *sar hor fun* (fried flat rice noodles) with seafood ingredients or *hoo moey* (fish porridge).

I still remember for *hoo moey* or *bak moey* (pork porridge) the *tong chye ang* (earthen container for preserved vegetables) or Milo-tin[7] that were utilized as containers for take-away street food during the pre-plastic days. The ticking sound of Ah Pa's bicycle's gear system was signal for us kids to be up and ready for supper, often about ten or past that late hour. With sleepy eyes we would eat supper and only gradually realize what we were consuming. After the mandatory gurgling and rinsing of our mouth with water I remember having a splendid sleep with pleasant dreams on a full stomach.

When we were on our own, meaning neither Ah Kong or Ah Pa were back home, we savoured Mamak's 'menu' prepared by Ah Chee. Home-cooked *bak chuuah* (steamed minced pork with salted egg), *tau chieh bak gulai* (pork belly soybean paste curry), *tau eiw bak* (pork belly in dark soy sauce, more diluted than Ah Kong's version), *hong bak* (pork belly in thick spiced sauce), *kiam hoo tau hoo th'ng* (salted fish with tofu soup), *oar-chieh chee-rempah* (deep-fried black pomfret stuffed with chilli spices), *stek* (pork patties, potato slices sautéed in gooey sauce), *bean chee bak* (stir-fried potatoes, carrots, lean pork, and onions less the deep fried-bread), *stoo* (stewed chicken or pork with potatoes), and many more. My all-time favourite, then and now, is *tau chieh bak gulai*: that I can easily savour with two full plates of rice.

AT WELLESLEY PRIMARY SCHOOL

I recall vividly when Ah Pa and Mamak came to fetch me after school at midday and I walked out of the classroom to greet them with untied shoelaces. I did not know how to tie my shoelaces. I do not recall how they became untied: perhaps there was PE (Physical Education) that day. Looking at my untied laces, both my parents had a smile on their faces as I approached them.

The one particular memory of my Standard One days was of the curly hairy legs of my female teacher. It did not bother any of us children but I could recall the mothers who stood just outside the classroom pointing and gesturing to one another about this rather unfeminine feature. I am glad Mamak did not bother to stand outside my classroom during the first few days when I started school unlike other mothers.

During this time – Standards One, Two, perhaps even Three – we had playtime when the teacher gave us plasticine, a kind of putty-like modelling clay to play. I tried to make a man but was often unsuccessful and ended making blobs with frankly no idea what they were supposed to be. I recall having to buy *kana*, some kind of preserved dried fruit for Mamak, Tua Ee,

Eng Ee, and my sisters. My schoolbag is full of *kana* upon reaching home. I don't recall my eating *kana* as I had an aversion of *kiam sui tee* (literally salty, sour, sweet) preserved titbits, thinking that they are women's foodstuff.

One year in primary school I underwent several horrific experiences. Whether it was for real or in the overdrive of my anxiety and imaginings there is this feeling of being locked in the toilet sitting on the bowl and staring at the four walls and waiting to be rescued. I don't suppose such a situation ever happened except in my overactive imagination. Second, and this is for real as I am occasionally reminded by my sisters was my spelling nightmare. "Cockroaches", "grasshoppers", and a third word I cannot remember, were words that I was unable to spell. Everybody lent a hand but mastering the spelling exercise appear elusive.

Then there was the experience of feeling 'cold' throughout the episode of returning with some other schoolbag other than mine! My schoolbag then was a rectangular suitcase-type bag that opened with two locking devices, and I could sit on it when placed upright. Only upon returning home and opening it did I realize that it was not my bag. Checking through its contents, Ean or Lian uncovered the owner's name and address enabling Kin Ee to drive over to the owner's residence, somewhere in Tanjung Bungah a distance from Clove Hall Road, to exchange the bags. I remember that it is more a case of pity, sympathy, perhaps even comedy with Mamak and my sisters and Kin Ee, and no reprimand whatsoever.

One last particularly "bad" incident involves a form of bullying relating again to my schoolbag. There is this classmate who sits in the immediate rear who keeps unlocking my bag which is placed on the back seat of my chair. He totally disregarded my repeated protests. I mentioned this while at home. Ah Pa took it seriously and appeared at recess time the following day. Upon my pointing out the culprit, Ah Pa took him aside for a word. No unlocking of my bag by him 'forever'. I was probably eight or nine years old then. It was perhaps at this juncture I vaguely recall Ah Pa wanting to teach me boxing or some kind of self-defence. I was not exactly enthusiastic at the thought of acquiring such 'aggressive' behaviour. I was already a pacifist back then. Probably Mamak dissuaded him from insisting that I learnt street-fighting skills.

During break time or recess, I recall playing marbles. The marbles were placed in a straight line and each player stood behind this line to throw a single marble; whoever throws the furthest gets the initial chance to roll the single marble back to hit the line-up: the further to left of the line-up, the more marbles one collects. 'Bank' is a marble game whereby each pundit will contribute three or four marbles to the pool that is placed within a circle known as the 'bank'. Each player utilizes a single marble to hit those within the circle; any that exit the circle belong to the hitter. If the 'hitting' marble itself lands within the circle, it is forfeited.

Miss Chuah, my Standard Four class teacher, took a fancy to me and I became her 'favourite' pupil. She was possibly the most beautiful amongst the female teachers. She was in charge of staging the annual school plays and I was given a role. In Standard Four the play was *Don Sancho*, some Spanish story of the hero Don Sancho fighting a dragon and saving a maiden and marrying her. I remember the role that I played walking around on stage with a fake apple in hand. I had no idea what I am supposed to be; we followed what we were instructed to do. Plenty of songs to memorise and sing. When in Standard Five, I was involved in some play in which I played a Red Indian Chief. I reprised my role as a Red Indian Chief in *Nostalgia*, the play that was staged when I was in Standard Six, the last year of primary school. All of us actors had to put on make-up. I disliked the gooey stuff put on my face, eye lids, etc.; a bit sticky and we are told not to scratch or rub our face. Somehow I got through this discomfort without undue protest as we studiously followed Miss Chuah's instructions.

Again it was Miss Chuah who spoke of great men like Napoleon Bonaparte, Julius Caesar, Genghiz Khan, Mahatma Gandhi and others that totally mesmerized me. I was hooked to these great personalities and their exploits; my initiation into the discipline of History.

KITE-FLYING OBSESSION

Between the ages of 10 and 12, I was simply obsessed with kite-flying including making kites and taking a a hand in 'manufacturing' glass-glazed strings. The large garden of Clove Hall Road presents an ideal playground for this outdoor distraction that earned me a tan and a slap. Firstly, the tan. Post-lunch windy afternoons spent at kite-flying made me rather tanned in my face and arms. Being dark skinned was inconsequential to a 10-year old who loves to have his kite up in the clear blue sky. It was only once that I ever 'won' in 'cutting' another line resulting in the vanquished kite floating away in the wind. Once when I followed others in chasing the fly-away kite, upon my return home, I received a tight slap from Ah Pa who was furious that I was involved in chasing a frivolous 20-cent kite that could endanger my life on the road. No kite-flying for a week or so, I think.

I dabbled in making glass-glazed strings. It is an exercise in patience that I wholly lack and I threw a mini-tantrum on my own. Looking on from the upstairs front window Mamak appeared amused at my impatience. Kite-making on my part was a more successful enterprise. I remember learning it from watching Tiau Kong, who in a sense, was my kite-flying buddy. During my kite-flying days, I had an aversion for bushes and trees that seemed to want to entangle my kites. Words like 'angkat', 'ulok', and 'lambong', all Malay-based, meaning 'pull up', 'release more string' and 'holding the kite for its launch', still bring a smile after all these years of boyhood enjoyment. Seeing one's kite in the sky gives a sense of accomplishment; an 'I-have-done-it' feeling that begs for more.

'THE ONE-ARMED SWORDSMAN'

Family outings during my childhood involved going to the movies followed by dinner. The six of us would take two trishaws to the cinemas, namely Rex on Burmah Road, Capitol, Cathay, and Odeon on Penang Road, and the furthest, Federal on Datuk Kramat Road. English movies from Hollywood were the main family attraction particularly spaghetti Westerns and James Bond, both Ah Pa's favourites. Despite being Anglicized from English-medium education, my parents and we children loved Mandarin movies of the sword-fighting genre. English sub-titles overcame the language issue. Wang Yu who found fame in *The One-Armed Swordsman* is our family's all-time favourite; other actors being Lo Lieh, Ti Lung, David Chiang, and Chen Kuan Tai, whilst female leads are Cheng Pei-Pei, Li Ching, Lily Ho and other tough swordswomen that escape my memory. Bruce Lee who ushered in the *kung fu* flicks emerged only in my adolescent years.

One particular experience, perhaps indirect, is listening to my sisters complaining of the smoky environment in cinemas and post-movie tobacco scented attire following an afternoon or evening at the movies, particularly prevalent after a James Bond show. It did not bother me at all then; it appears to me as a boy that all men smoked including Ah Pa and Ah Kong and Tiau Kong too. Since I had not witnessed any women in the household or in public smoking, my child-like deduction was that smoking was peculiar to menfolk.

Mamak whispers to Lian, she to Ean, and she to me that the movie proper has commenced. Pre-movie commercials are aplenty and we children are unaware whether it is the movie or just the run of advertisements. The Marlborough ads are rather 'confusing': we see the vast countryside with cowboys and don't know whether the Clint Eastwood movie has begun or not. The 'whispering' is a welcome cue. *Kacang putih* (a variety of nuts) in a paper cone is a favourite show time snack. *Kuah chee* (dried melon seeds) also took my fancy. Another favourite is *bak kuah roti* (sweetened grilled mincemeat in a bun). My sisters love *rojak* (cut fruits in an admixture of sweetened and spicy sauce); I only love a piece or two of the pineapple.

Another movie practice is the 'picnic' at the cinema. Being enthusiastic movie-goers, Mamak will pack dinner in Tupperware containers with spoon ready for consumption. It is a commonplace routine: movies often begun at 6:45 pm hence once we alighted from the trishaw returning from school, still in uniform, we are bundled into another trishaw with other family members to head straight for the cinema. Once inside the semi-dark, or if we are late, dark interior, each will be given his/her packed dinner. We quickly eat the rice with *tau eiw bak* in order that we will be ready to watch the movie uninterrupted or distracted by dinner. Those were indeed happy days that I joyfully recollect.

Especially when with Ah Pa along, the family will partake of a post-movie supper at one of the many food courts. Padang (Brown Gardens) were a family favourite, and several coffee shops along Penang Road when we were at cinemas there. Adjacent to the Rex, we often frequented the coffee shop where the servings of *char koay teow* and *sar hor fun* were I recall lip-smacking delicious.

Afternoon movies starts at 1 o'clock were problematic. Exiting at 3 o'clock into the afternoon sun brings forth a headache consequent of the temperature change between the air-conditioned cinema hall and the outside. Both Lian and I needed to pop two tablets of Dusil, a painkiller.

A HAPPY AND JOYOUS CHILDHOOD

Memories of growing up as a boy in 1960s George Town against the background of a loving, supportive, ever-attentive nuclear family and extended circle of household relatives are indeed pleasant. I recall being happy when playing with my toy soldiers, laying my head on Mamak's ample thigh, running into and 'bouncing off' Mamak's stomach, walking across Ah Pa's back (apparently therapeutic for him), eating this and that, and of course kite-flying.

NOTES

1. My father was a widower when he married my mother. He had a son and a daughter from his first wife; the daughter was my eldest half-sister.

2. See below.

3. Both my paternal and maternal families were of Baba Nyonya descents. The Baba Nyonya were of Sino-Malay extractions with a unique eclectic sociocultural traditions drawn from mainly Hokkien Chinese, Malay, and Siamese. While retaining Chinese culture and its world of beliefs and practices (Confucianism, Daoism, and Buddhism), the Baba (male) was a highly Anglicized gentleman owing to his English-medium education at the Penang Free School or Christian mission schools (St Xavier's Institution, Methodist Boys' School, etc.) with a clerical appointment in one of colonial bureaucracy or in European firms (agency houses, banks, insurance, shipping), or a professional (doctor, lawyer, civil engineer, architect). His counterpart the Nyonya (female) was more Malayanized adopting the Malay *sarong* (pareo), Malay-style eating with the right hand, and food preparation borrowing heavily from the Malay and Siamese kitchens. The Penang Baba Nyonya retained their Hokkien dialect but contaminated with much intrusion from English and Malay words and phrases.

4. Hainanese cooks who were employed by British households during the colonial period re-created Western dishes such as pork chops, steaks, chicken cutlets with a twist utilizing ingredients from the Chinese kitchen such as soy sauce, locally-made Worstershire sauce, etc. Those who ventured out to run restaurants introduced these unique sinicized English fare that were alien in Britain itself.

5. Originally a Malay creation, *nasi lemak* was appropriated by the Nyonya who tweeted some of the ingredients lending it a different, unique taste. Nyonya-style nasi lemak is served with a small pinch of sambal belacan, *assam hair* (pan-fried shrimps in tamarind marinate) or *assam hoo* (pan-fried small fish in tamarind marinate), a slice of boiled egg and garnished with thin slices of cucumber.

6. *Nasi kandar*, was and still is, a George Town delicacy. In its original outing it was served by an Indian Muslim man who carried a pole (*kandar*) with either end strapped with two big pots, one of which is steamed white rice, and the other, fish curry with okra. An additional ingredient was boiled eggs. It was cheap breakfast and lunch for stevedores at Weld Quay who needed ample amounts of carbohydrates (rice) for the heavy labour of loading and unloading onto *tongkang* (light wooden barge). Since the late 1960s and early 1970s, *nasi kandar* had become common amongst the general populace that consequently witnessed additional dishes to the hitherto limited menu, thus *daging rendang* (beef pieces in thick curry), *sotong rempah* (pan-fried squid in curry paste), *udang rempah* (pan-fried shrimp sautéed in spicy paste), *tau kuah* (bean curd in thick spicy sauce), *kobis* (stir-fried cabbages with turmeric), hard boiled salted eggs.

7. Milo is a chocolate malt drink.

My Childhood Memories

Hajar Abdul Rahim

THE TENTH CHILD

Being the tenth child in a family of eleven, my childhood was memorable for many reasons, not least because of the endless adventures I had playing, learning and living in a household with six brothers, and four sisters. As social beings, much of what we are, I believe, we owe to all the experiences, good and bad, we had as a child. In my case, there are many of them but whenever I reflect on my childhood, the central theme is almost always the bond that my siblings and I had growing up in an ever busy household. So I will allude to the experiences I shared with my family especially my siblings in two places that we called our hometown, George Town in Penang and Ipoh in Perak in Malaysia.

I was born in the early 1960s in my maternal grandmother's house in Kampung Sheikh Eusoff, a village in the George Town area of Penang Island. It is also known among the locals as Kampung Masjid, after the Sheikh Eusoff Mosque that sits near the north entrance of the village. Situated in the Dhoby Ghaut area of George Town, Kampung Sheikh Eusoff is bordered by Ayer Itam Road (Jalan Ayer Itam) to the north, Gopeng Road (Jalan Gopeng) to the west, Tramway Road (Jalan Tramway) to the east and a river to its south. As with many Malay *kampung* (village) in the George Town area on Penang Island, my *kampung* is essentially a village in a city. So living in a village in George Town means that whilst one enjoys the rural and laidback vibes of the '*kampung* life', downtown was practically a fifteen-minute walk from one's home.

Strange as that might sound, for many Penangites like me who grew up in a *kampung* in George Town, that was the only kind of *kampung* that we knew. Unlike the typical Malay villages in rural areas in Malaysia which are usually surrounded by paddy fields with houses set far apart from one an-other and water buffaloes, fruit trees as well as rice farmers as familiar features, *kampungs* in the George Town area commonly comprise houses which are built fairly close to one another with a little area around each house and narrow tarred roads. So, these Malay kampungs in the George Town area of Penang had the makings of a Malay kampung in terms of the traditional Malay houses that were found at the time, but the similarity between them ended there.

IT'S A KAMPUNG LIFE

Thus, it was in my grandmother's house in a village in George Town where I spent the first five and half years of my life before my family moved to Ipoh where my little sister, the eleventh member of my family, was born. Al-though I lived in Kampung Sheikh Eusoff when I was very little, I still have many vivid memories of my 'kampung life'. Central to all these memories is my family and our closeness as a family unit. Besides my immediate family, we had extended family members including uncles, aunties, first and second cousins who lived in the same kampung who were always stopping by my grandmother's house.

My grandmother's house (which still stands to this day) is located in the central area of the kampung with some land around it. For a Malay kampung house, it was medium-sized with three rooms, a living room, and a small veranda on one side. The house is elevated about four feet (1.2 metres) from the ground except for the kitchen which is on the ground level. Besides my grandmother's house, I remember how the kampung was in those days in terms of the flora and fauna, the neighbours, the houses and certain events that still come to mind in vivid colours. There was a little backyard where my grandmother used to rear chickens, and sometimes turkeys and geese. I still remember times when we had turkeys walking around at the back of the house and curiously peeking into the kitchen. There was a time when she had pigeons too but apparently after a python sneeked into the pigeon house one night and ate them: she did not bother rearing pigeons anymore.

A few yards from my grandmother's house was our great grand aunty's house. *Nenek*, as we called her, lived in the house with my uncle and his family. There was a yard between the two houses where we and our cousins used to play. There were two jackfruit trees on the yard, one that grew near my grandmother's house and the other nearer Nenek's house. The trees did not only bear boundless fruit over the years but were also very functional. I remember times when a string would hang across the yard with each end tied to the two trees and used like a net by my sisters and brothers to play badminton. They also cycled around the trees a lot. I played hopscotch and other games with my elder sister and cousins who were closer to my age under the tree near my grandmother's house because it was shady and cool in the afternoons. I also recall my mother and our aunty, as well as the neighbours who sometime sat around to chat under the tree.

There were only a few fruit trees around my grandmother's house but on a patch of land not too far away from our yard, my grandmother, being the industrious woman that she was, planted various kinds of banana trees and a few other fruit trees. We used to call it our *kebun* or sometimes *kebun Tok* (grandmother's orchard) because that was like our own little orchard. My grandmother would sometimes plan picnic lunches for us and our cousins in the *kebun*. That was always very exciting as we sat on the ground and ate rice with simple dishes on freshly cut banana leaves. Food, especially rice and curry, somehow always tasted extra delicious during picnics in the *kebun*. Sometimes, when durian was in season, we would have *nasi durian* (rice mixed with fresh coconut milk and durian).

The durian fruit season reminds me of a favourite food of mine, known as *lempuk durian* which my grandmother used to make for us. It is made from fresh durian flesh that is cooked with coconut milk and sugar until it reaches a dough-like state. It took a lot of time to cook but my grandmother never found an excuse not to make it every durian season. She would buy a trishaw[1] -load of durians that would be delivered to her house. The image of a trishaw fully-laden with durians at the kitchen door is still very clear in my mind. For days, the smell of durian would linger around the house as we ate them with bread, rice or simply on their own. My grandmother would select a number of the fruits to make the *lempuk* which she cooked in a huge wok in the backyard. It took her hours to cook the *lempuk* which had to be continuously stirred over a very hot clay stove. The *lempuk* tasted almost like toffee but with a rich coconut and durian flavour, and it was absolutely delicious.

Within my immediate family, as the youngest at the time, I was doted over but what I also remember very clearly is the way we did everything together. Because there were so many of us in the family, from the time I could remember my siblings and I shared food, living and sleeping space and clothes. With ten children to feed at the time, my grandmother and mother would cook every single day. Breakfast was usually bread, toasted with butter and sugar, or just dipped in fish curry (usually from the previous day). And there was always a huge pot of milk tea to go with the food. Some days, when my mother had extra cash, she would buy *apom lemak* (a kind of pancake) made from flour and coconut milk, from an Indian Muslim family who lived in a house across from the mosque in our village. Lunch was usually rice with a vegetable dish and fish curry. Once or twice a month, we would have meat or chicken. Late afternoon was tea time, usually with a simple sweet or savoury snack that my mother or grandmother would prepare from ingredients available around the kampung like bananas from the *kebun* to make *goreng pisang* (banana fritters), fresh coconut to make *roti nyiok* (coconut pancakes) and tapioca to make *ubi rebus* (boiled tapioca with sweet grated coconut). Dinner was usually re-heated food from lunch and we generally sat around for dinner quite late in those days, usually till around 8.30 pm.

Whatever meal my grandmother and mother prepared for us, we had to share. This was the same with the sleeping arrangement. The girls slept in one room and the boys shared another room and as far I can remember, we all had our own *tilam kekabu* (mattress made from *kekabu* a fibre from the pods of the kapok tree). These mattresses (and pillows) were made at home by my grandmother. Every night before bedtime, the mattresses would be laid out and the next morning, each one would be folded and stacked away neatly. And of course where clothes were concerned, hand-me-downs were not unusual in my family. We could only afford new clothes once a year for *Aidifitri* (the Eid celebration to mark the end of the Muslim fasting month of Ramadan) commonly known as *Hari Raya Puasa* (this literally means 'Big Day') in Malaysia.

During the month of Ramadan, the adults and teenagers have to fast from dawn till dusk. This duration, marked by the *azan* (call for prayers) just before the first light of dawn known as *Subuh* and another call for prayers at the beginning of dusk known as *Maghrib*, was both a strange and exciting time for me as a young child. It was odd for me then because I knew that the adults would get up in the early hours of the morning to have a meal and did not eat or drink the whole day. The exciting part was the hustle and bustle that went on in my grandmother's kitchen from late afternoon until it was time for those who were fasting to break their fast. There was always a lot of food on the table whenever we were all gathered for breaking fast. One dish that I remember vividly is the *bubur* (also commonly known as *bubur lambok*) a delicious spicy rice porridge, cooked at the village mosque and distributed to the villagers in the late afternoon (in many mosques the *bubur lambuk* is made every day throughout the month of Ramadan and packets of the porridge are distributed to those who come to collect them).

Of course the build-up to *Hari Raya*, usually the last three days of Ramadan, was even more exciting. The memories that I have of this particular time at my grandmother's house are not just images but also the aromas of *Hari Raya* staples in our family like the *Hari Raya* biscuits and cakes, the *nasi impit*, *kuah kacang*, *nasi tomato*, *ayam ros* and *bahulu* and the sounds of fire crackers, music and people. As with all religious celebrations, preparing for *Hari Raya* involved not just cooking large amounts of food, but also making sure everyone had new clothes and shoes to wear, spring cleaning the house and areas surrounding it, and decorating the interiors. *Hari Raya* itself was always the best day of all for me as a little girl. All of us queuing up to *salam* (salutations) and to ask forgiveness from our parents and grandmother is one of the most heart-warming memories I have of *Hari Raya* mornings, after the menfolk return from the mosque. My mother would cry, kiss each one of us and tell us that we were the best children - and this emotionally-charged event happened on every *Hari Raya* morning without fail!

Hari Raya was the best time for children, not just because of the new clothes and shoes, playing all day, enjoying good food, but also because of the *duit raya* (raya money). It is a tradition among the Malays for the adults to give money to children on *Hari Raya*, and this is not limited to one's family members. Living in a kampung means that once you are done enjoying your time at home, you get to go to the neighbours' houses to visit them and wish them '*Selamat Hari Raya*' (Happy Hari Raya). For children, this means collecting more *duit raya*. And one of the most exciting times of the day for me was when I sat around with my sisters and brothers counting and comparing how much *duit raya* each collected.

As a child growing up in a big family with so many older sisters and brothers, I did not really have to look for friends. Although we had neighbours, my siblings and my cousins were my playmates. And because we were not well-off, the games we played were usually those that involved simple things that were found around us. One fun game was being dragged around on the ground while sitting on a dried coconut tree leaf. We also played a lot of hopscotch on the ground around my grandmother's house and *batu tujuh* (seven stones which involves throwing and catching seven small stones with one hand). During the *durian* season, we played with durian seeds by stringing rubber band through and spinning the seeds. There were also some games that were seasonal like playing marbles, spinning tops and tossing rubber bands. I also remember going to the field in front of the mosque where my brothers and their friends played football in the evenings. During the windy season, my brothers and other children would play with their kites on the field. Even now, I still remember watching different coloured kites flying in the sky while I stood on the field with my sisters.

During the rainy season, the river behind my grandmother's house usually flooded and memories of waking up in the morning and seeing water surrounding my grandmother's house are very clear in my mind. If the flood water near my grandmother's house was not too deep, my brothers would jump in and play. But there were times when the water came up close to the floorboards of my grandmother's house. That was always a scary time for me, not just because it meant that water had risen to a dangerous level for me especially but also because snakes and frogs might find their way into the house. Thankfully, as far as I can remember, that did not happen and I was always glad when the waters subsided. Of course this means that the kampung was muddy for some time before the ground dried up completely and the river returned to its normal level.

During the normal season, I remember the river to be very calm and beautiful. The river water, when it was not flooding, was clear and not too deep. My brothers would sometimes bathe in the river but I never ventured to join them. As a little child, I used to stand by the river bank and looked at little fishes swimming at the side. The river also reminds me of the times when I would get to the edge of the bank to pick up fruits that fell from a tall tree with deep purple fruits called *keriang acheh*. The tree that I remember grew very near the bank of the river. Although other fruit trees grew along the bank, I remember the *keriang acheh* tree because of its fruit that I liked very much. I am not sure what it is called in English but the fruit was about the size of a large olive and was sweet when ripe. I remember picking them up (especially the very dark purple ones) from the ground and eating them, and getting all excited when my tongue turned purple from the fruit.

Because I was very little, my adventures in the *kampung* were limited to exploring the areas around my grandmother's house and playing near the house. And this was usually for much of the day except when it was raining, meal time, naptime, and after dark. However, the dynamics of being indoors changed a little when the first television arrived at our *kampung*. It was quite an event when one of the neighbours bought a television set and for some time, people just flocked to their house to watch television. Soon after that many other households began to either buy or rent one. I think the first television set we had was rented and this was in 1966/67. In those days, the television programmes started at 5pm and there were not too many shows to choose from. However, the television changed the way we spent our evenings. Friday nights were usually eventful because that was when Television Malaysia, the national broadcasting board screened a Malay film on Channel 1. The shows were in black and white but they were something that we all looked forward to every week. As the Malay film slot was at 9pm, Friday night was an after-dinner family movie night for us.

LIFE IN IPOH

When I was about five and half years old, my family moved to Ipoh, in the state of Perak, to be with my eldest brother who had got a job there. We lived there for almost eight years before returning to Penang in 1976. I consider the time in Ipoh as the second phase of my childhood with a different set of experiences mainly because of the place and being a school-going child. The rented house that we moved to was in the suburbs of Ipoh in a housing area known as Lim Gardens. It was a semi-detached single story house which was in a row of similar houses on Winter Road. It was our first *rumah batu* (brick house). And by contrast to Penang where we had extended family and Malay families as neighbours mostly, in Lim Garden our neighbours were mostly

Indian families. There were only a couple of Malay families who lived on our street and one family whose house was behind ours. Our immediate neighbour with whom my parents struck a long-lasting friendship was a Ceylonese couple, Mr and Mrs Silva. There was a sundry shop across from our house which was very convenient.

One of the first memories I have of Ipoh is the arrival of my little sister, a few months after we settled there. She was the first in the family to be born outside Penang and the only one in the family to be delivered in a hospital. With her arrival, I lost my status as the baby of the family, became a big sister and soon after that began my first year of school. Hence the beginning of what I consider the second phase of my childhood.

I went to Tarcisian Convent primary school, which is an all-girls school. Convent schools in Malaysia began as missionary schools until they were absorbed into the Malaysian public school system. By the time I went to school, most of the convent schools had become national schools. So unlike traditional convents, the teachers were not nuns. Nonetheless, the school exercised the strict regulations that convent schools have always been known for.

Because I never went to kindergarten, going to school was an alien experience for me and one that was daunting. So my memory of my first day at school is of my mother waiting outside the classroom until the end of the school day. And if I recollect, my mother did the same for the next two days. After that, I was brave enough to walk to school with my elder sister who was attending the same school. And just to make sure I did not run home from school, my mother had one of my brothers check on me during recess (break time). This went on for a few days until my mother felt that I was independent enough to be on my own.

I completed my six years of primary education at Tarcisian Convent and during that time I struck friendships with a few girls who were in my class, so it was at school that I really began to have friends who were not family members. We used to play before school started, would eat together at recess and sometimes played after school. Like my elder sister, I walked to school and back, rain or shine. The school was 700 metres from the house and for a child who was quite little in stature, 1400 meters in one day was quite a distance. Despite this, I enjoyed school, both curricular and extra-curricular. I had the responsibility of being the assistant monitor of my class in Primary 2 or Standard 2 as they call it in Malaysia, the opportunity to be part of the netball team for the school when I was in Standard 5 and my art teacher's favourite for being quite a good artist in Standard 6. One random memory that I have of primary school was the Milo[2] van. Once every few months, the Milo van would come to the school to serve the school children ice-cold Milo: so delicious.

The way we lived as a family did not change much in Ipoh. We still shared a lot of things together and still did many things together. However, there were some experiences, both happy and sad which stood out for me. One happy memory that is still vivid in my mind is the times when my eldest brother, who was already working, would take us out once a month for dinner and a movie in town. Because we did not have a car, he would take all of us on the bus to Ipoh town centre for *satay* and ice *kacang*. Usually, after that we would all go to the nearby Grand Cinema for a movie. Another memory of our life in Ipoh was our pet cat. He was our first pet cat, and not to be unoriginal, we called him *Pussycat*. All of us loved him very much but he seemed to love my eldest brother the most. As if he knew time, he would wait around for my eldest brother to come home from work. When my brother was at work or away, *Pussycat* would sniff at his singlet which usually hung on one end of his bed. Sadly, *Pussycat* got very sick one day. The vet said that he had been suffering from some incurable disease and to spare him further pain, he was put to sleep. When my brother came back from the vet without him and told us what had happened, we all cried uncontrollably. I was indeed really sad.

Hari Raya in Ipoh was just as festive as in Penang but different in some ways. We did not have extended family or neighbours to visit. Instead, every *Hari Raya*, we would have neighbours and friends visit us. We reciprocated this gesture when they celebrated their religious festivities like Christmas and Deepavali. Our immediate neighbour, Uncle Silva and Aunty Mary and their daughters particularly, who celebrated Christmas, would invite us to their house on Christmas Eve for a big dinner. Being in Ipoh and in the suburbs gave us the opportunity to begin experiencing the multicultural life that Malaysia is known for.

Another major memory of my childhood in Ipoh is the first wedding in our family. The eldest girl (who is fourth in the family) was the first to get married. It was the first wedding in the family and it was a new experience for us. The sights and sounds of the wedding which culminated in a huge dinner reception at our house were tremendous. The house was full of extended family members who came from Penang, days before the big day. I remember my poor sister who was not well at the time having to sit through various ceremonies, like the *berinai* (henna) the night before the wedding, the *akad nikah* (the marriage ceremony), the *bersanding* (sitting-in-state by the bridal couple), and the reception. The following week, there was another reception by the groom's family. There were so many memories of my sister's wedding but one that really sticks in my mind is dancing to the music on the table with my little sister after the reception was over and just enjoying the night.

CLOSING REMARKS

My childhood adventures began in Penang and ended in Ipoh. There are so many other memories of my life in Penang like the time I had the chickenpox and my sister falling from the front steps of my grandmother's house and breaking her arm, going to a funfair on a field just outside our village, walking to the market with my mother, visiting her friends, going on the bus to town with my parents and many others. It is the same with my memories of living in Ipoh. There are memories of going shopping for *Hari Raya* clothes with my parents, feeling terrified whenever the van from the dental hospital came to school (in case they called my name), the excitement of travelling back to Penang on the train during school holidays, the joy of the first day of long school breaks, the fun of reading comics and Enid Blyton novels, the boredom of sitting around the dining table with my sisters and brothers to study and do our homework every weeknight, the worry of showing my report card to my parents and many more.

We lived in Ipoh until I was about thirteen and half years old, after which we returned to Penang. As with my childhood, my teenage life was also one that was very much influenced and shaped by the relationship I had with my parents, six brothers and four sisters.

NOTES

1. A trishaw evolved from the jinrikisha that has three wheels whereby a rider cycles with two adult passengers comfortably sitting on the front carriage.
2. Milo is a cocoa based beverage that was and still is popular with both adults and children.

Where It Began

Kenelm Robert

On 5 April 1952, Brigadier Sir Robert Arundell, the Governor of Grenada in the British Windward Islands, was resplendent in his white plumes and feathers and being driven through the capital, St Georges, to an official engagement.

He was happy to have his headquarters in Grenada, a British colony in the Southern Caribbean where a population of some 100,000 enjoyed 132 square miles of lush vegetation and pristine white beaches.

His driver, Davis Robert, a 24-year-old policeman, had mentioned earlier that his wife was within two weeks of giving birth and that they were undecided on a suitable name for their first child.

"Ah, Robert", boomed the Governor when they reached their destination, "I have something for you that should help you and your wife choose a name" He passed a slim book of English common names and their meanings to the young officer.

Poring over the myriad of choices later that evening, Davis and Maude settled on "Kenelm", as they thought it both unusual and distinctive. They discovered that Kenelm was the English King of Mercia in 819 who, at the age of seven, met a painful and untimely death at the hands of his sister's lover. St Kenelm was later beatified and canonised by the Pope after the Archbishop of Canterbury conducted an investigation into his murder.

Thus, it came to pass that on 10 April, in the family house at Happy Hill, a small village just three miles from the capital, I was delivered by the midwife, Miss Elsa, and christened Kenelm, Joseph, Humphrey Robert. My grandparents, aunts and uncles visited in turn during the following days.

The first weeks were uneventful. Trinidad-trained Miss Elsa attended to all the needs of the children and infants in the village because the only hospital on the island was restricted to the most urgent cases of life and death. Only the most difficult births were transferred to the hospital, with the Head Teacher of the local school, Percy Hood, providing transport as he was the one person with a car.

Elsa was a superb midwife; despite the limited facilities for home births, the vast majority of her charges were delivered without undue alarm. One of the few complications she could recall was some six years earlier when attending the birth of the first child of Mr and Mrs Mitchell. Her invaluable expertise and knowledge ultimately ensured the safe delivery of Keith Claudius Mitchell, the current Prime Minister of Grenada, the island having gained independence from the United Kingdom in February 1979.

AUNTIES AND UNCLES

As the first child from my mother's side of the family I was a prized exhibit for my doting aunts and uncle. The extended family and friends were always available and afforded my mother unlimited assistance and encouragement, especially after giving birth to three children in as many years.

Aunt Audrey, already demonstrating the determination and drive that spurred her future career as an eminent and celebrated doctor in Washington, USA, was among the first women in Grenada to learn to drive. She often took me to town in her Triumph Herald to see films at the island's only cinema.

My other aunt, Theresa, whom I called Tante Nicks, began instructing me in the basics of the alphabet and, pleased with my progress, spent much of her free time teaching me reading and writing, for which I will be forever grateful.

Uncle Paul, twelve years older than me, was thrilled to welcome his first nephew and as soon as I was able took me to the beach, on fishing trips and to watch him play football at his school in the capital.

DAILY ROUTINE

Life in Happy Hill was unremarkable for the 600 residents who lived in the village. Most adults worked on their own land, growing bananas, corn and various fruits which were sold to passers-by on the main road or at the Friday and Saturday market in town. There was little or no poverty. Though many people were cash poor, the verdant vegetation and equable climate ensured ample growth of crops and a daily catch of fish from the Caribbean Sea. This was supplemented with meat from the goats, cows and sheep often found tethered by the side of the road.

My father was one of a number of professionals who worked for the Government in St Georges. The daily commute meant taking the frequent mini bus that operated along the 18 miles of undulating coast road from Sauteurs on the west of the island.

As a policeman working a shift rota, Dad was often away for days at a time. Despite these enforced absences I was quickly joined by two siblings, Reginald, in November 1953 and Junior, in June 1955.

Even in the mid-1950s Grenada enjoyed the highest literacy rate in the Caribbean with over 95% of children attending primary school at five and secondary school between eleven and fifteen. Education was based on the colonial English model, with frequent tests and exams to pass before reaching the next level.

I started my schooling as a three-year-old in May 1955, two years earlier than usual. Teacher Percy, who lived in a big house 100 yards away, suggested that my aptitude for reading would be enhanced if I sat with a teacher and listened to the class. Armed with a pencil and a colouring book and an eagerness to learn I joined the daily throng of children making their way to school about 800 yards away just after the Easter Term.

The facilities at Happy Hill Primary School were basic. Students had to provide most of their own materials including pens, pencils and exercise books. Although text books were available they were often shared between two or three pupils. Personally-owned publications were highly prized and rarely exchanged.

Corporal punishment was common and frequent; a leather strap was administered for misdemeanors such as lateness, forgetting homework or a simple inability to learn or grasp a task. A much-used saying, "a good lickin' makes you learn", was a popular proverb with parents and children. Teachers enthusiastically adopted it as the best method to guarantee control.

Sport and other recreation were encouraged, with regular cricket, football and athletics matches played on the nearby grazing pasture that doubled as a sports field. Cricket was the most favoured activity as the West Indies team had emerged as national heroes after their triumphant tour of England in 1950.

Attempting to emulate their success most of the young boys, supervised by their sports teacher, practised batting and bowling for many hours after school. The equipment was rudimentary; the only two bats were held in the Headmaster's office and only used against other schools. The palm fronds of coconut trees were passable substitutes and a forward defensive stroke was perfected because any deviation from a straight bat sent the ball flying to a fielder.

However, there was no shortage of cricket balls especially when oranges and plums were in season. By collecting as much of the fruit as possible a bowler could deliver many lethal balls to the other end knowing that a full-bloodied blow would often result in an explosion of orange or red. One memorable year the Headmaster obtained 30 tennis balls and distributed them sparingly over three terms.

Health and safety were of little consequence but as the school was perched on a hill with a sheer 200 yard drop to the sea, the instruction that it was dangerous to play near the cliff-edge was disregarded at your own peril. If a ball was dispatched beyond the boundary it was only retrieved if a fisherman below was passing the area

My six years at Happy Hill School were memorable and demanding. I pursued my interest in reading through some of the treasures from the school library. With no television and limited access to radio, my imagination was fired by the adventures of Enid Blyton's Famous Five, the Biggles books and Tim All Alone written and illustrated by Edward Ardizzone. These books were often sent directly from England, or given to children when a British warship dropped anchor for a diplomatic visit to the islands.

1955 HURRICANE

The annual Caribbean hurricane season began early in 1955, with a severe tropical storm in late July off the southern coast of Aruba, an island in the Dutch Antilles some 560 miles from Grenada. The weather warnings broadcast on local radio in mid to late September were heeded by the authorities, who assured the population that, while the imminent storm was predicted to be severe, it was unlikely to be life threatening so special precautions were unnecessary.

Disregarding this advice, the residents of Happy Hill and scores of other villages on the island stocked up on supplies. The more sensible headed for the churches, schools and other brick buildings while many others decided to remain in their flimsy, wooden shacks, putting their trust and safety in God and a favourable wind.

Hurricane Janet, the fifth major storm of the season, reached Grenada on 22 September with alarming intensity. It was the ninth strongest tropical cyclone ever recorded in the Caribbean at the time and winds of 175 mph tore through the whole of the island. Over 95% of buildings were destroyed and perilous flooding followed as rivers burst their banks, bridges were washed away and roads made impassable and unsafe. St Georges was the worst affected. The French-built town was devastated and, of the two main places of worship, the Catholic cathedral survived with a quarter of the roof intact whilst the Anglian church was totally demolished. It was proof, said the Bishop, that God was undoubtedly a Catholic.

Distressed and desperate, Mum, we children and the baby sought refuge under the family home, sharing the cellar space with five goats, a dog and some 20 other friends who gathered to shelter from the storm.

Dad, now a detective in the Royal Grenadian Police Force, was only four miles away riding out the storm in the safety of the police station with all his equally anxious colleagues, but, with all the telephone lines destroyed, contact had been lost with all their families throughout the island.

As the hurricane passed through the Caribbean, more than 500 people lost their lives before it reached Mexico where it declined and expired on 30th September. We were lucky; many of the badly-built houses were simply lifted from their foundations and were taken by the excessive winds to the treetops or even 300 yards out to sea. One unfortunate resident, fleeing from his home, was decapitated by corrugated iron sheets borne by the wind. Happy Hill residents suffered many injuries but luckily only a handful of fatalities.

When Grenada began to count the cost of the disaster all police leave was cancelled. Dad joined his fellow officers and a force of 500 soldiers in St Georges to support the authorities providing emergency assistance. Although they could survey the devastation from the Police Headquarters perched high above the harbour, the help they could offer was slow and laborious. All around were fallen trees and crumbling masonry and progress was slow and dangerous. The usually calm and tranquil Caribbean Sea had encroached over 100 yards inland and most of the city's streets were flooded and filled with debris.

However, as the day after the storm dawned bright, sunny and benign, thought could be given to those who needed to contact their families. The journey back home would not be easy. Blocked roads and pathways rendered most forms of motorised transport useless but, as the sea was calm and blue, coastal villages were best approached by sea.

Unfortunately the majority of small boats were either destroyed or lost their moorings and were floating in the harbours or roosted atop buildings or telephone pylons. There was no other choice but to slog north on foot and, armed with axes, cutlasses and anything else that could cut wood, to carve a way through to the furthest parts of the island.

They met many others similarly engaged and information and advice was shared along the journey. The three miles home, usually a 15-minute ride in the governor's car, took Dad five hours to complete because of the obstacles along the way.

Dead goats, sheep and cows littered the road and mango, coconut and banana trees blocked the way. With little help available, his sense of foreboding increased with every step. When he finally arrived in Happy Hill not a single house remained standing although he could see the carpenters already embarking on some immediate and basic repairs. Finally, a relative assured him that his family had survived but that he should be prepared for some disappointment.

Approaching his house he noticed the mango tree close by was still standing and had not destroyed the building. An even happier sight was the emer-
gence of his wife and three children from their makeshift and subterranean
shelter. His relief was palpable and only matched by Mum's joy at finding
her husband, from whom she had not any contact in two days, alive and well
and appearing miraculously from the ruins of a once familiar landscape. Only
then was she able to take some comfort after experiencing the worst storm in
living memory.

In the months and years that followed a major rebuilding programme was
agreed upon. Monetary and building aid was offered by Great Britain, Cana-
da and the USA, with Grenada becoming one of the first recipients of financial assistance from the decade-old International Monetary Fund.

Many houses were rebuilt with stronger and deeper foundations and, for
the first time, an increased amount of tiled roofing was used in the construction of official buildings. The destroyed and damaged churches were soon
rebuilt and many worshippers donated time, money and physical effort to
ensure they were amongst the first communal centres to reopen after the
hurricane.

Over the next six years 15 new schools opened and substantial repairs and
enhancements were made to damaged buildings. Two new markets, selling
fish and vegetables, were erected and from the destroyed bus station a modern transport hub, with improved facilities including main link roads to the
north of the island

Hurricanes in the Southern Caribbean follow a 50-year cycle and storms
can now be anticipated and emergency measures prepared. In September
2004, almost 49 years later, Hurricane Ivan struck with an equally terrifying
force. The 125 mph wind and accompanying rain was blamed for 15 fatalities
and 90% of homes in Grenada were destroyed. Dr Keith Mitchell, the Prime
Minister, suffered a double mishap. His official residence was flattened and,
with the Parliament building was completely destroyed, government business
was conducted from a Royal Navy vessel moored in the harbour. Lessons
were learnt from the past and with help and assistance from various international agencies the vast majority of residences, hotels and buildings were
repaired within a year, thus saving the all important tourist industry.

LEAVING FOR ENGLAND

A perilous economic situation existed throughout the Caribbean in early
1950s and Grenada was no exception. Since the late 1940s the United Kingdom had sought assistance from its dependencies and colonies throughout the
world to help rebuild the country after the ravages of the Second World War.
Answering the call, the Empire Windrush had sailed from Jamaica as early as

1948 with 493 West Indians and 60 displaced Polish women and in the following years a steady and increasing flow of young people joined the exodus from the region. Although the first workers from Grenada left as early as 1953, Mum and Dad waited until my youngest brother, Fitzroy, was born in December 1957 before they made enquiries in search of their fortune and a better life for their family in what was then the Mother Country.

It was soon clear that, despite financial assistance from other family members, they would be unable to take us children on the journey. They left in May 1960 and we four boys remained in the care of our Aunt Beatrice until our parents had saved enough money to pay for us to follow.

A long and traumatic 11 months passed. Mum was distraught leaving us behind, in particular Fitzroy, who was just two years old. Letters, parcels and money were sent and exchanged among the family because both parents had found suitable employment in London. Dad became a bus conductor in Ladbroke Grove and Mum as a cleaner in St Mary's Hospital in Paddington.

As they were living in a small room in Maida Vale, with a bathroom shared by four families more suitable accommodation was sought so that we could join them within the next 18 months.

Back in Grenada, Beatrice and her daughter Cildred looked after our welfare, following our parents instructions. Full time school or nursery was the order of the day, with religious instruction supplemented by attendance at Sunday school after morning mass.

Everyone eagerly awaited the monthly parcels from England of clothes, exotic foodstuff and shoes. When the delivery van was spotted at the top of the hill a race to the village Post Office followed, to see what surprises it contained.

In January 1961, just eight months after their departure, my parents had saved enough money for our fares so we could to join them. Cildred was chosen to accompany us because Dad had secured employment for her as a bus conductor with London Transport.

The process of preparing for departure to a new and strange country began. The necessary formalities, including obtaining passports, tickets and other travel documents were completed and lengthy goodbyes were said to aunts and uncles, some of whom we would never see again. All our clothes, toys and possessions that were no longer required were given to our friends and classmates. Keith Mitchell was well served. Although older than me he was of similar stature and he benefited from the shorts, shirts and shoes that I did not take on the journey.

On 12 April 1961, two days after my 9th birthday, we joined hundreds of others at the St Georges quayside to board the RMS Arcadia for the eight day voyage to Southampton. Berths in steerage within the bowels of the ship made for a long and uncomfortable week. Seasickness was experienced by the majority of passengers, many of whom had never sailed before.

Fortunately, a kindly Italian steward took pity on the lady travelling with four young children and supplied us with extra goodies from the main dining table. From him I tasted my first European apple, the fruit being unknown in Grenada, cheddar cheese and, best of all, strawberries and cream.

Our arrival at Southampton on a cold and foggy morning was marked by a sense of wonder and excitement but we were taken aback when tasting the air of our first sharp English spring and the steam exhaled when breathing was disconcerting.

Seeing our Mum and Dad for the first time in nearly a year was the best thrill of all. Two-year-old Fitzroy had forgotten who they were and was perplexed to receive hugs and kisses from two strangers. We older children were not so inhibited and regaled our parents with information about life in Grenada and our adventures on the ship. Then we headed for the train, sitting in amazement as, in a smoke-filled carriage, we watched a very different landscape slip by on our way to London, a city which we found was just a little bigger than St Georges.

From Waterloo Station Dad hailed a taxi that took us to 236 Ladbroke Grove, where he had persuaded the landlord to rent him the use of two rooms on the top floor, where we shared the second floor bathroom with three other families.

We did not begin school immediately after our arrival in London, a week after Easter, because Dad had arranged our admittance to Middle Row Junior School for the start of the summer term. Consequently, we were forced to hide behind closed curtains during the day, in case a zealous neighbour reported Mum and Dad to the local Education Authority. We passed the time choosing our new school uniform and visiting the library during the evenings and on Saturdays to familiarise ourselves with the sights and sounds of our new environment.

When our first day at school finally arrived my initial confidence and self-assurance were severely dented as I was introduced to my new class-mates. My soft Grenadian accent was not easily understood by everyone. However, my teacher, Ms Olivier, had taught in Rhodesia and Nyasaland, was quick to come to my aid and helped make my first term both exciting and enjoyable.

Life in North Kensington quickly surpassed all I had read from books and watching the Pathe News in the cinema back in St Georges. The Robert family were united once more and, with Mum and Dad in full employment, we began the process of integrating ourselves in the church, school and local activities.

A Reconquest of Memories

Georg Schmid

What most readily comes to mind is drabness and a sensation of dysfunctionalities. Of restrictedness and extreme humbleness, of the limits caused by discomfiture and the lack of basic things. But the seeming pureness of what may, now and then, seemingly out of nowhere, flash up for a short instance, is all too easily getting distorted by secondary rationalizations: once you engage in trying to remember, your mind starts to perform all kinds of tricks on you: it acts as a censor of what we consider to be our consciousness. Do you really remember first impressions at all or do you always, inevitably, remember memories, resulting in a cascade of memories of memories? This is a "theoretical" question (albeit an unanswerable one). But it is also quite simply a matter of personal experience: you cannot say with any certainty whether you remember this or that occurrence or impression or experience or whether you think back to previous instances of remembering. There is a lot of equivocalness.

Let's say, I remember my way to school. Just one block, along a main thoroughfare. This banality appears in a far from precise fashion in my mind; it is fragmentary and I have no way of knowing what parts have later been added by simply passing along the same street. I do seem to remember, however, that, after school sports, I regularly, much to my chagrin, had difficulties in tying my shoelaces. This stands out because of the embarrassing character of the experience. Also, I was very bad at school sports, another sore point, which did not exactly contribute to my popularity (and I never developed any liking for spectator sports either). I am not sure whether pleasant memories are of a comparable intensity.

Childhood, for me, took place in the immediate post-war period in *Mitteleuropa*, and, to say the least, that was no picnic. The privateness of memories appears to be co-determined by a general atmosphere of bleakness. Everyone seems to believe that childhood must be something not just precious but full of beauty, wonder, exciting discoveries and the expectancy of a future destined to become ever more marvellous (or, on the contrary, just utter despair of Dickensian dimensions). Both assumptions are platitudes, glossing over either shortcomings, failures, culpability or improvement and hope. And let's face it: childhood can also be boring.

The destruction caused by the war was, of course, significant enough in Vienna – although less so than in most German cities such as, say, Cologne. A lot of people were bombed out (*ausgebombt*), as were my parents. Air-raid damage was to be seen everywhere, and for quite some time to come. My father had lost a spacious *Gründerzeit* flat; until 1952 we lived in a cramped two room *Bassenawohnung* on the top floor of a decrepit tenement house (*Bassena*, referring to the waterline, just one per floor, meant that more than a dozen tenants had to share the water, cold, of course; there were no water closets, just latrines, and of course there was no toilet paper, you used old newspapers).

From this working class district we moved – I was an only child – to the periphery of the city. The new urban settlement there consisted of a large cluster of houses, each of which in turn being made up of four apartments on two floors each. There was a loo, there was a bathroom with warm water, there was sufficient space. The development was planned and built along the lines of Scandinavian thinking; it was aptly called Per Albin Hansson Sied-lung (Swedes, Dutch and Swiss had helped Austria along after both acts of the Great War). Getting to this *siedlung* necessitated long trips by tram. Route 67 took a long time to get to the outskirts, then you had to change to a feeder route, the 167. My father, an engineer (heavy industrial equipment), got a car very soon, it was the first in the shabby street in the 1900s district, then in the *siedlung*. Especially for his needs a telephone line, several hun-dred metres long, had to be installed: I imagine that caused quite some envy with the neighbours. Our new place was many steps up, but it was located in an underdeveloped area and, what was more, in the "Russian zone."

Austria, just like Germany, was occupied by the victorious powers, and Vienna, just like Berlin, was partitioned into four zones. It was considered to be preferable to live in a "Western" zone. The partition of Germany lasted much longer than Austria's; in 1955 a so-called state treaty (in fact a *Frie-densvertrag* which is still lacking for Germany where a simple accord among the great powers sufficed for reunification) was negotiated. Under certain restrictions, not least the promise of "eternal neutrality", that treaty re-estab-lished Austrian independence (of sorts: even as late as 1995 Vienna had to beg Moscow to allow Austria's accession to the European Union, and there were misgivings in Paris and even in London, too).

At the back of our house there were gardens (or, rather, at first just patches of rocks, sand, weeds) and beyond the fence Soviet soldiers would regularly patrol for reasons difficult to imagine. In a general way, Vienna was not systematically patrolled, with the exception of the first (central) district where *Die Vier im Jeep* (the famous Willys jeeps!) were to be seen constantly: Americans, British, Soviets and French. The Schönbrunn gardens, by contrast, were a favourite haunt of the Americans who leisurely promenaded their Chevrolets there. There seemed to be military vehicles everywhere: the three-axle GMCs or the Dodges were a familiar sight, even long after the occupying forces had gone, leaving the lorries behind which continued to be used years later despite their gas-guzzling engines. I remember that even the postal bus service adapted some of the smaller GMCs to compensate for the penury of serviceable buses (as in Switzerland, the *Post-auto* was omnipresent in Austria and still is, despite now being a subsidiary of the Federal Railways).

One of the most prominent recollections concerns the difficulties of getting from one place to another. There was a general lack of means of transport, and that made itself felt in quite unpleasant ways. When I mention dysfunctionalities I mainly refer to that; one could also say non-functionality. The supply of electric power was often insufficient; in fact, power failures were frequent until around 1950. Regional traffic often meant using old lorries with park benches mounted on their loading space. And the trams, predominantly very old cars (most of which had been built during the imperial period before 1914), dilapidated because of neglect during the war years, were overflowing with people, often riding on the running boards or even the couplers.

Train services were hardly better. Railway electrification (then still a privilege of the hydraulic power-rich alpine provinces) had begun early in the interwar years but had not yet reached the capital city of Vienna, where steam engines were used. And of course both locomotives and railway carriages were no less in disrepair than the city trams of Vienna, Graz, Innsbruck, Linz. The trains were always packed; often you could not get a seat even on long distance journeys. I remember (a shade vaguely, I must admit) our first holiday trips made by train, the extreme uncomfortableness, only much later achieved again in the cattle class of modern planes. Incidentally, in rural areas hotels and guest-houses sometimes still sent horse-drawn carriages to pick up the guests at the nearest railway station.

But at least there were holidays again. This is a point where I surely mix up my own observations and what I was told by my parents: born in the later war years, I had no way of knowing what holidays were like before the second act of the Great War but somehow I incorporated their respective "hetero"-memories. That surely is how interpolations get on their way: you observe things, you are told how they once were and how they changed, and you draw conclusions. And that is how memes come about.

Anyway, the fact that vacations became possible again – earlier, I had listened to stories about hoarding trips to the countryside, desperate search parties to get foodstuffs, usually of the most simple sort, perhaps just some lard – was a sign that things might get back to normal again. Indeed my mother often promised me that I'd just have to be patient: soon, chocolate would be on the market again and the bright lights of the grand department stores would signal that they were open for business. In the meantime, however, life remained decidedly dismal; I remember the food rationing cards (in use in Vienna until 1952); even relief meals were wonderful: for children, the British handed out *Semmeln* with whole triangular soft cheese pieces, a delicacy.

There were few joys and pleasures: they counted all the more. I read a lot, just about anything I could lay my hands on (early on I discovered just by myself the great Carl Barks Donald Duck comics, comprising brilliant texts by Erika Fuchs). There were excellent municipal libraries, several in each district. Around 1980 they were all closed down: my mother never forgave the social-democratic municipal administration. And there were cinema and radio. Broadcasts and films, broadcasts of concerts and operas, regularly listened to in my family, everyone glued to the wireless; there were radio plays, so-called *Hörspiele* (Germanophone writers made a rather good living by producing lots of them), plus all kinds of rather low-brow programmes. There were popular emissions of acceptable quality, among them the *Radiofamilie* (self-explanatory) or the *Kriminalrätsel* (roughly, crime enigma, the solution of the mystery was provided one week later; you could win prizes, books of course, by guessing who the murderer was).

And we rather frequently went to a *Konzert* (in the *Musikverein*, for example) or an opera performance (the *Oper* as such, just like the main theatre, the *Burgtheater*, the pride and joy of the Viennese, had been very heavily damaged by bombardments: both were only reopened in 1955; the Vienna Philharmonic Orchestra and the opera ensemble performed on alternate stages, the *Theater an der Wien* for example, later on concentrating on musicals: now it's an opera house again). My passion for music has its origins there. Very early I heard a performance of Beethoven's violin sonatas (in the *Konzerthaus* I seem to remember), and I think it was the Allegro molto of the A minor Op. 23 that really did it: the feeling of some incredibly intense, unfathomable pure joy which you could follow your whole life.

I would, consequently, give a misleading impression were I only to stress the drab sadness of those years. But we did not just do things differently then: there was the objective pressure of circumstances. Some of the things were done better than later; the major inconveniences were the result of material restrictions which only slowly subsided. In cultural and intellectual terms quite a lot was more substantial than in subsequent periods (there was an excellent satirical cabaret scene, in some way the precursor of the stand-up comedians of today). There is one qualification, though: in general, it was a largely conservative cultural landscape.

In a number of Viennese churches Sunday mass came with a musical performance: mostly Haydn and Mozart masses, free entry, quite often members of the State Opera performed. That meant first-class music, provided by first-class musicians; they were, by the way, extremely popular celebrities immediately identified wherever they went (the indicative whispering when they entered a café or a restaurant). I remember clearly that most Sundays my father and I were off to a well-chosen church: the announcements had been studied in the Saturday papers, and we went to a part of the city I was not all that familiar with or didn't know at all. Ceremoniously, I used to tell my mother to prepare a nice lunch, a *Mittagessen*, which (even more than today) was the main meal of the whole week (comparable to the English sunday roast). I was hardly ever disappointed: my mother was a good cook although she worked, too, as a master tailor.

Meals and restaurants were, at least for me, more comprehensible than religious things such as churches and masses. Both my parents were entirely non-religious which in part explains why I completely misunderstood the true purpose of that Sunday exercise. I took it to be just another concert, a matinée, and as my father used to invite me to an early brunch (frankfurters or a small goulash: the Austrian churches were surrounded by pubs) during what I thought was an intermission, I failed to understand that the "entr'acte" in fact was the sermon (perhaps the pubs surrounding the Austrian churches were in fact there for exactly that purpose: they filled up with gentlemen, nearly all of them smoking, while the ladies remained inside the church for the homilies). Yet I by no means dislike churches: on the contrary, I have a particularly soft spot for the Tyrolean ones with their slender spires, often high up on a mountainside. But my interest remained purely aesthetic: the little I know about religion comes from my knowledge of art history. Strangely – one of my more bizarre recollections – on high ecclesiastical festivities such as Corpus Christi the children in our socialist (!) district were made to march along the tram tracks by the school authorities and pray (?) at specially decorated places: I never figured out what that was all about.

Sundays increasingly involved some elaborate planning. In summer, trips to the countryside were de rigueur; that often meant long tram rides beyond the suburbs. Indeed the termini close to the more popular places for excursions were served by something like a dozen tram lines going directly to the different city districts enabling the day trippers to avoid transfers between different routes. The same applied for the immense open air public baths close to the Danube, on the big river's lateral branches, unused except for the purpose of festival enjoyment. And that goes for the enormous main cemetery too, the *Zentralfriedhof*, no doubt one of the biggest of its kind in Europe. (The tram route regularly going there was and is the 71; when someone died in Vienna one used to say, he/she took route 71.) What was going on at that Central Cemetery, mainly on and around All Saints' Day, easily surpassed any kind of public festival, and I think no one was under the impression that it had much to do with religion. The "tram announcer" high up on a traffic tower (informing of departing trams' destinations well in advance) behaved like a humorous master of ceremonies, and the ritual consisted of a well organized ballet of three-car tram trains. Many dozens of such trains were kept in a so-called *Stapel* (endless rows of trams parked on normally unused track, reaching the next small town outside of Vienna) for the evening rush hour when the cemetery would close down.

The simple pleasures of the past. Not all of them were more than just a shade morbid. At any rate, after visiting the graves, one did not necessarily take the tram back home immediately but preferred to repair to one of the pubs and restaurants on the other side of the street. It is justly proverbial to say that eating and drinking play a major role in Vienna. And it did so even during the hard times on which we had been falling. Did I sense, in my early childhood, that things were beginning to slowly improve? If I did at all, it was probably due to a slow amelioration in all things concerning gastronomy. But it must have been a laborious process. In fact, one could say it was a restoration: it was about trying to recoup the traces of happier times and somehow make them work again.

So now I have stealthily arrived at politics. I am certain that, as a child, I early on comprehended quite clearly that something had gone very wrong very recently. It would have been difficult not to suspect something eery: the comments on the difficulties life presented saw to it. In my family and among our friends and acquaintances it was not about war narratives but about something atmospheric: it was constantly, if obliquely, referred to. I do not think that all of Vienna consisted of nothing but a bunch of Nazis, but a stigma hovering there was palpable. The conversational approximations by the adults resulted in the conveyance of an imprecise feeling that something was out of kilter.

I have said that I was an only child – and as I had no childhood friends (a surprising and dismal factor, particularly in hindsight) I was nearly permanently in the presence of adults. So I quietly listened to what the grown-ups had to tell each other and no doubt in the longer run something stuck. There were allusions to what had happened to this or that person, sometimes someone dropped a hint that he or she was connected by marriage to a Jewish person ("*versippt*" was the key word). There was, perhaps, a feeling of injustice: a kind of "cling together, swing together" had led to the bitter fate of being reprehensible but there certainly was also a perceptible feeling of guilt.

At this point I have to emphasize that my narrower family no doubt was a bit of an exception. Both my parents were, I'd say, viscerally anti-Nazi (which, even long after 1945, was by no means self-evident). My mother came from a milieu of pure Socialist creed whereas my father was a conservative, albeit a non-believing one (as a rule, conservatives in Austria were staunchly Catholic). The "Sozi" and the "*Kaisertreuer*" – that made for a nice intra-familial political education. My mother, however, had no sympathy whatsoever for the communists (the commies, in Viennese called the *Kummerln*), my father, in turn, was no royalist: it was just scoffingly said that the conservatives had never shed their devotion to the House of Austria. You have to realize that there were (since before 1914) three political camps: the conservatives (the so-called People's Party, *Christlichsoziale* of old), the Socialist Party (later the Social-Democrats) and the ominously called *Drittes Lager* (which meant the *Deutschnationalen* who later on in their overwhelming majority became Nazis). "National" in Austria meant *deutschnational*. For people used to Anglo-Saxon thinking this must be close to incomprehensible. Whereas in regard to Britain one speaks of one country consisting of four nations, English, Scottish, Welsh and (Northern) Irish, in *Mitteleuropa* it was thought that there was one German nation, split into four states (West Germany, East Germany, Austria and, in a sense, Switzerland, in its large majority Germanophone too).

Can a childhood be influenced by such circumstances? Oh yes. Because there were countless incidents where you were, in a very practical way, confronted with that state of affairs. Just a couple of examples. In school sports – at the age of ten I had entered secondary school – we for a time had a gymnastics teacher who apparently had not got it that the Third Reich was over. We had to stand in rank and file, obey military commands, listen to nice war stories.

On the occasion of one of the teachers/parents meetings my father and some others brought that up and it made for a nice little scandal. On another occasion, at a dinner invitation, the host got himself extremely worked up with the crassest antisemitic comments; all of a sudden, my father jumped up, threw his napkin on the table, and announced: that's just about enough, we'll be going. And we did.

There were lots of other political clues. I've referred to the occupation already. The west and the south of Austria were occupied by western powers, the east by the Soviets. Styria and Carinthia were British, Salzburg and Upper Austria were American, Tyrol and Vorarlberg French (at the very end of the war the French were, as we all know, granted the status of a victorious power which not only handed them over a large chunk of south-western Germany but also the west of Austria where they were still well remembered from the Napoleonic period). That meant that Vienna was surrounded by the "Russian zone" although, as said, Vienna itself was also partitioned into different administrational districts.

We moved again, to a better *Bezirk* (part of a non-Russian sector) where good schools were located. My new one was a so-called *Lateinrealschule* (meaning I had no Greek but Latin, and lots of maths and natural sciences) which would automatically enable me to go directly to the *Technische Universität* which, as my father was an engineer, was sort of expected of me; on the other hand, this choice of school also opened up the way towards the humanities. The move to the new apartment had been possible because of my father's political connections (he knew the then minister of finance and economics, of the People's Party, quite well) – just as the previous abode was a result of my mother's good contacts in Socialist Party circles. That's how you learn about politics. The specifics of how that worked was in Austria referred to as *Proporz* which, roughly, meant that practically all posts were given to partisans (or indeed party members) of the existing political parties, i.e., proportional to the membership and (up to an extent) the voting patterns of the parliamentary elections. This system (largely still in place) meant that the lion's share went to the "reds" and the "blacks," the *Sozi* and the *Volkspartei*, although some posts, not least at the universities, were reserved for the *Deutschnationalen*; bizarrely, even the communists were included in these games of distribution.

Political apprenticeship, then. I think that from an early age you were thus enabled to pick up on lessons life would, maybe much later, have in store for you. Whether you were, so to speak, trained to comprehend that the Austrians were felt to be of lower value than the Germans (the *Reichsdeutschen* as it was expressed during the Nazi period – and long after –); it was, and in part still is, impossible for an Austrian to become a full professor at an Austrian university: Germans are a priori deemed to be better. From a historical point of view – and this is, surprisingly, something I intuited very early – this is part of the ongoing question of "the supremacy of Germany."

I remember well that my father, when asked why our weekend excursions only were in westerly directions, responded, that in the east there is nothing. Which, of course, meant nothing of interest or attractive. We all knew quite well that there was a lot: it was felt to be uncanny, disquieting and, surely, not all that accessible (which many felt was all for the better). Another Austrian, of another generation, Gottfried Heindl, began a book on Vienna by reminiscing about a suburban tramway by which you could go from the city centre directly to Pressburg (or Bratislava, as it is called now, for a time it was also known as Pozsony). After the war the tram was cut off at the frontier with Czechoslovakia; henceforth the line quasi literally went nowhere. The demarcation line between Soviet-occupied eastern Austria and western-controlled regions such as Tyrol or Upper Austria, for instance, always reminded you of, to say the very least, unpleasantness. I may have been, as a child, a particularly oversensitive specimen; I don't hesitate to admit that I pretty regularly soiled myself when we got near that *Zonengrenze*. There was no real reason: nothing untoward ever happened, and I wasn't educated anti-Russian (on the contrary, my father always emphasized that he had a good working relationship with the Soviet authorities). It was an atmospheric matter. Just as something seemed to be lacking (a part of geography, so to speak), some other thing was there all right: the Iron Curtain. The word by itself sounded menacing, and as I was an easily impressible child both term and presumable reality played a disproportional role for me.

Both my parents were, at my birth, relatively old; my father had been born in the 19th century. The constellation only child / rather absent father (he constantly appeared to be supervising the opening of a new steel plant or some such thing) / possessive mother (as they say: "vee analysts like to look to the muzzer") were not exactly favourable starting points.

For me, friendships started very late: only in adolescence when, after having changed classes at the age of fourteen, I was, to my pleasant surprise, finding myself surrounded by equally or at least comparably "misconstrued" fellow students, very much given to intellectual pursuits. Early friendlessness also meant, as I've said, no sports; enthusiasm for sports was and remained incomprehensible. These limitations made me physically quite maladroit (which, of course, I early on tried to compensate by more intellectual techniques, even before I knew what "intellectual" meant). During one of our holidays, I remember vividly, my father did a very nice side vault over a barrier (he must have been around sixty): I tried to copy him, both parents yelling hysterically, don't!, and of course I took a terrible fall – even before having reached the obstacle. Mr. Hardy takes a terrible fall. Some such things happened not infrequently, and my mother took pains to assure me that when I stumbled I always put my arms backwards and fell flat on the face. (Perhaps I tried to save my precious fingers? For the piano? For the typewriter?)

A certain clumsiness (later on to be cleverly hidden behind a fence of attempted elegance) accompanied me my whole life; in practical things I always remained unskilful (with the exception of cooking, a very "girly" thing back then, thankfully not any more); I only prided myself that I was a good driver and could immediately point to some even minor quirk or weakness of a car, nobody believing me at first although, after some checks, my hunches and diagnoses were proven correct. But I couldn't repair anything: I was unable to change spark plugs, and I mastered a spare wheel only together with my father (and since his death long ago never since). This ineptness probably manifests itself best in what I think might well be my earliest memory. I nearly drowned – in a children's pool. It happened in a nice open-air bathing establishment in the Vienna Woods, and I recall that, eyes open, I sort of contemplated the world outside of the water. I do not remember, however, who lifted me out of the water. Still, later on I became a passable swimmer (though big rivers such as the Mississippi or even the Gironde are still frightening, as is the Danube). A contender for "earliest memory" must be even less tenable: born in early 1944 I surely cannot remember the wailing of the air raid sirens? I must have picked that up from radio plays and movies or I "re-employed" what my parents narrated, somewhat along the lines explained by Oliver Sacks (who was certain of a specific recollection which, as it turned out, couldn't be his own after all).

Yet the basic question remains: how can I be sure of this or that, especially in terms of remembering, how can anyone? There simply is no controlling instance. And even thorough thinking about probabilities can help you only so far. In my most recent book (*The Mind Screen*) I present an example: when I saw Hitchcock's depiction of Cary Grant's train ride along the Hudson River in *North by Northwest* I was duly impressed; some years later I also took the 20th Century Limited. And for the hell of it I cannot figure out what my own impressions were and what I adopted and adapted from the movie.

What I remember well are frequent illnesses during childhood. That meant staying in bed and getting a bit spoiled. But I tended to develop fevers, often with extravagantly high temperatures, and some nightmares during delirious phases have haunted me long afterwards. They were of the kind impossible to describe, even to oneself: there are just very vague images, suggestions of unspeakable horrors. Medical treatment was not easy in the immediate postwar period, and it was often unpleasant. (The most amusing episode: I was supposed to drink some awful-tasting medicine and my father, trying to show me that it wasn't so terrible after all, took a demonstrative trial swallow and immediately threw up. He was a red wine aficionado.)

My frequent illnesses also – as my mother kept assuring me – often ruined our holidays. Once (that must have been around 1950, before we had a car) we had to return to Vienna because I had had to go to some isolated provincial town hospital my mother had no confidence in. In order to see to my comfort we travelled first class, usually it was second (there were still three classes then). Only my father, nervous as he was, had thrown out the tickets (cleverly kept in a cigarette pack) by the window. Do I really remember stays in a children's hospital where I certainly was desperate? Or are all the respective impressions also in their entirety based on narrated bits and pieces? What I seem to effectively remember particularly well are the holidays. But such remembrances are by definition a pot-pourri of separate though not really differentiable impressions. In other words, it is a question of an amalgam of individual perception and "social narratives" the component parts of both having long since been completely compounded. There is a transitional zone of collective and individual memories, its interface characterized by a high degree of the interchangeability among the respective experiences. Mountaineering, eating out every evening, picnics, motor car excursions are much the same for everyone.

Automobilists would tell frightening stories about some Alpine pass, and naturally you would compare these to what you yourself had witnessed. My mind's eye provides images of very bad roads, and the Austrian auto touring club each year published special maps on road conditions, some didn't even have blacktop and were in a terrible state. My father always had two spare wheels in his car, and even that didn't always work out satisfactorily: three flats, game over anyway. The steepest street in the world is thought to be Baldwin Street in Dunedin, New Zealand (at 35%); but a well-known mountain road between Styria and Carinthia, the Turracher Höhe, sported a 36% gradient, nearly impossible to conquer as it was just a dirt road. Bus services by the Austrian post (the *Postauto*) used the four-wheel drive version of the renowned Steyr 380. Owners of front-wheel drive cars (DKWs for example) tried to ascend such passes by going in reverse; conventionally built cars, the overwhelming majority, hardly stood a chance.

At any rate, motor cars soon began to play a major role in social life. Close to everyone drove a Volkswagen, there were also lots of Opels (Vauxhall was still something completely different then) and Fords (sold as "Taunus"); the gentleman's ride was a Mercedes. Or was it? Of course you knew that it had been the favourite make of the Fuehrer, so some people, particularly in the more prosperous districts, rather chose Humbers, Rovers, Wolseleys, some connoisseurs tended to Lancias, there were some *tractions* Citroëns, the odd Nash, and I clearly remember two Jowett Javelins, near Schönbrunn palace.

Vacations were, of course, not just about mountain climbing by car; you rather did it on foot. My father was an avid alpinist. He complained, however, that at the refuges you only met Nazis. The generalization was hyperbole, the substance of the statement was far from incorrect. The Alpine mountaineering clubs had been founded (for the most part jointly) by Austrian and German associations when being *deutschnational* did not yet simply mean to be Nazi. As a historian I can vouch for the fundamental accuracy of my father's assessment (as late as in the mid-sixties university graduates who were members of the socialist (the socialist, not the "national-socialist"!) *Akademikerverband* used to greet each other, at least in Salzburg or Upper Austria, by intoning the so-called *Hitlergruss*).

Sometimes I wonder how some such negative experiences influenced our choice of vacation resorts. Early on, we would turn to Italy, surprising in itself as my father had fought on the Austro-Italian front during World War I, in the Dolomites; the truly astounding thing was that he was quite Italophile, and I should add that we by no means only went to South Tyrol (now known as Alto Adige) which had been a part of Austria for centuries and was (and still largely is) Germanophone (Margaret Macmillan referred to the South Tyroleans' unpleasant surprise to suddenly find themselves in Italy, a vexation which turned into embitterment when the country became fascist in 1922), but also to the medium-sized north Italian cities such as Pavia, Piacenza, Parma, Reggio, Modena, Bologna, Faenza, Forlì, Verona, Brescia, Bergamo, the lot. So, there you have it: a bit of *distinction*, in the sense of Bourdieu, because nearly all the other Austrians went to Adriatic seaside resorts which became proverbial (and abhorrescent) exactly for this reason.

In any event, Austria, maybe particularly Vienna, was given to much politicizing – and not exclusively of the unsavory sort. Political debates (not least in the cafés, the *Kaffeehäuser)* between friends and acqaintances were a matter of course. It is not true that there was no intellectual life worth mentioning in Vienna after 1945 (although the Jewish element was sorely missing). Indeed often passionate political debates took place; satirical-political cabaret was extremely popular, to a large extent this rather specific type of cabaret relied on remigrated Jews. Listening – to the cabaret artistes or *Kaffeehaus* conversations, to the adults, then – you could learn a lot.

Yet another point has to be made in regard to the cafés and restaurants. You often ate out, and going to the *Kaffeehaus* was an everyday routine; the plenitude of such premises was amazing, quite a few of them even survive today. In a way they were the backdrop to all this talking; it benefited from the impressive number of newspapers the *Kaffeehäuser* offered to their customers for free. I took that to be standard, "normal" (but it only is in Vienna) – that all the papers were there, from the most radically different political camps, and everybody read the extremely varying, often contradictory editorials, leaders, commentaries. And there were of course the foreign language newspapers as well: in English, Italian, French, a number of other languages, and not just one of each country: even *Pravda* and *Isvestija* could be found. So you realized early on that there were different political opinions and different languages in different countries.

I always liked to dine out (you used to have lunch at the restaurant, too). That was easier back then because of the enormous choice of establishments; you also could choose from a very large number of items on the menu (*Speise(n)karte*); and what one took for granted at that time is simply surprising nowadays. There are things that stick to your memory which originally appeared so natural that only much later they would stick out as extraordinary. Many restaurants, regardless of their reputation and price level, offered three "classes," just like the railway. There were different saloons: first class with white tablecloths, second with red-white checkered ones, third class having wooden tables only. The bizarre thing was that the prices usually were the same everywhere (with the exception that you paid less for your wine or beer when you simply remained standing at the bar). People did not so much choose the class according to their social status but rather according to their prevailing mood, how they happened to be dressed, whether they were alone or in company, etc. In this specific case we observe a class society being, paradoxically expressed, not obsessed with class; things were rather fluid – maybe particularly in the cafés where different social strata mixed quite beautifully.

My personal recollections would suggest that class distinctions and divisions were less easy to stage back then: all those who had no car (or no car yet) had to stand in the same dilapidated tram carriages or even on running boards and had to pay the same price for the ticket. Things were easier differentiated in the cinemas. There never was a uniform price: better seats cost more than those with a disfiguring perspective.

Both the Vienna trams (which always had something iconic, somewhat like the Melbourne ones) and the movie theatres are connected with some of my most pleasant childhood memories. When I was about five, my mother permitted me for the first time to go by tram alone. Right around the corner, there was route J, one of the longest in the system. So one day I boarded a tram and installed myself on the front platform, right behind the motorman. Soon after, it began to rain heavily; I figured the best solution was to stay on, go to the terminus and take the same *Garnitur* back. Naturally, it appeared different to my mother who no doubt already saw me minced to death.

All the same, I was allowed to go to the movie theatre just by myself. That was facilitated by the fact that my paternal grandfather (born in 1874 and retired long ago) had, in order to increase his meagre pension, secured an additional job as an usher in one of the larger cinemas. So I grew up with Laurel and Hardy, Gary Cooper, Bob Hope, Fred Astaire, Humphrey Bogart. I felt as though I became part of that universe, and films in fact remained, *tout court*, one of the mainstays of existence. There was a kind of hereditary factor involved. My mother was a film buff if ever there was one, and customarily we went to the movies more or less every other weekday, plus practically all Saturdays and Sundays.

Almost exclusively we went to see American (or British) movies. It was way below us to watch German ones: perhaps my parents recalled all too readily how many stars had already "served" during the Nazi period in the Ufa-films. This certainly made us stand somewhat apart from the other cinema-goers although I am sure I remember correctly that, among our friends and acquaintances, US-films were considered to be of another class, at least in terms of intrinsic cinematographic qualities; I think they were considered to be more respectable which would disprove what otherwise raised its ugly head time and again: anti-Americanism.

To hold that in check, a number of newspapers had been founded, and of some of them it was openly said that they were CIA papers. Then again, the so-called *Volksstimme* ("The Voice of the People") was financed by the Soviets. Two consequences: even as a child I could quickly learn to compare different opinions and see how arguments were developed; and my family's unambiguous Western orientation contributed decisively to my increasing distance from my contemporaries. Indeed anti-Americanism is easy to remember but it was, in a manner of speaking, unevenly distributed, along the lines of social classification, above all in regard to the respective feelings of

"German-ness." Back then, the liberals were less given to automated anti-Americanism.

German, as "standard language," was taught in school but the very term (which you'd find in any dictionary) is seriously misleading as it was and is a characteristic of German that there is no real standard that is in practice truly observed: that is just a pious fiction. The differences and distinctions are at least as important as in English and its wildly diverging ways of pronouncing, choice of words, melody and intonation, etc. While in school instruction was in *Schriftsprache* (standard language), *Umgangssprache* (informal or colloquial speech), seen by many as to be of inferior value, was current, too. Generally, Austrian German has been rather distinct from German German, but today much of the former is forgotten, even expressions such as *Schönbrunner* or *Prager* or *Laibacher Deutsch* are close to incomprehensible. Anyway, I belong to a generation which learned practically two languages in parallel: "Austrian" and "German." I caught on to the fact that you adapted to any given situation by choosing either one – or indeed any transitional form. Perhaps that made it easier to comprehend the nature of hierarchies: Germany may have lost the war but Austria was even beneath it, be it only because Hitler had been Austrian. Among the first things you were taught was the proper response to that: yes, he was by birth, but he became chancellor and Fuehrer in Germany.

Against all hope I did not become an engineer but a historian, a fact I ascribe to my weakness in mathematics (I still adore engineers which probably not least allows assumptions about my father fixation). But my vocational choice turned out to be a lucky one. It helped me to see things in perspective. At the beginning I mentioned the feeling of drabness and limitations and despondency. (Could it be the reason that Christmas often was such a disappointment? For years I desperately longed for a model railway but never got one.) Although I am sure that, though not really unhappy, I somehow took part in that collective feeling of deprivation, I also realize that this assessment is influenced by my historical knowledge. Dissimilarity between what one feels and what is objectively there is too obvious a thing to merit long-winded comments. Some things are certain, though. The Iron Curtain *was* some forty kilometres east of Vienna, and when my father said that beyond it "there was nothing" he actually meant that there was something there all right. It bottled us in, you could only turn west or, to a degree, southwest (some fifty kilometres to the north there also was the Iron Curtain). And even if you did turn west or south-west, until 1955 there was still the "demarcation line" (*Zonengrenze*) at the river Enns or at the Semmering pass (when you tried to gain Italy).

Vienna was grey and depressing; as a child you hardly knew anything about nature (you might have assumed that the cows on the pasture in the holiday places were there solely for the vacationers' delight and edification);

even the filling stations were of a uniform drab dark blue. Minimal signs were sufficient to express – relatively – more freedom, for instance the colourful "western" filling stations such as Mobil, Esso, BP, Shell, etc., etc. (In the Soviet zone there was just one chain, inelegantly called ÖROP, as indeed the crude oil output in eastern Austria was tightly controlled by the Soviet authorities; Austria, incidentally, had to deliver large quantities of crude and many other products as war indemnities.)

The child's impression that eastern Austria was worse off than the western provinces is born out by facts: only as late as 2013 did Vienna reach the wealth level of the western *Bundesländer* such as Tyrol or Salzburg. How prosperity is felt is not absolutely dependent upon such objective indicators but still it makes you think to what an extent Vienna (and the entire Austrian east, that is to say, apart from Vienna, Lower Austria, the Burgenland and the northern part of Upper Austria, too) were held back.

For a child, all this was puzzling and confusing, despite the explanations or, paradoxically because of them: each and every explained thing has to be incorporated into a general picture, an entirety of secure knowledge enabling you to put it into perspective. Possibly, apart from the drabness, the latent feeling of loss was the most prominent. It was conveyed by countless disjointed narrative bits referring to "Old Austria." Small wonder that after the liberation in 1945 there was a serious barrier to collectively remembering what had happened during the last two or three decades: only catastrophes, terrible losses, awful crimes. These are circumstances enabling politically committed parents to facilitate a child's entry into the world. Taking this into consideration, I'd say my parents didn't do such a bad job. For example, I quite early on was let in no doubt what Nazi Germany of which Austria had exactly been a part had done to the Jews. In consequence, my relations with the whole of society had to be – I now tend to think – affected in a quite negative way. The fact that I had no friends until my adolescence can probably at least in part be explained by a generally well-founded mistrust which had been, somewhat osmotically, handed on to me. (Much later when I was, already an adult, teaching in the United States I received the only letter my father ever wrote to me. I had informed my parents that I intended to marry a young woman from Wels in Upper Austria upon my return to Vienna. My father warned me that someone, very teutonically named Sigrid, from that town, from that province, should be evaluated with utter scrupulousness: they're all Nazis there, he wrote. That didn't turn out to be quite true, and I am very content to say that Sigrid, privately referred to as Marie, and I have been happily married for a half century.

I can facilitate the present argumentation by simply quoting what an English teacher of mine once said: Oh, how much we would have loved to be English. (I'm not sure whom he meant by "we"; whatever he had in mind, he had learned the hard way, he had lost an arm at Stalingrad.) I have mentioned my cinema-going from a very early age on, much facilitated by my usher grandfather, and I've also stressed that we routinely watched American and British films. That was not only fascinating because of the depicted milieus (let us think less about Westerns than drawing room comedies and the like) but also because there always was the moral high ground. Always. Sure, it was personified by the super heroes of the Westerns, but it was also implicitly there in every genre, be it only because it went by itself that decent people either had had a "good war" or had suffered atrociously at the hands of the Japanese or the Germans. And of course I understood that I somehow was part of the latter: in for a war, in for the guilt. (The paradox of my existence is that I was born a German as in 1944 the *Ostmark* (Austria) was still a part of the Nazi Reich.)

It seems to me – but even now, in old age, it is still a slow realization – that I envied people who could draw on that moral high ground. I suggest that it is not so much about *what* we remember but *how* we do, and it is a question of the moral system in place providing decisive parameters. While I remember well the food rationing cards and the promises concerning all the marvellous delicacies which would, hopefully, soon turn up on the market again, I understood less well the causality of deprivation, poverty and distress: my country had not only lost, but had also caused, the war. For a child things like these are far from clear. I am driving at "context-dependency". In that respect the food ration cards can somehow appear to represent a kind of (due) punishment; reversely, for those occupying the moral high ground they mark but a transitory phase, and the inconvenience can be traced back to the adversary anyhow.

Such interpretations may well be the result of professional deformation. After all, I chose to become a historian (I now flatter myself I didn't do so solely on the grounds of being too weak in mathematics and natural sciences). At any rate, I think it worthwhile to consider the following hypothesis. "Soft sciences" – you can consider historiography to be one – force you to think very carefully. In some respects the lot of the scholars practising them is more difficult than the one of the "hard scientists": considerate cerebrations have to stand in for truly provable or disprovable data you can fall back on in, say, chemistry or engineering. In history – and by extension in biography and autobiography – there are no such thing as absolute certainty, or hardly. There are objective inconsistencies but some conclusions have to be arrived at by interpretation. On the one hand, we were assured that Austria belonged to the West – but what were you to make of the banners hanging over entrance gates of factory buildings in eastern Austria? These banners, not all that dissimilar from the ones in the communist countries, were all red, with yellowish script, and they proclaimed yet another victory of the workers in mastering their ever-increasing work quotas (or at least a respective promise). Remember, Vienna and the whole of eastern Austria were Soviet-occupied. Even when I was very young, I realized that that had something to do with "Stalinplatz," "Tolbuchinstrasse" or "Brücke der Roten Armee" (Red Army Bridge), words which were to be seen daily on the destination blinds of the Viennese tramways. But there was no Churchillstrasse. And there wasn't even an avenue de Gaulle (which would have been in keeping with certain French obsessions) or a place Napoléon in Innsbruck, the capital of the French zone.

Yes, the Red Army liberated Austria. It was, however, not alone in achieving that. Living in the east, you could, I presume, get the impression that it was *just* the Red Army. Contrasts, contradictions and inconsistencies can lead to anguish: the fashionable expression "cognitive dissonance" expresses it in a standardized way. In any event, you have to be very careful with propositions that intend to qualify in a general way. And childhood memories (in fact any kind of memory) lead you only so far: they impart little knowledge and transport it badly. Memories become useful when fitted into "securitized" and generally accepted knowledge. And even that is judgement: there never really is complete concordance. There is no *absolute* certainty either.

Memories, reversely, seem authentic – and are still channeled, guided, directed by often only alleged certainties which, moreover, are in a state of constant flux. It may well be that there is a strange correlation of mutuality: historical learning certainly provides the framework for putting memories in perspective, it rectifies, perfects, provides indispensable information. Conversely, memories, based on feeling and sensing, represent emotions reaching far back to earlier sentience and perceptions. Simply because they exist they cannot be discarded. But only by reconciling them with safe bases do we have a chance to hold on to them without negating a general consensus.

Divided Austria

Sigrid Schmid

I was born in 1946, in Wels, a middle-sized town (40.000 inhabitants) in
Austria (which, as only few people seem to know, was divided into occupation zones exactly as Germany until 1955, when a peace treaty was signed).
My mother was a primary, my father a secondary school teacher. As a former
member of the Nazi party he was not allowed to teach, so he worked in a
rather lucrative building material enterprise until 1955. I have one brother,
six years older than I. Both he and I ended up teaching at the university, he in
botany, I in literature. My mother died young, at 56, of skin cancer; my father
remarried and lived to be 90.

Trying to remember, really to remember and not only to recall stories
being told in the family, brings me to a rather strange experience I had about
twenty years ago.

When driving with a friend to a conference, we passed an area where my
mother's sister had lived with her family, and where we had spent our holidays up to the time when I was seven: I am so sure of the dates because from
1954 on we spent our holidays at the Adriatic seaside, and we never returned
to that village Schiltern in Lower Austria.

The family – he was the director of the local primary school and they
lived in the school-building – had long moved away; a new school had been
built in the meantime. When we arrived at the village, I did not recognize
anything, but when I saw the old school building, which now serves for
administrative purposes, all of a sudden the whole thing came back – I could
draw a map of the rooms, could picture the furniture, the garden in three
terraces… It had been a strange building – though typical for country schools
all over the Austro-Hungarian Empire. There were two street-side entrances,
each leading to a hallway that went all the way to the court-yard behind the
house – one leading to two class rooms on the right and the left, the other

leading to one class-room on the right and the headmaster's apartment on the left. This consisted of a large kitchen, a living room (which also served as study as shown by the big desk), a bedroom and a children's room. The toilets were situated in the back yard, just four plain latrines; their smell – this mixture of urine and faeces and of hot, sun-beaten wood - still comes to my nostrils when thinking of it. The hot-wood-part is the nice component of the memory – when it was raining, the whole thing was worse, since the backyard was not only just plain dirt, but was also populated by a number of chickens. I still have a skin (and scent) memory of chicken shit getting stuck between my toes when playing there.

I was totally surprised by the precision and details of the memories that emerged when seeing the place again, from the outside only –we did not enter, it just all happened in my head.

I do not have any specific memories of what we did during those vacations, it is almost exclusively the topography that re-appeared, and some sensations.

We travelled there by train, and once again I recall a strange emotion. The station of St.Valentin was the border between the occupation zones and everybody was controlled by Russian soldiers. Though obviously much too small to understand anything I still remember the atmosphere of fright and terror that descended on the train during these controls – I have no memories of anything ever happening, but to this day St. Valentin for me isn't a station like any others.

I was born after the war, and yet, as I have often noticed, for me war has a reality that is different from that of people only a few years younger than I am. Across the road from the house we lived in there was a ruin that, for some reasons of proprietorship, was one of the last ruins in town. Our own house was pock-marked with pieces of that house; parts of it could be found in the attic, too big to be carried down, and despite all kinds of repairs, the ceiling of our kitchen always showed the part where it had been hit. Though repaired and painted in the early fifties the white arrows pointing to the bomb shelter (marking where you had to dig for possible survivors) re-appeared after every new coat of paint.

The important part about the ruin across the street was less that it was a ruin – there were quite a few around at that time – but that not going there was one of the few commands that were obeyed without exception. We were given the rational explanation that there were unexploded bombs down there, we were told that the dead bodies were never salvaged because of that – but all that might have only stirred our curiosity: again, it is the memory of a feeling, a notion of real danger, that not only kept me and my brother, but everybody else out of that area – I cannot remember ever having seen anybody there, even when bushes and trees were already covering the decaying walls. Our house – and the "our" means both lived in and owned – was a block of a large settlement of a type of council housing – as often in Austria and Germany it was not built and run directly by the city, but by a – supposedly – private non-profit association. Some of the blocks had to be sold off during the depression: that's how my grandfather managed to buy them

They were four attached houses, each comprising four flats of about 50 square metres, consisting of two rooms, a hall and an indoor toilet and a pantry. Strangely, this toilet was the only display of modern sanitation– there was neither a shower nor a wash basin nor water in the kitchen – the water for cooking, doing the dishes and for your personal toilet had to be fetched from a public faucet on the staircase – it could, however, be disposed of in the private toilet. In each of these two-room apartments lived families with two children – nowadays that would hardly meet the living standards for fugitives – but at that time, everybody lived like that and it was quite normal.

Our apartment was even fuller – because we had an "auntie" living with us whose main occupation was being my nanny– both my father and my mother were working. She was no relation to us, just a friend, who had taken the opportunity to move from the Russian to the US zone, nearer to her boyfriend/fiancé. She stayed with us for five years, when they finally did get married. It was not even a room of her own that she got, but just a place to sleep in the kitchen and I guess some pocket money; but a roof over your head was worth a lot at that time.

If I think back now, I just wonder how people managed, how they arranged their things. I have no idea where aunt Steffie kept her personal stuff – many people did not have much of that – but even where her bedding was kept during the day escaped my notice.

The focal point of our lives was the kitchen table – it was the place to eat, to work and to play – especially in winter. The kitchen was the only place that was heated – by a large stove that also served for cooking and for providing warm water. It was heated by wood and coal – if there was enough of it. There were people in the house who could not afford coal, so they used special saw-dust stoves instead which were rather tricky to manipulate. And I still remember the repeated complaints of people that coal was stolen from their cellars.

Heating was not only expensive – coal was rationed as was food – but it was also rather messy – coal to be fetched from the cellar, ashes to be taken out – but it also had its special advantages. Coming in from the cold you could warm up right next to the stove, putting your freezing hands on the warm parts and letting your wet clothing dry on its railing. You could toast a slice of bread on its edge, roast an apple in the oven, and watch the flames through the little door. All those advantages turned into nuisances in summer, however, when the additional heat was more than superfluous. The first "modern" convenience that entered our universe thus was an electric oven with two plates for cooking in summer.

I remember long winter afternoons on the week-ends, when we played cards – usually Canasta – and I think I learned to count and add here and not in school. I also see my mother – and later on my father – correcting tests and homework. It was also in the kitchen that the few books I had were read to me, over and over again. Knowing them already by heart and learning to make the connection between the words and the letters. I never let anybody change the words or skip a part – it had to be read as written. There was however one book that I never wanted to be read from - I always hid it at the bottom of my little pile – I still can see it, its cover was a sickly red and it showed a girl tied to a chair and had the title *Merk dir das, mein Kind (Remember that, my child)* – inside were various similar "pedagogical" stories. I remember just the one from the title. A girl was alone at home, the parents had told her not to open the door, but when somebody knocked that was exactly what she did; they were robbers and they tied her to a chair. I really was afraid of that book, though I was never afraid of strangers or of opening the door. I did not mind other "classics" of the genre, like *Struwelpeter* or *Max und Moritz* by Busch, in which awful things happen to children – their fictional character was obvious – but that other book was deadly realistic and I hated it.

Talking about books' being few – because of paper rationing – I come to one of my earliest memories: I am sitting on the floor in the kitchen, with scissors in my hand, and am cutting the newspaper into squares to be used as toilet paper – and I try very hard to keep my mouth closed, but it always works in tandem with the scissors, I just cannot yet separate the two movements.

Shortage and rationing of almost everything were a fact of life. I do not remember ever having been hungry, but meat was something for the week-end only; in the middle of the week we usually had some sausages with vegetables: that was all the meat you could get on the rationing cards: 100gr per person and week. Otherwise we were – by necessity, not choice – vegetarians, or more precisely, we were eating a lot of sweets/pudding which the central European kitchen knows so well to prepare; they were not dessert, however, but the main meal. Vegetables were provided by one of the families in the house who owned a *Schrebergarten*, a small allotment used to grow vegetables in. It was amazing how much you could get out of such a small space, they not only grew enough for themselves but sold quite a lot to the other families in the house. The vegetables at that time were usually smothered in floury gravy – to be more nourishing, and I detested them and was granted the privilege of eating them raw – the rest of the family ate the cooked version. That was a precursor of much later nutritional fads.

We were lucky to live in a mid-sized town: the situation in Vienna was much worse. The rationing there in 1946 and 1947 was less than 1000 calories per person, and even that could often not be provided. In the countryside everybody had some relatives or friends who had a garden, raised some small animals, were real farmers. A cousin of my mother came to visit us every month and in his rucksack he brought a large loaf of bread, some lard, a chunk of black-smoked bacon – our regular evening meal. Sometimes he even brought some eggs and, luxury of luxuries, some butter. (The normal bread-spread was lard.) It was, of course, all black market stuff, but everybody had some link like that to fill up the meagre official rations.

I also can still picture the pantry of our apartment: on the right hand side were the jars of home-made jam and canned fruits, on the left hand side a large earthen pot filled with lard, the bread in a tin-box and flour, sugar, dried peas etc. On the wall hung the bacon, ready to be cut into very thin slices. We also had a large cellar, where we kept wood and coal for heating, but also the apples and pears from our own garden, potatoes, jars of home-made pickles, jars of eggs conserved in sodium silicate for the long winter months when hens did not lay eggs, and a real keg of cider – it was cider country we lived in.

The kitchen was also the place for knitting socks and mittens and pullovers and jackets for the whole family, and of the unravelling of the old ones, a task where my brother and I were also employed. Wool being as rare as everything else, it had to be made good use of. So if a sweater's arms couldn't be repaired any more by a leather patch, the parts that were worn thin would be cut out, but the rest of the wool would be carefully unraveled and used for something new– either a smaller piece for the children or one with two or three colours for the adults. The same thing went for dresses or pants – they were carefully unstitched (using old razor-blades), not ripped, the various pieces washed, the threadbare parts cut out and the rest brought to a seamstress – nobody in our household had the necessary abilities – to be made into something "new".

I was the youngest girl on our whole block. Gerti, who was two years older, was the closest friend I had before I started school. I remember that we had a ball and that we could play endlessly with it, throwing it against the wall and catching it again, then clapping once, or twice, or turning around before the catching, etc. When one did not catch it, the other one took over. In hindsight I pity the poor people living behind the wall that we used.

We also used to produce large quantities of rose-water – by tearing up the fallen petals of a huge rose-bush in our garden, and letting them soak in water – it had a nice smell – but was thrown away each evening, only to be re-made the next day. I had three dolls, the oldest one home-made: the body, arms and legs were sawdust sewn into cloth with a papier-maché head: and every year, when the head was already pretty beaten up and the body rather dirty, it got a new head and the body was newly covered with old, torn nylon-stockings – a regular resurrection. When I was ten years old, large teddy-bears (about 60 cm high) hit the stores and every girl wanted one for Christmas. I still don't know how and where, but my father got a special teddy-bear that had been made for a window-decoration – and that was even bigger – so I had – and still have – the (at that time) biggest teddy ever.

Winters in the late forties and early fifties were much harsher than they are nowadays: looking at photographs confirms that memory, and I used to have a toboggan even before I started school. A railroad embankment near our house provided a wide ditch of about 5 to 6 metres depth that served as our toboggan-run. I remember spending many winter afternoons there, dredging up my toboggan and sliding down, running up half-way on the opposite side if the speed was right, which made the way up much shorter – you really had to choose the right spot to achieve the best speed without hitting too many icy patches. I think there were about forty children playing there – with no grown-ups around, the trains passing by. If you crossed the rail-tracks, you could reach our house in a good five minutes; if you took the prescribed under-pass, it was more than a quarter of an hour. This was one of the commands that could be broken: when we were already late we would –carefully – cross the tracks, which was not easy with a toboggan to pull, but nothing ever happened.

The railway underpass leads to another isolated memory. When I was five years old I desperately wanted to attend school. So my mother took me with her on her bicycle and let me sit in in the beginners' class of one of her colleagues. As my mother had to stay longer I had to make my way home alone – no big problem, I knew it well. For some reason or another I fell in the underpass that was full of coal-dust – the railway was still running on coal - and hurt my knee. It started to bleed: everything was red and black. I made it home and auntie immediately took me to another aunt next door, who happened to be a nurse. She obviously took pity on me and used hydrogen peroxide as disinfectant to spare me the stinging pain of alcohol – and all of a sudden the red and black mess turned white: I can still see it. But I have no memory of the school-day before, of bandages, of pain afterwards, just this marvellous changing of colours.

Before I started school at the age of six, a big change in my life occurred, because Auntie got married and moved to a different city. I visited during the vacations, but that was something different from living together: it was the first great loss of my life.

I was lucky to go to school in a brand new building that was less than ten minutes' walk from our home. Though new, it followed the old pattern: boys to the left and girls to the right, no idea of co-education yet. But the interior was amazing: we had tables and chairs (in different sizes), not the old fixed benches, and we had changing rooms on the ground floor – we left our coats and shoes there and changed into house-shoes, which altered the smell of the class-rooms considerably. There were forty two girls in the class and I had a choice of friends for the first time. Discipline was pretty strict and/or we were rather well-behaved. While waiting for the doors to open at the beginning of the day, everybody lined up in pairs according to the class they belonged to and then entered the building in an orderly way. In the great break everybody got a quarter of a litre of milk and a piece of bread, courtesy of the US. Every girl (and boy) had to bring their own small metal mug and was served from a large milk-can by the janitor.

School in Austria lasted (and still does so) only until noon, so the afternoons were free – with the exception of the short time it took to do the homework. I remember that we were a number of friends who spent their time together, not in the apartments of one of them – that hardly ever happened, they were all too small – but on the outside of them, in the gardens, on the streets. What we actually played I do not really remember, hide-and-seek, playing with a ball, in winter the toboggan – I just know that I often forgot the time and my brother was sent to bring me home. As children did not own watches – they were expensive and you usually got your first one as a confirmation-present – this lack of punctuality is understandable. What I do remember is that my territory at that time was quite large, covering a good square kilometer.

The only time that I remember that children were invited into the house was to the celebration of my/our birthdays – my brother's and mine were combined with the carnival (*Fasching*) season. Our living situation had been improved in the meantime, my parents having managed to build two additional rooms, a *Mansarde*, under the roof and one of them was the children's room. Concerning the celebration of the birthdays I have to rely on the photographs, nothing has been imprinted on my memory, with the exception of the fact that the room was decorated with colored paper attached to the ceiling (the ceiling was rather low, below regulation heights) and that they were carefully rolled up every year to be preserved for next year's festivity.

The Christmas present preceding my sixth birthday was very important – I got a red children's bicycle. As the roads were icy I learned to bike in our attic, my father standing on one side and giving be a push, my brother on the other, stopping me and turning me around, till – rather quickly, I seem to remember – I learned to pedal hard enough to avoid falling.

Bicycles were the main means of transportation in towns the size of ours. No public transport was available, and cars were only for the rich. On our whole street, there was only one car; if you considered the whole block, there was just one more, belonging to the doctor. Cycling as a green ideology came much later. Before I got my own bike, I was sitting first in a seat in the front, later on in the back of either my mother's or my father's bicycle. In summer we very often took rides to the country-side, visiting some castle, looking for berries or mushrooms in the woods, and often meeting friends at a country inn.

If you can remember a lack of something, it certainly was the lack of refrigerators that marked our lives. As shops were plentiful – there was a grocer on our street – that posed no great problem; you could by a quarter of a liter of milk or fifty grams of butter without anybody thinking that strange – and you went to the store daily. It was a job that was I was entrusted with very early, at about the age of four, and I was very proud that I not only always remembered what to buy without having a slip of paper with me as most of the other children had, but also that I was entrusted with the money to pay directly. Most clients had accounts with the grocer that were kept in a large ledger and were paid only once a month on pay-day. On hot summer days I was also entrusted to go to the inn one block from our house, carrying a large glass pitcher and buy beer on tap for my father and sometimes also my mother. I was much smaller than the counter, but people knew me and I was served without any problem, carefully balancing the pitcher on my way back home trying to be as quick as possible to keep the beer from getting warm.

My parents took their first real holiday in 1953 – travelling to Rome for Easter, a city that meant a lot to both of them, antiquity to my father, a Latin teacher, Christianity to my mother, a devout Catholic. Auntie had left us in the meantime and had been replaced by a young girl, a former pupil of my mother. Once again, her situation was something in between a maid and a warden to learn good house-keeping – a task well fulfilled, for she too married a colleague of my father some six years later. Her parents lived nearby and she stayed on living with them, just coming to us for the day.

My parents' trip left the three of us alone at a crucial time of the year – Easter was the time of the great spring cleaning and we decided to do it without them, as a surprise at their return. This does not sound like much nowadays, but at that time cleaning meant something. All the furniture had to be moved, to get to the dust and the cobwebs behind them, afterwards the closets had to be emptied, all the clothes aired in the spring sun, beaten and brushed, the pockets turned inside out; in the library, all the books had to be taken out, opened and thumped together to get the dust out of them, the curtains taken down, washed and ironed etc. etc. We were working all week long and our parents were duly surprised on their return.

I generally remember that cleaning was rather important – in the absence of vacuum cleaners the carpets were beaten once a week, the wooden floors waxed and polished, the brass door-knobs polished, the stone stairs washed. Even the rooms were painted by professionals every two years – I admired them greatly when they walked around the room using the ladder as a simple extension of their legs; the windows got a new coat of paint every other year too, the only work in the house that my father did.

Looking back I wonder whether all that cleaning was a psychologically motivated cleansing of guilt or whether the times were really dirtier than today. With all the heating and cooking done with wood and coal, with hardly any roads paved and with the amount of building and reconstructing going on, the latter is not improbable. Add to this that the materials used were often old and very likely did produce more dust and dirt.

The trips to the cobbler were quite frequent. The shoes got new soles, or just new heels, or little metal supports were added to the front and the back to make them last longer – they always got lost pretty quickly and had to be replaced. The frequency of these repairs can probably be explained by the fact that we walk a lot, because walking and cycling were our only modes of movement, and the shoes were all leather, no plastic soles that would last longer.

A rather unbelievable memory comes with shoes. In the centre of town was a large shoe store, where the mother of one of my friends worked. In the sixties they installed an x-ray machine in the store, you stepped on it, put your feet in the aperture provided, pressed a button and then you saw the bones of your feet and the outline of the shoes and could thus check whether they fitted correctly or whether your toes were bent. It was fascinating to see into the inside of your body and we used this machine whenever we passed by: there was no security around it, no lead protection, nothing. I must have surpassed a life time's allowance of radiation there.

My brother and I were – and are – very close. It has always been mentioned that we never quarrelled. He considered me as something of his personal property and I was very willing to go along with that, as it opened opportunities for me that other girls did not have. I was the only girl who was not only allowed to play with an electric model railway, but who even owned half of our rather impressive outfit. Auntie's husband was a railway-fanatic, he had 100 metres of track, 30 switches, 30 locomotives, 100 carriages – quite a large number of them hand-made by himself, out of sardine tins, old parts of airplanes etc. – and soon after he got married, he decided that he did not need this hobby anymore, but they needed the room it was taking up in their tiny apartment, so he sold it to our parents as a Christmas present for both of us – and some Christmas it was.

I also was taking part in my brother's biological pursuits. At the age of 14 he became an almost professional entomologist, a collector of butterflies. As usual I was fully enrolled in this task. It does not sound like much, but the butterflies you catch with a net – which we did in the beginning – were usually already quite a bit damaged, so the real collector raises the caterpillars in special cages, lets them turn into chrysalis and kills them as soon as they have turned into a butterfly – still perfect. Thus our room was turned into a caterpillar-farm. As anybody who has a garden knows, caterpillars are both voracious and rather picky about their food. So we had to provide them with their special diets every other day. Unfortunately for me an ersatz diet that quite a few accept is nettles. Another food accepted by some exotic species are leaves of walnut trees. How he did it, I don't know, but my brother managed to order (long before the Internet) butterfly-eggs by mail, which we raised afterwards. Unfortunately, in our area there were just three walnut-trees: I guess the gardens were just too small. When we tried to be honest and asked for a few leaves every other day for our caterpillars the owner of the tree told us rather agitated that he had just been spraying the garden to get rid of them, and he was certainly not willing to help raise them. So we had to resort to stealing the leaves every other day. Luckily, we never got caught.

But to watch a chrysalis turn into a butterfly, slowly pumping their equivalent of blood into the wings that unfold and grow within a few minutes to their full size and become stiff very quickly was worth all that risk and bother. Killing them was another problem: one method was cigarette smoke – you blew it through a small hole into a well-sealed large glass with the butterfly in it and it would die in two or three minutes. Maybe that experience is the reason why neither my brother nor I ever smoked. But the two minutes were too long: the butterfly could damage its wings in that time. So we resorted to the quicker and more professional method which was cyanide. Once again I have to admit that I do not know how my brother managed to talk people into doing things for him: I do know where or from whom he got the cyanide. There was a factory producing enamelled pots and pans, and cyanide is used in the process, and that's where he got it. Put into a glass jar with a lid, it kills a butterfly within seconds. My parents were unaware of the presence of this poison in their house, we knew quite well what to tell them and what not.

Insects bring back two earlier memories. The potato-bug had been accidentally introduced into Europe. To fight it whole classes of school-children were sent out into the potato plots to collect them. They were still few and hard to spot – quite different from today when you really can't miss them.

Other bugs you were encouraged to gather to be killed were cockchafers – every four years they became a real plague, and we collected them in shoe boxes and brought them to the collection points. No problem to fill a box in one evening – you had to bore a few holes into the boxes to let some air in – before they were killed the next day anyway – the boxes were humming and vibrating all the time.

My brother dominated my life to a large extent, but there were two connected areas where we differed, where I managed to hold my own. One was school, which I liked and which he neglected as much as possible, repeatedly just scraping by to have his vacations ruined by having to learn for a fall exam. The other was reading. I was – and still am – a voracious reader; the only books my brother read were reports on explorations into strange lands. For the required reading in school short resumes were enough for him, or he talked my father into telling him the main points the evening before his exams. I, on the other hand, read everything – old fashioned girlie-stories and boy's books about Red Indians. Books were always part of the gifts we got for birthdays and Christmas, but they did not suffice. I started to consume the library at my mother's school, then the one at our parish, then the local branch of the public library. At the age of twelve I was hooked on the books of Karl May, a well-known 19th century author of novels about the Red Indians and the Arabs, who, in real life, had never left Germany. It was a fad that practically the whole class shared, but there was one friend who was almost more enthusiastic than I; the two of us challenged each other to read all his 50 novels, each well over 300 pages – and we managed to do this in one year – besides our regular activities and readings. Very soon I started on the classics in my father's library, and then, at about 12, I was given the books that he himself read.

So my parents had a rather difficult job of getting one child to read and keeping the other one from getting completely lost in fiction. Strangely enough one strategy was to warn me that reading will ruin my eyes. Another one was to turn off the lights in our room at 10 PM, which only lead to my reading under the blanket with a small torch – now maybe that really was not too good for my eyes.

My mother being a devout Catholic, religion played a big part in our lives. But it was not only my mother. After the war religion saw a revival that manifested itself clearly in the building of new churches. Our town already had three churches, one Gothic, one Baroque and one neo-Gothic: now three more were added. The first one was right across from my primary school. The building itself was really ugly, but it had a rather attractive modern priest. There were four masses every Sunday that were full, with people even standing – which makes, on a rough count, around 500 to 600 people going to mass regularly.

I liked the old Gothic church much better, although we had to walk more than half an hour to go to it – which we did every Sunday. My parents went to an early mass and my brother and I went to the later children's mass. The attraction was not only aesthetic, though, because on our way home we were allowed to visit the Non-Stop-Cinema – they showed the three different news-reels, but between them there were some cultural one-reelers and the funnies – Tom & Jerry etc. – and you could stay as long as you wanted – so you could see the funnies several times – two for us, to be exact, because we had to be home for Sunday lunch.

Sunday mass was not the only church service my mother made us attend – in May there were the daily five o'clock *Maiandachten*, short services in honour of Mary. I rather liked them: they started and ended with some hymn in honor of Mary, and between them there was the list of names attributed to Mary read by the priest and followed by the injunction "Pray for us". The strange names, repeated over and over again, exerted a kind of fascination, because most of them were utterly incomprehensible – morning star, ok, but why, star of the seas, or, even better, House of Gold, Tower of David, Arc of the Covenant?

The only attraction the afternoon rosaries in the October held, though, was the speed with which the old women – they were the only ones to attend – managed to say the Hail Marys, it just took them one long intake of breath for the first half, the shorter second half was finished by exhaling.

What was attractive, however, was the procession on Corpus Christi Day in May, a public holiday in Austria to remember the victory over the Turkish invaders at Vienna in 1683. "Public" meaning in that context that it was not only a Catholic holiday, but it also was a demonstration of imperial power (up to 1918, as is manifested by a number of famous literary descriptions, e.g. by Josef Roth), which continued on into the republic – to this day the conservative members of the government take part in the procession in St. Stephen's cathedral in Vienna. But processions took and take place in every parish.

The priest carries the monstrance with the Host through the streets – right ahead of the priest go the small girls, dressed in white and carrying little baskets full of flowers (daisies and peonies mostly, due to the season) and throw the petals onto the street so that the Host "walks" on a carpet of flowers. The doors of the houses are decorated with fresh birch trees, and behind the priest the rest of the parish marches in hierarchical order. Although the day is a public holiday the schools took place in this procession, too. I remember that the only time my mother, who did not care about clothes too much, was really upset, was when she and a colleague from the same school happened to wear the same hat for this procession.

From 1954 on we spent our summer holidays in Italy on the Adriatic beaches. The first time we spent in Grado, a resort that was already popular during the monarchy – our hotel was appropriately named *Hungaria*. On the evening of the first day – the first time to see the sea (though a very tame and flat one) for our whole family – I ran a high fever and started to vomit, so a doctor was called – luckily my father spoke Italian rather well. It turned out that I did not only suffer from a severe sun burn but also from a sun stroke: nobody had thought of sun lotion, of sun hats and the like. So I spent my first seaside holiday in a shaded hotel room: only on the last day of the week did I venture out again to the beach. And here is, once again, one of the memories that must be real – everything that I have related up to now has been told many times in the family and I have no way of knowing what I really remember. But I do remember this last day, going to the beach, where my family was, and that I could not get in, because in Grado the beach was fenced off, with an entrance where you had to pay to get in – different from all the other beaches I got to know later on. I remember the iron fence and the gate, and the strange square huts for changing, with cloth that could be opened and used as a sun-shade on all four sides – there are photographs of the beach and the huts, but none of the fence and the entrance, so my mental pictures of them must be real memories. I managed to attract the attention of my parents and spent this last day on the beach, smothered in sun lotion with a huge hat covering my head.

The next year we changed location to Chioggia, staying in a *pensione*. For reasons unknown even to myself I categorically refused to eat cheese as a child. This had been no problem in the rather posh international hotel in Grado, but it did in the typical Italian *pensione*. When I discovered that they put parmesan (sitting on every table next to salt and pepper, olive oil and vinegar) not only on the various pasta dishes but also on the soup and on some meats and salads, I refused to eat anything but *caffé-latte* with the delicious white bread (*cornetti*) soaked in it and fruits. I became the concern of the whole *pensione*, the cooks, the guests, everybody. They offered to cook something special for the little *bambina*, they did not want me to starve, but I did not trust them, I stuck to my diet. And so from the next year on my parents found a place where my mother could cook for us: as this was cheaper, we also could stay longer, usually four weeks. All this happened at the very beginning of the wave of Adriatic holidays that hit Germany and Austria – and Italy – in the fifties, so I still remember some of the *Italianità* of the place.

We stayed in a house where a traditional fisherman started to invest in the future. He still ran a boat with 10 men out every night to catch fish and sell them on the local market, but he saw tourism coming. On our first visit the house consisted of four rooms on the ground floor, plus a dining room and a kitchen, where there were four gas burners to cook on. There was one shower and one toilet shared by everybody, but each of the four bed-rooms already had a wash basin with hot and cold water. The owner's family of six slept in a small corridor off the kitchen where the *nonna* washed everybody's dishes all day long. In the next year, there was already one room on the first floor, and when we stopped going there, about five years later, the whole thing had turned into a full-fledged, four floor hotel.

We were the only foreign guests; the other rooms were rented out to young Italian mothers with one or two small children, chaperoned by a grandmother. On the weekends the fathers came from town to visit, impeccably dressed in suits and shining shoes which they never took off, not even on the beach, watching their children play in the sand and the water. The grandmothers also never took off their black garments, not even when they lay covered up to their neck in the hot sand – a procedure that was supposed to alleviate rheumatism. You went to the sea for the air, not for the sun and the water.

Italy at that time was a prosperous and modern country in comparison with Austria. We admired the roads, the modern architecture, the fashion.

And we did not only go there for the holidays, but also to buy things that you still could not get in Austria. The Italian elegance counted, too: leather bags and shoes were so much more stylish than anything you could find in Austria. At that time we were fed up with natural and organic materials, and longed for the synthetics the Italians had to offer – drip-dry shirts, pants and skirts that did not wrinkle, socks that dried overnight, sweaters that did not scratch – all those modern amenities were sold on the markets in the Italian resorts, and we bought all that we dared to smuggle through customs, wearing as much as we could without suffocating.

A big change in the lives of Austrian children takes place when they are only 10-years old – the decision has to be made whether they will, later on, have a chance to go to university or whether they are destined for more practical jobs. Of the 40 girls in my class, only three tried the entrance exam to the *Gymnasium*, and only two passed it. The ratio for boys was somewhat higher, but still only around 10%. Things have changed in the meantime, but the first splitting up still takes place at that age. For me that meant that I lost all my friends – I might as well have moved to another city. We could have easily met in the afternoon, but that just did not happen. I think subconscious social pressures were decisive: I had moved from their sphere to something "higher", and both sides kept to their circles.

It was a bitter, not-understood experience for me, the more so as I did not fit into the new circle. The new class was made up by a central group of girls from the town's "elite", doctors, lawyers, important shop-keepers – all of them having shared the same primary school, all of them interrelated for centuries, all of them rich. The other forty percent came from the surrounding area, they had to travel by train or bus to get to and from school; sociologically they represented the same circles – only on a smaller market-town scale, with a few girls thrown in, whose teachers had insisted that they go to the *Gymnasium* because of their good grades. Girls like that from the town itself made up the rest. The commuting girls quickly formed a group of their own, due to the time spent together in the waiting room of the station, and "elite"-girls kept to themselves anyway. It was not as if I were really isolated; I quickly understood that to be accepted, you had to make yourself useful. That was easily done. I always liked to learn, so I had the homework done, and I let the others copy it; they soon depended on me for help with tests and exams, I was even elected speaker – and yet that all was completely different from the natural, non-profit relations I had had with my friends in primary school. It never felt like us: it was always them and me, a difference that I interpreted as my being, smarter, more intellectual, more serious etc. which probably did not help my fitting in, either.

Apart from this social aspect, the school itself was a kind of shock, too. It dated from 1910 and had not been renovated since, which meant that it still had fixed wooden benches. We did not change before going to our classrooms, but just hung up our coats on hooks on the wall – the smell, especially in winter, was obvious. The floors were wooden boards, soaked in some black oil. The benches bore the inscriptions of generations of students before us, either in ink or carved with knives: it was hard to find an even place to write on. Complicating things was the lack of school-space. The rooms had to be used in shifts. One week it was the boys who had classes from 9 to 12:45, the girls came in at 13:00 and stayed till 17:45, the next week the shift changed, girls in the morning, boys in the afternoon. Originally, it was a nice example of the Habsburg Empire's *Gymnasium*, with special class rooms for chemistry and physics, where you could do experiments, a special room with large desks for geometry and drawing, a large hall with a stage and two pianos for diverse festivities. But space was so scarce that there were always two forms that had to move every hour from one room to another. When class A had a chemistry lesson, the itinerant class moved into the regular room of A, which it had to vacate again to move someplace else freed by its regular occupants because they were in the gym or in the music room etc. Being an itinerant class was fun, but also rather stressful, and you had to be pretty well organized.

The question of how the past was dealt with is easy to answer: it wasn't. It was obvious that there had been a war, and everybody agreed that wars were bad, especially if you lost them. And the Nazis were in some way involved with this war, so they had been stupid, but most of all, they were rather vulgar, uneducated and inelegant. There were still some of them around - you could hear them at the *Stammtische* (reserved tables) in country inns talking about their war adventures – but you would not want to associate with people like that. The problem with that attitude – not clearly expressed, but certainly prevalent – was that it was so similar to the one expressed towards the Americans– they too were vulgar, had no education and no manners – so where was the difference?

In school the history of the 20th century was never reached – because of lack of time; all history lessons ended somewhere at the end of the 19th century. When a young and very progressive history teacher did talk about the 2nd World War in our class (we were twelve years old), it was about his personal experience in Stalingrad – being in the trenches for weeks, standing literally in your own piss and shit that tended to freeze on you, being eaten by fleas and lice – it was very drastic, we all could not eat our lunch that day, and it impressed on us that war was really awful – but we heard nothing about why they were in Stalingrad. This Austro-German chiffre for the war remained as isolated as before.

We read *The Diary of Anne Frank*, but it had about the same moral impact and personal relevance as *Uncle Tom's Cabin* – you wrote essays about it, but there was no connection to your family, your teachers, your everyday reality.

People had to go on living and to go on living together, so they preferred to pretend to know nothing of others' past. And the compromises would have been difficult to explain. In my school we had a few real Nazi teachers, one of them was my Latin teacher, ex-SS and proud of it – he transferred Nazi ideology to the old Romans, so nobody had to complain. The head-master of the school was a known alcoholic, and when somebody complained about that, the answer was, well, you must understand... I always assumed that you must understand what he went through in the war, only much later did I find out that he was a survivor of a concentration camp putting up with the Nazi teachers. That could make you an alcoholic.

Another ex-SS man– though he at least did not talk about it – an uncle of mine, was the head of the Catholic hospital; he was saved by the church from being sentenced in return for letting the hospital be run by the very able and ambitious Mother Superior; to this day, Wels, though in the meantime among the 10 largest cities of Austria, does not have a public hospital.

I could go on with examples like that – bits and pieces were mentioned from time to time, but it was hard to piece them together for a child or adolescent, and to develop a consistent picture of the past. The one lesson that we did learn was that war was bad; what was left out was that it was caused by humans and was not a natural disaster.

When I was sixteen I spent a year as an exchange student in the US. It was quite a challenge, not only the cultural change, but also a social one: I lived with a blue collar family. On top of that, it was the year of the Cuban missile crisis – so I became acquainted with a different attitude towards war – it took quite some time to be digested – childhood was definitely over. But it took the Vietnam War (and the movement against it) to make me and the young Germans and Austrians ask the relevant questions about our own war.

Memories of My Childhood

Kobkua Suwannathat-Pian

It seems almost impossible to remind myself that in a long, almost forgotten but happy past I was once of those same beautiful, carefree and innocent ages as my three grandchildren, doing and enjoying life with no concern that could dampen the "now" and the "good life". Naturally what makes their happy life and mine so personally special is totally different. As I see it, theirs is firmly grounded in modern and up-to-date electronic gadgets the complexity of which is still beyond my poor sagging mind and slow aptitude; mine was of course very much grounded in outdoor activities and lot of DIY stuff. Maybe looking back into my own distant past would at least serve one good purpose—a personal record of the bygone way of life and the socio-cultural values extant in Thailand more than half a century ago.

COMMUNAL / EXTENDED FAMILY ENVIRONMENT

It is hard to pinpoint the age where my own memory can without external assistance recall events or significant experiences of childhood. Nonetheless, I can recall with clarity that by the time I was four years old I was living in my paternal grandfather's home together with my siblings and numerous cousins of more or less the same age range. The old house had a vast com-pound and a number of buildings surrounding the main residence where my grandmother (my grandfather had passed on before I was born), my uncle's and my own families resided. Other buildings were occupied by families of uncles and aunts and other relatives. It was a warm and happy setting for children. We were a roaring, unruly gang of naughtiness and free spirit. I could not remember being constrained by any set of physical or mental barriers that would curb our free-spirited activities especially during school holidays when all bigger/older cousins would be around to organize or invent games or frowned-upon activities which would normally take place at further corners of the compound, away from the prying eyes of grown-ups. Open-air and space, inventions of games, pastimes, and/or toys were our life style. Some favourite games in our collection include *I-mon son phaa*,[1] *Ling ching lak*,[2] *Ai kei Ai khong*,[3] *Khi ma song muang*[4] and kite-flying (naturally we made our own kites) and, among the girls, *moh khao moh kaeng*,[5] or fighting-fish rearing for the boys. My second elder brother was apparently an expert on this last mentioned pastime. We hardly stayed indoors because all our fun was conducted in an open space; in fact, one of the most "cruel" punishments that I remember was being ordered to stay inside the house for a specific time span. It was a most suffocating experience.

Living in a communal family home meant there was no secret, no privacy, and a lot of topsy-turvy and make-do situations. But then we were not really aware of any other style of a home-life nor such "strange" concepts as privacy. I remember well my father routinely opened my sisters' mails to make certain that no "subversive elements" would be passed on to them. And if my sisters were not happy with such privacy invasion, they never protested nor displayed their unhappiness. Imagine what kind of a family war would be waged in my own family if I were to adopt this parental care in dealing with my daughter's jealously-guarded private domain. Generally, whatever happened to a family member or a nuclear family would naturally become common knowledge to share, to criticize, to analyse, and to be used as a point of future reference within our communal circle. Luckily for us children, we were spared this unsavoury side of our communal life. For us, living in a big compound meant a common space to share whether it was food, fun, family happy time (now referred to as quality time) or parental attention. I personally benefited a great deal from my communal upbringing. I became well-versed in Thai classical literature such as the *Ramayana, Inao, Phra Aphai-mani*, and the *Romance of the Three Kingdoms* at quite a young age, even before I could really read well myself. I was also introduced to the world of modern/popular literature—such as the works of Dok Mai Sod, the then very "in" novels such as *Ban Sai-thong, Photjaman Sawangwong, Prisna* and *Sii Phaendin* before I reached my teen years. A habit of reading was instilled in me through a communal activity introduced by a senior aunt. This particular aunt loved to have all the classics and the modern/popular literature read out to her in the evening (this was before the age of television), and encouraged her young nieces and nephews to join her as members of this literature soiree, listening to elder cousins or other relatives taking turn reading these precious works.

The fact that my father loved the classics and would recite some of these works especially the *Ramayana* as part of his pick-me-up in the morning or, whenever he felt inclined, as a tease or lesson to his younger siblings, somewhat completed my "classics education". As far as I can remember I grew up loving reading and appreciating the outdated classical literature.

Some fond memories of good old times that I truly cherish from my childhood include the annual merit-making day in memory of the passing away of my paternal grandfather which fell on November 10th, the summer *khao chare* day(s) for the family sometime in April or early May, and some other communal activities such as wreathe or wedding-gifts making.

November 10th was a most important day in my childhood calendar. Not only because the Suwannathat clan would come together and take part in this filial and family devotion to its ancestors: it was also a day that served as the clan's annual gathering whereby members would spend part of the time catching up with their updated news and extended family developments or simply enjoying one another's company. Joy, affection, patience, tolerance and compassion were flowing in plenty among elders. For children, it was a heavenly time. Actually, the fun and indulgence began even before the day itself namely during the preparations for the occasion. For a few days prior to November 10th, the compound of the house was temporarily turned into an open-air cooking arena where many types of dishes, including the family specialties, and all kinds of traditional desserts were being prepared for the great day. It was great fun to witness the activities: the construction of a huge stone stove for cooking rice in an enormous metal *kuali* (wok); the making of flour from rice using a manual stone-grinder (no ready-made flour was good enough for the required recipes); the selection of ingredients for certain dishes that got various "chefs" including my mother, to argue with one another with their lively repartees; and the presence of practically all kinds of utensils and food stuff in big quantities—vegetables, meat, poultry, eggs, sugar (both palm and cane), and others.

The memorial service and the merit-making rite took place not at home but at a royal temple built in honour of Phranang Chao Sommanat-watha-nawadi. Known commonly as Wat Som, the temple was, and still, regarded as the temple of our ancestors, as Queen Sommanat, Rama IV's first queen who died in childbirth, has always been identified as an "honorary" member of the clan simply because of the fact that her mother came from our clan. Impressive family history aside, for children such as myself, the whole day was our red-letter day because it was the day of almost complete freedom with non-stop happy, happy fun time. The fun started with the trip from home to the temple (most of the time in a huge transport full of food contain-ers and enveloped in deliciously pungent fragrance of a variety of flowers). The vehicle was spacious enough for us to while our time playing some of our indoor favourite games such as the five stones or *i-tag*. Once we got to the open space of the temple (visiting the temple these days, no one would believe it that once the space surrounding the main pagoda was large and perfumed by the sweet scent of *dok phikun* from trees hemming the temple compound) and performed our obligatory homage to the ancestors' ashes beneath a statue of the Buddha, we were free to roam around, climbing or rather running up and down the steps of the pagoda and enjoying all the good stuff the day had to offer. It was a perfect time.

For our family, *khao chare* was, still is, a summer affair when the weather was hot and almost unbearable. Remember that those were the days before air conditioning had been introduced, and though Bangkok was very much cooler and more pleasant than it is now, the temperature could become un-pleasant especially during the months of April and May. My family never had *khao chare* at any other time of the year. Again the fun of the *khao chare* day was not so much in the consumption of the dish, though that was, I must admit, a great culinary joy for me, but in engaging in the preparation of it. I most enjoyed watching my elders exhibiting the art of carving chili, cucum-bers and spring onions among other fruits and greens into leaves and flowers and whatever other artistic shapes and sizes. So what is *khao chare?* In sum, my family's *khao chare* is a special set of dishes composed of rice soaked in cool and fragrant water, stuffed *prig-yuak* (big chili stuffed with minced meat marinated with spices), *kra-pi* (actually a mixture of prawn-paste, *kra-chai* and spices, dipped into beaten egg and fried), fried shallots stuffed with a mixture of *pla-haeng* and other ingredients, and served together with a side dish of fresh and cold variety of fruits and vegetables all carved in beautiful shapes of leaves and flowers. As we only had *khao chare* in the summer which coincided with the long school holiday, *khao chare* always reminds me of those happy, carefree and contented days of childhood.

FAMILY AND UPBRINGING

I was born into a fairly conservative family, meaning that throughout my childhood my father was the sole breadwinner and my mother a housewife who focused on the well-being of her husband and children. This responsibil-ity must have been hard going for her in spite of the help afforded by the traditional communal family living. There were at any one time at least four of the young ones in her care. Yet in spite of her very traditional upbringing and the expected role she played so well as wife and mother until the death of my father, my mother entertained an amazingly liberal outlook—a little too advance for her time in fact—and was open-minded when it came to gender issues. She wanted her daughters to have as good an education as her sons; she wished all of her children to have a career, be masters of their chosen life and of independent means, regardless of gender. In fact, she insisted that her girls should not be brought up in the traditional mold like herself. Naturally they should learn to cook and clean so that they could take care of themselves and the family they would one day have, but, more important to her, they should be educated, have a career of their choice and make something of themselves.

When my father unexpectedly passed away I was finishing my *mathayom* 3. There were five of us still schooling. My mother took the shocking decision to join the work force in order to make sure that all of us would complete our education without interruption. She would not hear any talk/advice that tertiary education for girls was a waste. She'd rather give us a choice whether we wished to be a fulltime housewife (and thus "wasted" our hard-fought training) or a career woman, or both. To her being a mother was not an obligation, but rather an option that each of her daughters should make themselves. I am so grateful to her for standing up for her daughters. I also take pride that I have inherited many aspects of her then blazing-trail stand and determination on gender in general and the right of a woman to freely choose how to live her life.

Yet all in all, I grew up basically in a strict sociocultural environment where discipline reigned supreme. Strangely as it seemed for the generation of macho men to which he belonged, my father chose to get involved in our upbringing ever since we were small. For one thing, my father was truly determined to instil in his children the traditional values of good manners and of being respectful to elders. To him it was an unforgivable sin and evidence of poor upbringing if we ventured to explain disputed issues at hand to our elders, be they our aunts, grandmothers, uncles or senior cousins. There were "rules" of good manners and good behaviour: one needs to refrain from rebutting your elders, from portraying a defiant look, to be ever obedient and respectful of one's elders. In short, to just keep quiet with one's head down if in trouble with grown-ups. We all soon learned to know our place in the hierarchy of grown-ups. My father was also very conscious of the healthy mental growth of his children. I vividly recollect the "must" routine we were required to perform every Buddhist Sabbath day (which occurred every week according to the lunar calendar). On such days, my immediate three siblings and I would join my grandmother in front of a radio, listening to the Sabbath sermon delivered by a reputable monk and broadcast on the national radio service. At the time, we were all livid and thought such an exercise a waste of our precious playtime. We even thought it was one of subtle punishments my father loved to churn out every time we were perceived to have committed a "wrongdoing". Looking back, I have to admit that these sermons had been informative and useful. For me, my personal and basic understanding of right and wrong, good and not so good, compromise, humility and compassion were nurtured and sharpened by these sermons.

Maybe to soften my father's strict and disciplinary stand, my mother took every opportunity to balance it with a more laissez-faire approach to kids practised by my maternal grandparents. I remember my countless visits and long stays at my maternal grandparents' home. There we were allowed to talk to—compared with being talked at by—our elders and were forever forgiven if ever we should commit wrongdoings through curiosity or pure naughtiness. Though my mother would never go against my father in front of us, she must have often taken him to task in the privacy of their bedroom. When this happened, we would notice our father becoming more playful and letting his guard down, at least for a few days.

SCHOOLING

As far as I can recall, schooling began almost the same moment that I was conscious of being. In fact, I am unable to clearly look back into my pre-schooling childhood days. I recollect the unhappy feeling of always being pressured by my father's constant scrutiny of my school performance, in spite of the fact that I always did well. I started schooling at the tender age of around three years old when my maternal grandmother sent me to a Chinese school near her place. It was hoped that the school would put some discipline into the child who appeared loud and bordering hyperactive (not that the term was then in vogue: very naughty and impossible to discipline would be how I was described). I loved the experience as there were many friends and toys to play with and therefore I was more than willing to start a proper school soon after this. In truth I took to school as a duck to water. As it turned out, though I could not really quite grasp it then, I was lucky to catch a pedagogic attention of one teacher who understood and successfully handled my bound-less energy, curiosity and precocious intelligence. Instead of forcing me into the tight class structure and discipline, she won my "cooperation" by allow-ing me to entertain myself after I got all the class and some extra work done. Without much effort, I seemed to have done pretty well throughout my primary education and was awarded a "promotion", that is allowed to skip one standard, which resulted in my passing out of primary education in three years instead of the four years prescribed.

The Thai educational system of my time i.e. the 1950s and 1960s required children from an average age of 5 years old to an average age of 18 years old to attend primary (4 years), secondary (6 years) and pre-university (2 years) schools before they could proceed to any tertiary educational institute. Urban children would normally be sent to a kindergarten for one or two years prior to primary schooling. Compulsory education first ended with completion of primary education, but later was advanced to the completion of the *mathay-om* 3 of the secondary education. A secondary school certificate holder could proceed to a vocational college of their choice, subject, of course, to their individual ability, for a period of three to five years, or continue with the pre-university programme and enter the academic world of university. There were at the time two main universities in Bangkok namely the prestigious

Chulalongkorn University, the choice target of practically every pre-university graduate, and the people's Thammasat University with its then most prestigious Law and Political Science Faculties.

As there was no official hard and fast rule about school attending age, and most likely because I was a nuisance at home, I was sent to school when I was very young and because of my ability to read and write well beyond my years, I completed my primary schooling a few years ahead of the primary school average age. By the time I reached my twelfth year, I had finished my lower secondary school level. I loved school and all the facilities and activities it provided. Inexplicably, my father chose to send me, alone among his children, to a small private primary school owned by a Christian couple on the Si Ayudhya Road. I am not certain whether my parents realized that every Friday—I think it was Friday—the school would arrange a special session propagating Christianity—its history, philosophy, the Bible and amazing episodes of Jesus's life told with colourful illustrations and at times dramas, or special sermons on God, Jesus Christ and the Trinity among others. Most children attending the school were Buddhists. I do not recall anyone among us converted to Christianity. But we all loved and looked forward to these special sessions because to us they were more an entertainment than religious propaganda. My happy memory of the school owes much to my standard two class mistress who set the tone of how to deal with active and vocal pupils such as myself. I remember none of us was ever punished for our nonconformist attitude to learning. As long as we did our work well we were allowed to "retire" to the back of the class and did whatever we fancied without disturbing or interfering with on-going class lessons or our classmates.

School life was the best part of my childhood. Undoubtedly.

EXTERNAL ENVIRONMENT

The world of my childhood, Bangkok of the second half of the 1940s and early 1950s, and Bangkok of the twenty-first century are, to state the obvious, worlds apart. The Bangkok I grew up in had more big trees than high-rise buildings, more canals than roads, better clean air and clear canal water, no air-conditioning and few cars and buses: children had no trouble crossing roads without minders. It had slow but safe and charming trams as a part of public transport. The tallest buildings that I can recall were the exotic and glittering spires of the Grand Palace which are now towered over by many less individualistic skyscrapers that dominate contemporary Bangkok's skyline. There were canals and big trees (mostly rain-trees, tamarind and mahogany apparently planted during the reign of King Chulalongkorn) lining both sides of the two-lane roads everywhere. There were also proper footpaths under the shade of these trees making walking pleasant and fun. My paternal grandparents' home was hemmed in by a canal and a modern road lined with beautiful and shady rain-trees. I recall happily skipping to school with my elder sisters along the Phyathai road footpath with a row of rain-trees on one side and a clean and clear canal on the other. It was indeed a happy idyllic living in a clean, cool, safe, serene and beautiful Bangkok that has definitely long disappeared or is simply relegated to a distant past, and lives only in nostalgic memories of Bangkokians of my generation.

No far from my home was the Sa Prathum Palace, the residence of Somdet Phra Phanwassa, the Queen Grandmother (and one of Chulalongkorn's chief consorts). It was also my cousins' and my own happy playground. In those far-gone days of the 1950s security issues did not command such a strong presence as presently. The Palace gate was always open and though there were guards around, the public seemed to have no difficulty moving in and out of the Sa Prathum Palace. One logical explanation was the fact that the Queen Grandmother had many farm and orchard tenants and their family members lived within the enormous compound of her palace. The palace compound proper was huge and filled with mature trees, and small buildings. It seemed unlikely to us children at least that anyone could disturb the tranquillity of the palace. Nonetheless, one cardinal rule we learned was to make ourselves "invisible" and "voiceless" when we passed the main residence where the Queen Grandmother resided (she disliked noisiness of all kinds, we were told). I look back with disappointment that in spite of our countless adventures to the Sa Prathum Palace, we never came face to face with the Queen Grandmother or any of the dignitaries who resided there.

Usually, whenever my cousins and I could sneak out from our place without notice of our minders, we would visit the Sa Prathum Palace. We never tired of admiring the great pond with its unique-looking water lily, the Victoria lotus apparently imported from Latin America, together with its enormous and amazingly tray-shaped leaves. I remember wondering whether these enormous tray-shaped leaves would be able to take our weight if we were to try to sit on one of them. Apart from the main attraction of the Victoria lotus, my cousins and I were most mesmerized by various fruit trees found in the orchards of palace tenants. With a few baht payment to orchard owners, we were given freedom to pick fruits from the trees ourselves. Every trip to the Sa Prathum Palace would usually end up with us coming home with handfuls of guavas, Siamese apples (*pud-sa*), jackfruits (*khanun*), kra-thon[6] and mangoes. The fun was not so much about the fruits per se, but was more about spotting the right fruits in the groves and the challenge of tree climbing to get them. Considering how young we must have been—no more than ten years old—it is a wonder that such foolhardy adventures did not end in one or more amongst our gang members being seriously injured.

One of the highlights that I vividly remember and cherish was lining up with members of my big family and others along the Phyathai road waiting for the King and Queen to pass on their way to the Sa Prathum Palace, the National Stadium or Chulalongkorn University. We knew the King would be passing our way because policemen would be standing along both sides of the royal route and traffic would be stopped at least half an hour before the royal convoy appeared. We loved looking at, and waving to, the royal couple who would smile (the Queen) and wave (the King and Queen) and acknowledge our presence. It was a great day every time we had a chance to see the King and being acknowledged by His Majesty and the Queen.

I also loved journeys to visit my maternal grandparents in Thonburi, the capital of King Taksin's Siam, situated on the opposite side of the Chao Phraya to Bangkok. It was fun, challenging and exciting to sit in a small boat, a kind of sampan, rowed by one man, across the seemingly huge and endless body of water. The rower expertly navigated his tiny boat against the rather lively currents of the Chao Phraya and amidst the endless on-coming floats of teak logs, big commercial carriers of rice and other goods from up-country regions and other types of boats, all appearing much bigger than the one my mother and I were travelling in, and all vying for their space in the mother of all Thai rivers. Yet I truly preferred the boat trip rather than a land route across the Rama I Memorial Bridge which was not only much longer but also a rather boring journey. Nothing ever happened on the road. Everything about the Chao Phraya enlivened my curiosity and, curiously, I had an enormous sense of triumph every time we landed safely at the Khlong Sarn jetty. These boat trips, exciting and animating as they were, were truly haphazard at best. But what other alternative was there that would indelibly impress upon a child to love, respect and appreciate this great body of water, the then main life-line of the kingdom?

The 1950s was not a good time as far as politics and the stability of the country were concerned. It was the time of seemingly endless coups and counter coups, of rivalries and power struggles within the ruling clique itself, of the Cold War ideological rivalry and of sociopolitical instability. Yet this sociopolitical environment had few negative effects on us children who remained immune to the ugly situation created by grown-ups. In truth, I found Prime Minister Field Marshal Phibun or rather his pictures in perfect creamy-coloured and well-tailored suits and always with a friendly smile, most reassuring. In school, we wholeheartedly learned to sing all politico-patriotic songs such as "Ton Trakun Thai", "Rak Muang Thai", "24 Mithuna" and others. Strangely enough I was not intimidated by a show of force during any coup, such as the rolling out of tanks, soldiers with guns walking the streets and bunkers set up with machine guns at strategic points in the capital. As one of the true-blue coup kids that I turned out to be, a coup atmosphere seemed a fun/*sanuk* time for me and most likely for many other children of my generation. We could befriend the soldiers who patrolled the streets and would often be allowed to touch the weapons on display. I grew up with good feelings about soldiers and *coup d'etats*. Like other children of my generation, I had no clue, nor did I bother, about politics and justification of the military political role or for that matter the rule of democracy and elections. Elections were a fun time because most trees along the road to school were pasted with posters and handbills of slogans and faces that I did not know except that of Chomphon Por. In my childhood ignorance, I did not quite get the reason for general or any kind of elections. After all, what was the fuss? Chomphon Por was our leader and he would always be there for us. It was not until in my university days that I unconsciously and belatedly began a process of sociopolitical awareness and understanding.

Then life became complicated and growing up was no longer fun.

NOTES

1. *I-mon son phaa* is a kind of children's game that involved a number of players (the more the merrier) who, except the one with a piece of cloth, sit in a circle while the one with the cloth, the runner, would walk or run slowly behind the circle and stealthily places the cloth behind one of the players who forms a part of the circle. The aim is for the runner to run around the circle fast enough to return to the person behind whom he/she has placed the piece of cloth before that person realizes that there is a piece of cloth behind him/her. If the runner succeeds, he/she would pick up the cloth and start hitting the person who fails to redeem the cloth behind him/her, and after completing a round of the circle, he/she would take the place of the loser. The loser becomes the runner and the game starts all over again.

2. *Ling ching lak* is a pastime game whereby all players stand touching their selected pillars while one of them acts as a 'monkey' without a pillar. The purpose of the game is for those with pillars to exchange their position without their pillar being snatched by the 'monkey'. If the 'monkey' succeeds in catching one of the pillars, the erstwhile owner of that pillar automatically becomes the 'monkey'. And the game continues. Obviously the best avenue for such a game is a corridor or an open yard with a lot of pillars.

3. The game of *Ai kei Ai khong* involves an unspecified number of players where one of them acts as a 'crocodile' in a river with a well-defined demarcation between the river and the river banks. The idea is for some players to engage the 'crocodile's' attention in order to afford their friends to cross the river to another riverbank without being touched or caught by the 'crocodile'.

4. *Khi ma song muang* is a horse riding and racing game that requires players to make their own 'horse' from banana leave stems, and the one who 'rides' the fastest 'horse' wins.

5. *Moh khao moh kaeng* is play-cooking using miniature saucepans and charcoal cooker made of clay. It is usually more fun if real charcoal fire and real foodstuff are allowed such as eggs, vegetables, and rice.

6. *Kra-thon* is a local fruit that can be eaten raw or made into an elaborate dessert dish.

Fair-haired Cherub

Nicholas Tarling

Schooling should perhaps provide some time-lines for a child's memory, but my earliest years in inter-war England cannot be quite cudgelled into chronology. They bring my elder brother – born in 1927, a little over three years before me - into focus, because we both went by bus to Frays College in Uxbridge, Middlesex. But we also went to the Butterfields' dame schools, he to the senior one run by an elder Miss Butterfield in Iver village, Buckinghamshire, opposite Coppins, the walled dwelling of Princess Marina, and I to the junior one on Richings Park estate, run by the younger Miss Butterfield, under whose tutelage I have a vivid memory of playing with plasticine. Did the Frays phase precede or follow the Butterfield phase? I cannot recall, and Mike is no longer around to put his brain to the test. Uncertain recollection suggests that I went to Uxbridge after the plasticine period, but went back to the young Miss Butterfield when I became more literate. Certainly Frays was very inadequate. Searching for a better education – initially of course for Mike – was to be decisive in our parents' decision in 1937 to leave Richings Park for somewhere with a better school still within commuter range of the City of London, where Dad was an accountant for a firm with South African interests, Central Mining.

If plasticine sticks in my memory of the Richings Park phase, a prime memory of Frays College, I fear, is the boys' lavatory: it was utterly filthy, the floor itself covered in excreta. The teaching should be more in my mind. It was done, I recall, in a very large room, probably containing three different classes. It must have been there that I somehow learned to read at about five years of age and presumably to write, glorious skills that I thankfully can still exercise, though others [and sometimes I myself] have been testy over my illegibility. What happens in Chinese schools, where writing is an art? I cannot recall any art teaching at Frays, nor indeed at the Butterfields'. I am amazed at what children can now achieve in primary and intermediate schools in New Zealand and in Singapore. Do we knock too much out of them later on?

Most of the time, of course, I was not at school but at home. It seemed to me on a visit only a few years ago that Richings Park was almost frozen in time. The same block of shops – presumably in different hands – still stood at the end of Thorney Lane. Our house was still there, though I could not decide which of two similar buildings it was. The name Mum and Dad had given it – houses were always given names – was no longer in use. That was 'Manana', applied, I later learned, because whenever they asked the builder when it would be ready for occupation, he replied 'Tomorrow'.

My recollections are less of Dad, or even Mum, than of the context: I suppose they were taken for granted. I do not even recall the appearance of a third son, Francis, in 1936, let alone the international crises of that year. There was no radio, but there was a piano, made by Weidig in Leipzig, on which Mum played, as she continued to do in later years until, she claimed, she had become so long-sighted she could not longer reach the keyboard and read the music at the same time. Both Mum and Dad, I learned subsequently, had taken classes at the Guildhall, and, I suppose before children supervened, went to shows in London, *Chu Chin Chow, The Maid of the Mountains, The Immortal Hour*, which remained a favourite with Dad. He sometimes deployed his pleasant baritone on the prologue to *Pagliacci.* We joined in when Mum went down-market to Ketelbey's *In a Persian Market.* 'Backsheesh! Backsheesh! Allah!' we yelled in childish disregard of the yet unknown perils of 'orientalism'. Sometimes one of the dogs contributed an occasional howl, whether in sympathy or protest. There were two, Kai and Punch. When they died, two more replaced them, establishing a family tradition that Francis sustained.

The front garden was quite small. In our day it had a curved path leading round to the front door, which was at the side. It was outside that where my pram and I, well wrapped up, were placed for fresh air. But later I could see out of the front windows who was coming to the door and even join Mum in 'answering' it. It might be the milkman, who did not deliver bottles, but sloshed his product out of a churn. Or, more sinister, it could be a 'gypsy' woman, with a tray of wares, such as clothes pegs, that also included little bits of wood that you could put in your raspberry jam as pips to enhance its apparent authenticity. The postman came to the door, as he still does in Britain, and each door had a letter-box in it.

The back garden I recall as large, and, after what must have been an initial burst of heavy work, Dad rather gave up on it. He continued an interest in the asparagus bed, however. Adjacent to that, right at the far end of the garden, was a somewhat dilapidated shed.

Mike had a friend, Don Dement, an Australian boy with a metal stump on one leg, who thought that was a place to try out smoking cigarettes, then, of course, an entirely fashionable practice in which my father indulged, but which was supposed to be known to the young only by the remarkable cards that could be found in each packet and could make up whole collections to stick in books of British or Empire cricketers or soldiers or railway engines. I suppose Don rolled his own. Perhaps he was nine or ten, but this six-year old did not care for the puff he took.

Our mischiefs seem to have been fairly mild. Another I recall Don probably had a part in: was he at least incipiently a Richings Park larrikin, I wonder? If you scrambled over the shed roof, and dropped down the other side, you could find what was in the neighbouring yard, sheds or garages belonging, I suppose, to the builders of the estate, full of odd tiles and collectables of that kind.

Don was the nearest we got to someone exotic: there were no black, brown or yellow people in Iver or Richings Park at the time, and not many, I suppose, even in neighbouring Uxbridge or Slough. There were what were thought to be jokes about exotic people, most, I think, about the Chinese, prominent after all in the East End which, before the first war, had been a place to which Cooks organised tours. Were the Jews exotic, too? I have no recollection of them at this time, though later we came to know 'Mr Stern', a genial young man in Dad's office at Central Mining, who had a fast car: a family friend, though Dad might still refer to him as a Jewboy. And I had no sense that those in Ketelbey's Persian market were real people, let alone Muslims. Religion of any kind was in fact absent. We were, as documents show, christened, but we did not attend church, my parents writing CofE whenever called upon to indicate their religion. The fact that they named all their boys after saints – three of them had two 'Christian' names both those of well-known saints - seems to have been entirely accidental.

Mine are Peter Nicholas, Nicholas being the most used. Mum told me she [or they] chose it because she and Dad had been to a play and the star spoke the name so beautifully. Nowadays I have to hang on to it in face of software obviously developed in the US, where the use of first names is almost de rigueur. I cannot travel by air without being called 'Peter', and I am addressed, with the spurious intimacy of almost every contemporary business, as 'Dear Peter'. How Mum would have hated it! she thought her Christian name, Doris, should be reserved for the most intimate occasions; otherwise she was 'Mrs. Tarling'. The children certainly never addressed their parents by their Christian names, as was even then an occasional middle-class practice. They were firmly Dad and Mum. I cannot recall how they addressed each other. Nor indeed at an early age was I conscious of any tension between them, though in retrospect I have concluded that there was.

Maybe the cinema was my source of the exotic. Films seem to me now –
after years as a historian looking, necessarily in vain, for authenticity – such
lies, though the source often of enjoyment or even what might be called, if
such a paradox is allowed, a moderate kind of catharsis. But then you realise
that *Lawrence of Arabia* was filmed in Spain and the two people apparently
engaged in conversation were filmed, perhaps separately, several times over.
And now of course much of the stuff we swallow – infantilisation being a
powerful marketing tool – is 'virtual', the product of clever computer manip-
ulators.

Richings Park had the Plaza cinema, on the right hand side of the road
leading to the station where Dad caught the train to Paddington. In those days
there was a Saturday morning serial, which I think Mike used to go to on his
own. I recall going only with my parents, and what is now called 'parental
guidance' was certainly needed, though not provided. We saw *The Lives of
the Bengal Lancers*, and I seem still to see something in flames. I was quite
terrified by the film of Rider Haggard's *She*, though I cannot recall anything
but the terror.

There were other moments of real-life terror. Once I was somehow lost, if
not to myself, then to my mother. All I was doing was playing with friends, I
suppose from Miss Butterfield Jr's, but we went on rather late, and it was
some way across the estate: probably not very far, since distances are exag-
gerated by the very young. Somehow I had lost the sense of time. Another
rather dim memory is again of a kind of bewildered participation, which this
time alarmed my father as well as myself. We were, it seems, at a large party
for children, maybe a Central Mining do. I joined a procession that was part
of the entertainment, then suddenly wondered where I was, and where indeed
my father was. The details are obscure, the fright remains. Another occasion
in which memory seems to offer has already been 'consolidated' by a mention in *History Boy*. I am in a push-chair, visiting London Zoo with my
maternal grandparents, Grandma and Grandpa [as we called them] Bibbye.
Entering the giraffe house, where those gentle animals were standing in
stalls, I was peeling a banana bit by bit. A giraffe bent down and neatly
removed the content, leaving me with the skin.

The Bibbyes were, unusually in the family, car-owners, a Vauxhall with
the famous V-bonnet. I think they once took us to Burnham Beeches, a wood
in Buckinghamshire, but my close association with them belongs to a later
phase. Dad's mother, Grandma Tarling, I cannot recall at Iver at all. Grandpa
Tarling, it seems, no longer existed. We knew nothing then, and know not
much now, of that side of the family, if indeed there was one. It seems likely
that Grandpa Tarling was had more than one liaison, and that Grandma
Tarling was a rather beautiful Edwardian lady who adopted some of the
Edwardian fashions. Much later, it seems, Dad was made conscious that he
was illegitimate – had he known before? –when he tried to get a passport. We

used to be told he was born in New York 'unexpectedly', whatever that meant. He certainly had a half-brother, Uncle George, with a different surname, Andreas, and it seems a half-sister who was said to have married the archdeacon of Buenos Aires. How much all that was valid it is hard to tell. Grandma Tarling did maintain a correspondence with 'Aunt Doris' in Argentina. We could see from the stamps.

The 1911 census is only partly revealing. Admitting illegitimacy was surely a more questionable step than it is now. Family members have not been genealogically inclined. The few Tarlings around – only one other in New Zealand, and one or two in the British Library catalogue – seem to have no connexion, though I occasionally get letters from lawyers or others who are seeking such links. No one has studied the Bibbyes, I think, though I remember in a later phase puzzling over a rather lovely photo portrait of a Grace Bibbye who had the 'fuzzy hair' [as we called it] that suggested maybe that there was 'a touch of the tarbrush', perhaps from Sierra Leone. Grandpa maintained – one of his jokes – that he was descended from a Welsh Jew, on the principle that he liked neither Jews nor Welshman. Grandma Bibbye's side of the family had the distinguished name of Nevill, without an 'e', which was Mum's second given name. The genes were marked by longevity, evident in her case, but also with other great uncles and aunts. For Grandma was one of nine, born to an East End shoemaker as Dad sometimes sniffily said, and Mum had aunts, like 'Aunt Olive', younger than herself. Having such large families was a latter-day version of Victorian attempts to keep some alive as well as a testimony to lack of contraception. Now they lived, and Mum had no brothers or sisters, though going on to produce five children of her own, rather unusual by the 1930s.

But this is to go ahead as well as to go back. We had other 'aunts', 'courtesy aunts', as they are called. The neighbours on one side of 'Manana' were Mr and Mrs Burrows. He kept a garage in Slough, not far off, though more or less inaccessible to the car-less: how little we travelled – how little most people travelled – in those days! We saw much more of 'Aunt Maud', who may have been, I think, one of Mike's godparents [such we had, though I cannot recall any attempts by any of them to exercise their Anglican role: they were a source of presents not prayers]. My recollection is that she used finger bowls at table, though, sensible as they are, they had become rare, and are now occasionally visible in stately homes or conceded by seafood restaurants. 'Serviettes', as we middle middle-class people called what upper middle-class people called 'table napkins', were, however, a requirement. Each of us had indeed a silver serviette ring with our initials on it.

Other courtesy aunts included 'Auntie Gladys'. Mother and I and maybe a small Francis used to go round to her place for afternoon tea. Some trauma had hit her, and she always set an extra place for 'absent friends', though it was never filled. Then there was 'Rabbo', my childish rendering of Miss

Rambaud: she does not seem to have the title of aunt. We also had tea with 'Auntie More' [why did I not use her Christian name? Aunts seemed to have them and grandparents not] and 'Uncle Jack' [he got his]. They were my godparents, and we played in the 'Rec' [the recreation ground] that their garden backed on to. 'Mrs Hoey' was another prominent figure, though not an 'aunt'. She kept the drapers round the corner, past the post office. Like other drapers, she talked of things by the yard at, say, one and eleven three. That was one shilling and eleven pence and three farthings, a kind of teasing precision still with us in another form when we are offered goods at nine dollars ninety-nine cents.

There were a few other shops further on, including a grocery. All I can remember of that, besides the soft drinks, is the jam: Robertsons, with a paper 'Golliwog' at the top of each jar, and the nearest we got – not very near – to the current practice of itemising the components: the best, I think, was called 'full fruit standard', which meant that it really had raspberries in it. Perhaps the uncanned items were fresher than they now are: bacon was sliced for you, butter patted: you were served, rather than serving yourself. There was no call for, perhaps no capacity to provide, the preservatives so alarmingly present in supermarket goods that lie on the shelf until you pick them up. I do not recall a separate 'sweet shop', still a feature of British main streets. There were, however, plenty of sweets, some still well known, like Bassett's liquorice, Rowntree's wine gums, Fry's and Cadbury's chocolates. Ice cream, of course: cornets, as we called them, not cones, the art being to get through it before it melted and savour the mingling of the cream and the wafer at the bottom if you had managed to push it down with your tongue.

I had no bike at Richings Park – I did not manage one till years later – nor even a tricycle: I did have a pedal car, though I could not manage that either: unable somehow to get my feet to push – maybe I lacked physical coordination even then – I always wanted someone else to do the pushing. The brothers had other toys, of course. We all had, as children still have amid their mountains of plastic, some 'soft' toys, usually avian or mammalian, that had to go everywhere with us and we could not get to sleep without. My sister still preserves my all-time favourite, Belisha. This was a bird-like creature, fashioned substantially like the beacon standing at pedestrian crossings, with an orange head and a long neck ringed in black and white, and rather rudimentary wings. It – she, perhaps – was called Belisha after the Home Secretary who introduced the beacons, Sir Leslie Hore-Belisha. Mike had a very large teddy bear that could not be taken to bed, inherited, I think, from the Bibbye family, maybe dating back to the time of Teddy Roosevelt, after whom teddy bears were named. Francis was to become very attached to a pink rabbit, though after a while it ceased to be very pink.

Later, but not, perhaps, at Iver, we were to have Dinky toys, wind-up Hornby trains, Brittain's toy soldiers, then made of lead, a dolls' house, and rubber Minibrix. Memory suggests that I did, however, have a toy stove at this point, in which there were little burners, so that you could actually cook a minute pancake. For some time I treasured the idea that I might be a chef when I grew up. But I have certainly failed to develop any skill I might have had and cooking for oneself long ago curtailed any wish to try. Other burners were those put in bedrooms when you were ill: vapourising what? We had little lamps, 'night lights', when we went to sleep. I cannot recall any dealings with the doctor while at Iver, though I was evidently circumcised. Remedies in those days included things also found in Otago University's publication on patent medicines in New Zealand. Maybe children throughout the empire were subject to California Syrup of Figs or paraffin oil, their cuts treated with Zambuk and Dettol, surviving despite or because.

Between Richings Park and Iver village the road crossed the Grand Junction Canal. I do not remember that as at all active: maybe the industrial disuse of canals had not yet been succeeded by the leisure use. Just on the estate side was Mr Wells' farm. That was one of the destinations of a Sunday walk. He was, as a farmer should be, a genial sort. I clearly remember the thrill of collecting the eggs. His chickens really had a free range, not the measly concession now offered those uncaged. So eggs could be found in one of the barns or in the straw, and collecting them was something like a treasure hunt.

Occasionally we went to London, and Westbourne Park, the penultimate station before Paddington, stuck in my mind. There, I conceived, an imaginary person called Micalooloo dwelled, though whether she was benevolent or malevolent I cannot recall. Was it on that piece of railway that I became familiar with the numerous signs on the walls telling us of the virtues of Virol: 'anaemic girls need it.' The walls, of course, were sooty, the trains steam trains: I do not think there were long tunnels on this line, which made you close the windows and reposition the leather strap, holes in which enabled you regulate the opening. Our objective was usually Mother's objective: shopping for clothes mostly, I fancy, for us. We went to Barkers and Pontings, department stores in Kensington, or to Selfridges in Oxford Street. One year we saw the Lord Mayor's show in the City, though I am not sure that it passed the Central Mining building on London Wall.

The first annual holiday of which I retain a recollection – maybe it was absolutely the first - was at Cowes in the Isle of Wight, I think in 1935. I have quite a distinct memory, perhaps reconsolidated over the years, of clattering down a staircase to breakfast, and Grandma Tarling complaining of the noise I made. I also think we took a boat trip: another distinct picture emerges of stokers sweating away to keep the pistons going. Mother used to tell me I was the subject of admiration from German tourists on the island: I suppose they were tourists, though Portsmouth is of course very near. Allegedly they exclaimed in Aryan fashion over the fair hair I then had, though I had been bald for my first year or two.

The next holiday I place at Paignton in 1936. I remember even less about that, though we did go to Torquay and see the 'palms' that grew in its mild climate, in fact New Zealand cabbage trees, I later learned. In 1937, memory suggests, we stayed our three weeks at a hotel, the Wyche, in Bournemouth, with other family members also there. I suppose it was from there we took a 'charabanc' trip to Cheddar Gorge to see the stalactites and stalagmites. I can remember them, and also how sick I was at the rear of the bus.

Our 1938 holiday was at Worthing. But that was reached by quite a different route, for by then we had moved to St Albans in Hertfordshire in search of better schools for Mike, who was just under 11 by then, and later for Francis and myself, and later still, of course, for Julian and Fiona, who entered the world in 1939 and 1940.

A child, we are told, sees things 'without judgment or understanding', as a character concludes in Stephanie Bishop's novel, *The Other Side of the World*, as he looks out of the train window when travelling through the appalling slums of Delhi he knew as a child: 'he would simply have seen children and animals, women washing'. [Sydney: Hachette, 2015, p. 190] Experience, expanding knowledge, greater consciousness, lead us to go further, some more than others. But one facility children deploy is a skill which some see as valueless and others as the foundation of learning. Children imitate; they also learn by rote. I can readily recall the nursery rhymes we picked up; I heard some of them the other day when overhearing a school party in Takapuna's Bruce Mason Centre. And there were family sayings that, a bit like comedian's jokes, were instant triggers of fun and threat.

The house in St Albans was 'Ninefields', 136 Clarence Road. It is still there. I have passed by twice in the past fifty years. Once it looked as if it been 'done up', but recently it looked quite distressed, as if it were occupied by flat-dwellers who did not care. It is unlikely, however, to be pulled down. The rest of the road had hardly changed at all since I left there in 1957. It is presumably protected. It lay on the fringe of Edwardian St Albans, adjacent to Sandpit Lane. On the other side of Sandpit Lane there were inter-war houses and unbuilt areas still with clumps of trees as if in the grounds of a great house. I believe the land had belonged to the Spencer family.

The house in Richings Park Dad owned, or at least had a mortgage on. The new home was rented. It belonged to a coal merchant, Pullinger. He was unwilling to do much to it, and in the second war and post-war periods, when rents were controlled, he did even less. It was thus as dilapidated as it now again looks. The damp course no longer worked, so that the walls were wet, and it was never painted, inside or out. Presumably Dad could not afford to buy a large house in such an area when we left Iver. He had to meet school fees, too. There was, however, some new furniture, and also some new bedding. Mike's was green, mine was pink, and Francis's was blue.

Though the house in retrospect seems to have been a bit of a wreck, it did not seem like that to the children who colonised it. The bells, of course, no longer worked: there were no servants to summon anyway. Nor were they there to bring coal up from the cellar under the kitchen for use in the coal-fire places that were in all the major rooms upstairs and down. Dad installed a number of gas-fires in the bedrooms. Downstairs only one big room was heated in the winter by a coal fire which had to be replenished by taking the scuttle down to the cellar and round which it was necessary to crowd if you were to keep warm. The kitchen was warm most of the time, since it contained an 'Ideal' boiler, which heated the water, and had to be fed by bringing coke up from the cellar, too. The rickety board on the wooden cellar steps had to be negotiated with care, whether with coal-scuttle in hand or coke-hod.

Beyond the kitchen was a scullery where the gas stove operated. That little room, also containing the sink, got very hot, even in winter, when the Sunday joint was in the oven. It was then that the Greek tortoise, bought off a counter in Woolworths for sixpence, decided that summer had come, hibernation was over, and burst out of the old meat safe in which he was supposed to pass the winter and sped across to the back door on a suicidal mission to reach the frosty garden. The scullery also contained the mangle, which had to be operated by hand, or indeed by both arms: it was hard work getting the clothes through. There was no washing machine, no drier. No refrigerator either: milk and meat were kept down in the cellar where it was cool at all times of the year. Things could still 'go off', given the otherwise happy lack of preservatives.

Downstairs the house included an entrance hall, out of which a passage led to the kitchen and the cellar stairs, and two large rooms, the one at the front called the drawing room, the one at the back the dining room, though most of the eating was done in the kitchen.

Stairs out of the hall also led up to the first floor, where there were three large bedrooms and one smaller one, together with a very run down bathroom, and a temperamental lavatory. Up another flight were a boxroom, an airing cupboard, and right at the top an attic, presumably once servant's quarters. For many years it was a children's playroom. It was later where I wrote my PhD thesis.

There was no garage. Indeed few of the houses of the time had garages. There were virtually no cars on the road. The coal was delivered by a lorry, but the milkman came by an electric van. The rag-and-bone man – who collected unwanted items too large to go into the dustbin – came by horse and cart, calling out as he came by. Ice-cream was sold by men on a tricycle with a refrigerated box at the front. They rang their bell to get attention. If you wanted Walls's ice-cream man to call, you could pin a card 'W' on the front gate.

The back garden consisted of a large lawn, surrounded by rambler roses and garden beds. They dated from the building of the house itself, and some had seen better days. Beyond the lawn was a weeping ash: it was trained to weep, rather than weeping naturally. Under it were winter aconites, snow-drops, and crocuses. And beyond that were fruit trees, equally old and very large. The apple tree could be climbed. It produced the best apples I have ever tasted, but they were very easily bruised, and never available on the market. You had to try to pick them. They bruised at once if they fell to the ground.

It was at that end of the garden that the children were given a plot of their own to tend. I became quite an enthusiast in the subsequent years, tending to go for the unusual, rather than the obvious. Dad brought me a red clematis, and I also took pleasure in trying out the packets of seeds you could get at Woolworths for a few pence, though the results only rarely lived up to the promise of the coloured packet. As I grew up, I got more ambitious, and in the war years I became increasingly responsible for the whole garden. The gardener Dad had employed when we first moved to St Albans joined up. Dad and Mike focused their attention on the wartime 'allotment', a very intractable piece of land carved out of a field further down Sandpit Lane that had to be broken in.

Moving involved, of course, a different school for me as well as Mike. While he went off to St Albans School, I went to Lyndale, a private school that took girls up to the adolescent years, and boys up to about the age of 9 or 10. It was what might be called a 'dame school', though two 'dames' were in charge. One was Miss [Elizabeth] Sheehan, a rather formidable little lady in, I suppose, her late fifties, though she seemed very old, and the other Mrs [Teresa] Walker, larger and younger and less formidable. Some of the class rooms were in a big old semi-detached house, still there in Hillside Road, now apartments. The Walkers occupied one half, the Sheehans [Elizabeth had a sister, Kate] the other half, along with the elementary forms [classes] and Form 3 upstairs. The other classes were located in a purpose-built 'Big Room' without permanent partitions between them. Behind the two buildings were the remnants of a garden. There was a lawn where the girls could play rounders. And beyond that the so-called spinney, the central feature of which was a large horse-chestnut tree. The maturing of the 'conkers' so that their polished brown outside was revealed and subsequent 'fights' between conk-ers with a string threaded through them were two of the harmless pleasures of boyhood.

Games themselves gave me no pleasure, and never have done so. For that purpose, and maybe for others, the pupils were allocated into 'houses'. All of those at Lyndale were given the names of bishops of St Albans, where a bishopric had been created at the time in Queen Victoria's reign when the old Abbey was subjected to a neo-Gothic restoration and turned into a cathedral. My house was Claughton and our colour was green. We sang hymns every morning, Anglican ones, which after all, like the Devil, have most of the best tunes. One of the teachers – usually Miss Hitchcock – thumped out the accompaniment. Hymn tunes stick in the memory, I find: I suppose repetition stores them away. And there was a great deal of rote-learning, including chanting of the mathematical tables: 12 12s are a hundred and forty-four, we would end in triumphant chorus. At the time, of course, there were twelve pence to a shilling, and a shilling was worth something. And eggs were sold by the dozen, as they often still are.

Miss Hull taught the youngest downstairs in the old house. We put on the plimsolls we had brought in our school bag, and sat in two at very low desks, using slates. From her preparatory endeavours we moved to another part of the room, where, besides chanting tables, we learned to write, dipping pens into inkwells in the right-hand corner of the desk, and using a copy book, with firm downstrokes and lighter upstrokes. A blot was a terrible thing. I do not think corporal punishment was applied for that, though Miss Sheehan did use a cane on the hands, and her stinging efforts could reduce a child to tears. I was a goody-goody, so it did not happen to me. I now had quite a mass of hair, and Mrs Walker once memorably described me as 'the fair-haired cherub who could do no wrong'. Whether Miss Sheehan saw me in the same way, I do not know. It did transpire that she thought I should enter the Church. I do not think I ever shared that ambition.

From that part of the old house, which was lit in the winter by gas-mantles, we moved on to a class in the Big Room. Of that I remember rather less. It seems that it was then we began to study history. That meant the history of Britain, starting more or less with the ancient Britons, and going on to 1066 and all that. The third class I attended was upstairs in the old house. Two teachers still come to mind, Miss Shilvock, an elegant lady who taught geography, and Miss, or was she Mrs Quiggin, an enthusiast who taught French. I still find it surprising that so old-fashioned a school could do something so enlightened as to teach a foreign language to eight year olds.

In 1939 the seaside holiday – undertaken this time by the nuclear family alone, no grandparents or aunts, though it had recently been augmented by the fourth son – was at a then rather remote, even desolate, resort in Sussex, West Wittering. I have two memories of it. It was the first occasion in which I have narrowly escaped drowning. Unlike Mike, I could not then swim, but I was happy playing in the sand. On this occasion, I had built a kind of sand-boat in which I sat, well out on the long more or less flat beach, and my idea, I suppose, was that I would abandon ship as the water eroded it. Suddenly, however, a wave came over my head, and another followed. I can still in my mind's eye see the swirl of the water above me. I was not afraid, but in retrospect I doubt if I could have survived much longer. I was in no position to shout for help, and Dad and Mum were well back on the beach. It was Mike who saw me and hauled me back to safety. So I think I owe my life to my late elder brother, though he never made a point of it.

The second memory was of the radio. The family did not have one, but there was one in the seaside house they rented. And Dad and Mum were glued to it in the evenings, for the news was, as I have realised since, of the Nazi-Soviet pact and of Hitler's threat to the Poland whose independence Britain and France had guaranteed. Indeed the holiday was shortened by a week, and we returned to St Albans. There we found Grandma and Grandpa Bibbye sticking brown paper strips on the windows, which was the recommended precaution against their shattering when the bombs began to fall. Dad had taken another recommended precaution. He had not built an 'Anderson shelter' in the garden, as many did: a kind of concrete bunker. He had, however, had the passage from the hall to the kitchen strengthened by heavy wooden planks. That, as I remember, was where we went when the first air-raid siren sounded, not long after Chamberlain's announcement. Nothing then happened. It was only in the following year that what was called the 'phony war' came to an end, and, after France surrendered, the Luftwaffe and the RAF engaged in the 'Battle of Britain'. It was then, I think, that we took shelter in the coal cellar. Sometimes we slept amidst the coal or coke.

St Albans was, however, rarely bombed. It was said that its long Cathedral was too useful a pointer for German planes on their way to smash the Midland manufacturing towns. Unfit for military service, Dad joined the Auxiliary Fire Service, going off in the evenings after a day's work in his City office to join the other fire-watchers. One morning he went up to London and found the City office was no longer there. A gas-main had been bombed and it had played on the Central Mining buildings all night. Nothing was left but the iron girders and on them the safes for each floor. Their contents burst into flame when they were opened, Dad said.

My memories of this period focus on family and school. The major family event of the early years of the war was the birth of Mum's fifth and last child, the first girl. Fiona was born in 1940 on 20 April, Hitler's birthday, too, as we too often reminded her. It can have been no fun being a sister to four older brothers, but she has always made the best of things.

The other major event for me was leaving Lyndale and going on, as 'Tarling ii', to join 'Tarling i', Mike, at St Albans School. That was over the other side of town, and since I did not at first yet ride a bike, I went by bus, the circular route, 354. From the town centre, I walked down French Row, a block of 18th century houses that had held prisoners in the Napoleonic wars, past the Clock Tower, built where there had once been an Eleanor Cross, across Verulam Road, down Fishpool Street to the School.

To the left was the Cathedral, more often called the Abbey, and the sixth form in fact occupied the gateway of the monastery, of which little else remained. The school claimed to have existed since 948, but its continuity is exposed to doubt. It had, however, been re-founded after the dissolution of the monasteries and chartered as a grammar school under Edward VI. Now it had become a 'public school', which, in the wayward style of the British, means in fact a 'private school', inasmuch as it was not state-controlled. 'Public schools' themselves had more status than 'secondary modern' schools, but there was also a pecking order among them. St Albans was not Eton or Harrow. It was a 'minor' public school, its headmaster, W.T. Marsh, a member of the Headmasters' Conference, the qualifying factor.

Looking back on it, I think it was a good school, and did a great deal for me. Not so far as games were concerned, of course. My focus was on the academic side of things. I was not good at every subject, but good at the major subjects, including English and Mathematics, and they were given special weighting in the overall assessment of one's position in the form that took place at the end of every term until you entered the sixth form. I was invariably top of the form, in the term's work and the examinations, through-out the whole period. That must have been maddening for the rest of the class. But it had its positive side. I was, for example, able to pass, I think in 1941 or 1942, what later was called the 'eleven-plus', a state-supported ex-amination that entitled you to remission of fees. So Dad no longer had to shell out nine guineas a term. And the school diversified a bit. As a 'direct grant' school, its roll was half scholarship and half non-scholarship students.

I was still 'doing no wrong'. Just as well, too, for corporal punishment was still applied by prefects and form masters, as well as the Headmaster. Some of the masters were World War I veterans, and not always very stable, I think. At Form 1A Major R.O. Sanders absolutely lost his cool with a boy on one occasion. Now, of course, it would be regarded as – what it was in fact – an assault. Other masters were much milder. One I recall was 'Beery' Webster, who taught English, and found a way to make grammar interesting, and even entertaining, something now often absurdly deemed impossible and, even more absurdly, unnecessary. During the war, too, the 'masters' came to include women as well as men. Miss Cooper also fascinated me. She taught what was called 'Nature Study'. We drew birds – the essential shape is that of an egg, and you draw that first – and flowers, too, with pistils and cotyledons. We were taught Latin from Form 2 onwards, but, though the Headmaster was a Classicist, not consistently, so that, when the time came to go to University, I had to swot it up as it was a requirement for entry.

At times, too, we were to be taught 'Divinity'. The school was Anglican, but religion – like sport - was more taken for granted than enjoined or expounded. Some boys were Jewish, and they joined the school assemblies that began each day after the Headmaster had said prayers and we had sung a hymn from the Public School hymn book. We did not march in like the school children I later saw in Brisbane, nor did we sing the national anthem. Twice a week we trooped across to the Cathedral that the German bombers spared, for a service that included a sermon by Dean or Deputy Dean, prayers, a couple of hymns, a 'lesson' - some verses from the Bible in the King James version - read by a prefect, and a voluntary from the organ as we came and went.

In the early years of the war, the buildings were shared with another school, Hastings Grammar, which had been evacuated from a part of England immediately exposed to the Luftwaffe. We worked a long morning of some five hours, and they took over in the afternoon. We had homework to do, and two afternoons a week I was reluctantly on the sports field, then at Belmont, at the foot of Holywell Hill. The very junior pupils played Soccer, all the other forms played Rugger, but I never knew what either was all about. Nor was I an athlete, though decades later I found, like other ageing men, that I could jog for a long time, though whether I should have done so is questionable. Belmont also boasted a cold-water swimming-pool. Boys who could do two lengths wore black costumes, those who could not wore red. I never graduated from red. Now I like swimming, though I am not good at it. Then I hated it.

With other afternoons more or less free, I found plenty to occupy myself, besides homework. Reading was, of course, one of my pleasures. There was no school library, but the City library, then in a Carnegie building at the top of Victoria Street, had a junior section, and I read the Arthur Ransome books and a great many stories in the public school genre where bullies met their due punishment at the back of the fives courts. I gradually acquired a few books of my own, *The Wind in the Willows*, a book of Russian stories called *The Glowing Bird and the Grey Wolf*, and the *Rupert Bear* books and annuals: my favourite character, perhaps significantly, was the Wise Old Goat. I was keen on the Disney film *Bambi* and read other novels by Felix Salten, though not, of course, his pornography. We read 'comics', too. Mike had *Hotspur* each week, and I had the *Mickey Mouse Weekly*. I had my water-paint box, and I used that on colouring-in books, now again in fashion for grown-ups in search of an escape from cell-phones and I-pads. Dad sometimes operated an old Magic Lantern, and I worked on card-board cut-outs for a slide show up in the attic. At some point I also began to inflict a kind of house magazine on the family, called *Surprise*. Dad gave me an old duplicator discarded by the office at Central Mining, and I cut wax stencils and inked through them with a hand-roller.

I did not spend all the time indoors. I can recall some very snowy winters that I would not want to repeat, though I enjoyed sledging down the next street, Sunderland Avenue, which has a satisfactory hill. Often I would take Julian and Fiona out for a walk in a green pram, in which they were strapped in facing each other. I developed a series of routes that I followed as if I were a bus company: down Sandpit Lane, through the 'rec' opposite Beaumont Avenue; or across to Faircross Way, where house-building had stopped for the duration, and there were the remnants of bluebell woods, and you could also gather sow-thistles for the rabbits we began to keep on the back verandah. Another walk was down to the Fleetville shops, where you could still buy cakes – a ten-penny thin jam sponge for example – at Miss Goodey's. I am still rather surprised that not only could a young boy take a public bus or walk to school on his own, but also quite safely push a pram with two small children round the streets. There was, of course, very little traffic, especially given that petrol was severely rationed, and there seems to have been no such fear, or paranoia, about child molesters as there now is.

"There is no depression in this house. We are not interested in the possibilities of defeat. They do not exist." Queen Victoria's statement printed on a card was stuck above the hall seat as you entered No. 136, pushing aside the blackout curtain that spread at an angle across the front door. I am not sure how conscious I was at an early age that the conditions the war imposed were so abnormal. Food was rationed: that was obvious, even if only because you could get only one chocolate bar a fortnight; and even then I marvelled that sausages could be advertised 'guaranteed no meat', so that buying them did not use up your meat coupons. Blackout was obvious, too: not only the front door, of course, but all the windows. Sometimes we did not burn coal on the one fire, but the tarred wood blocks from bombed London streets. Out of the back upstairs bedroom window, you could see a glow at night, which I fancied were the fires in London. Sharing a bed-room with Francis, we built up stories about an evil Nazi called Savenstrop. Quite often Dad would bring a uniformed soldier home for a night: someone he had perhaps met in the pub near the station – the Midland – whose leave was too short to enable him to get to his own home and back. But, not much bombed, St Albans continued to function, and what was abnormal seemed normal enough to a boy for whom after all everything was more or less a new experience in any case.

Was It All Those Years Ago?

Lorraine Wheeler

'To Joyce (nee Coupar) and Robert Heywood, a daughter, Lorraine Joyce. Born 26th February. Both well. Grateful thanks to Sister Darling.' So read my birth notice in the *West Australian* in February 1932.

I was born at home, No 4 Gallipoli Street, Victoria Park in the state of Western Australia. It was a comfortable, brick and tile house situated on a corner block. My parents had bought the land because of its proximity to the railway station and had the house built ready to move into as soon as they were married in 1927. We had no car in those early days, so it was important that my father had easy access to his work in the city. As a small child I would tell passers-by that the Battle of Gallipoli was fought right outside our front fence. I remember being terribly offended when people laughed. I was sure it wasn't a laughing matter.

Victoria Park is only 3 kilometres from the capital city of Perth to which it is joined by a causeway across the Swan River. We could either go to the city across the causeway by means of electric trams, or catch the train across the river, a much more pleasant journey with glimpses of open countryside as we chugged along. I can still hear my mother's warning: "Don't put your head out the window! You'll be sorry if you get a cinder in your eye." And of course I did ... and I was!

At the time I was born, our family consisted of my mother, father and my paternal grandmother. My grandmother died when I was ten years old, but I still remember her with great affection. In later years I asked my mother if it had been difficult always having Dad's mother living with them and was delighted to find that for the most part they had lived very harmoniously, although apparently Grandma did have a fit of the sulks occasionally if she disapproved of something Mum did.

I don't remember a lot about those very early years – just a few memories kept alive by photos, but I do remember snippets of holidays we had at a Guest House on the banks of the Murray River about 60 miles from home. My father would dive and swim while my mother, grandmother and I sat on the bank and watched. Sometimes Dad would row us out on to the river to fish while at other times he'd disappear with his easel, paints and brushes to return later with some charming little scene captured along the river. I still have a water-colour painting of my mother, sitting in the boat with her umbrella.

My father always loved the water – not so my mother! The furthest she ever ventured into the water was to paddle in the shallows, but even that became fraught with danger after my father stepped on a cobbler. The cobbler (or Swan River Catfish) is a bottom dwelling fish during the day and is known for the sharp, venomous spines on its dorsal and pectoral fins. When he trod on it, one of these spines got stuck quite deeply in Dad's foot causing instant and agonizing pain. Poor man! We made our way back to the guest house with great difficulty - Dad in agony, Mum in a panic and with me sobbing loudly behind. The spine was removed by our sympathetic host as quickly as possible and the local remedy applied – the foot plunged into a bowl of very hot water until the worst of the pain subsided. … We didn't go back to the Murray.

In 1935 my parents took me with them to Sydney. I think I remember crying bitterly as we sailed off on the *Katoomba* leaving Grandma waving on the wharf (although maybe it's just something I've been told). Snatches of shipboard life come back aided by photos. My mother and father dressed up in evening clothes (most unusual) and celebrating my birthday on board (most exciting).

The Sydney Harbour Bridge had not long been built when we arrived and Dad joined the throng who were invited to write their names on one of the pillars. Dad wrote mine. We also stayed at Katoomba in the beautiful Blue Mountains and in my mind's eye I can still see Dad sitting in one of the spectacular Jenolan Caves engrossed with his easel and paints as Mum and I watched as the painting came to life. It wasn't often that we got to see him work.

We returned to Perth by train: a non-event for me, apart from the fact that the train stopped on the Nullabor and Dad bought me a mountain devil from one of the local aborigines. This event was not notable so much for the mountain devil as the reaction from my mother as she realized the thorny creature had somehow to be got home.

Our house in Gallipoli Street had two bedrooms with a large room added on the back for Grandma. There was a lounge room which was called a 'sitting room' which wasn't used much at all. I guess there was not a lot of time for 'sitting' in those early years. This room had a bay window with long curtains that could be pulled right across. Not only could we curl up there and read, it was ideal for our childhood concerts. The piano was in this room and music was a major part of our lives. Grandma was very musical and used to play the 'mood music' at the picture theatres in the days of silent films. She also gave piano lessons and in due course taught me.

My aunts and uncles would often come over to our house in the evening. One of my aunts was much in demand at the piano as she played very well by ear. They would all sing along for hours and as a small child I would lie in bed and listen. Dad played the piano by ear too (he also played the trumpet, banjo and euphonium), but Auntie Jean was better, so it usually fell to her to play for most of the evening, and she loved it.

There was a gramophone as well in the sitting room, one that had to be wound up and would go faster or slower according to the winder. This was great fun for small children who would sneak in to play with it when there were no adults to notice.

Looking back, I'm astonished at how many of our goods were delivered to the house. The milkman in his horse-drawn cart would call during the night and we would leave our billy cans hanging on the gate with the money in the bottom. The iceman would deliver blocks of ice wrapped in thick hessian sacking and place them in the top of our ice-chest. And the baker (also in his horse-drawn cart) would cheerfully call out "Bake-oh!" as he arrived at our back door with his basket filled with freshly baked loaves. His horse meanwhile would amble down to the next house and wait.

Any other shopping was mostly done in small shops. There was the corner store, almost opposite, that supplied most of our grocery needs. Then there was the butcher, the haberdasher (for our needles, cottons, laces etc), the bootmaker where we went to have our shoes mended and stores with sawdust floors where such things as grain and hay could be bought for folk who kept horses or fowls.

On Sundays we all went to church dressed in our Sunday best. We worshipped with the Methodists as their church was within easy walking distance. We children found the church services pretty boring, but the music was something else. The women would sing the tune and the men would join in effortlessly to provide the harmony. It was a joy to my young ears. Wendy and I attended the Methodist Sunday School too, but the singing there was not nearly as enjoyable either to sing, or listen to.

Occasionally the church would have visits from missionaries and those were exciting occasions as they always brought with them their lantern shows. We would sit enthralled as we watched the black and white, very shaky photos appear as though by magic. It didn't seem to matter much what they had to say, or whether they had come from far away China, India or Africa. If there was a lantern show, we would be there.

These were the years between the Great Depression and World War II, but in our little household I seemed quite safe. If there was talk of poverty and war it didn't reach my pre-school ears.

School was a major upheaval in my life, mainly because of one small girl in what would now be called year 1. She was a terror and pinched unmercifully. During the year, she contracted diphtheria and died and I can remember feeling very guilty indeed because all I could think of was how wonderful to be at school without her to pinch me.

Victoria Park Primary School was (and still is) a beautiful old building not far from the Swan River. Because of its historical significance, it has now been listed by the Heritage Council of W.A. It was a fair walk, but that didn't worry me. The worst part was that I had to pass the Catholic Church and nearby school. There was, at that time, an ongoing battle between the Catholics and Protestants. "Proddy dogs stink like hogs!" would chant the Catholics. "Catholic dogs are worse than hogs!" shouted the Protestants. On my six-year-old legs, I scuttled by on the other side of the road, across Albany Road (now Albany Highway) and so on down the hill to school. Some sixty years later, two of my granddaughters very happily attended the same school.

It was during my first year at school that my sister Wendy was born. Even though there was six years' difference in our ages, Wendy and I were always close. Music was a bond and we would sing and harmonize around the house, especially when we were doing the dishes. Dad could usually be heard either singing or whistling in the background. He had a fine tenor voice. Mum was very reserved and I had no idea that she ever touched the piano, or sang, until I came upon her doing so in later life. That was the first and last time I ever heard her play, or sing.

Swimming was a very important part of our lives as we grew up. Victoria Park Primary held its swimming lessons on the river at Como, small in terms of distance – massive in terms of execution! Getting to and fro by trams with huge classes of children must have been a nightmare exercise for teachers.

A favourite school activity was the Gould League of Bird Lovers. Named in honour of John and Elizabeth Gould, it was started in an endeavour to protect native birds and discourage the collecting of birds' eggs. Subsequently it has been credited with much of the environmental work done in schools.

And then there was the war. In the beginning it didn't seem to affect my young life at all. Dad wasn't exactly rejected as a serviceman. He had hammer toes, which for some reason the army found unacceptable. The way they dealt with this was to have them cut off. Dad was to get his toes removed and then spend his days in the army sign-writing their vehicles. Dad's boss was furious. "If they wanted you to go away and fight I'd understand it," he told my father. "But mess up your feet just so you can sign-write their vehicles? Over my dead body!" And he had him man-powered. This meant Dad stayed to run the business in Perth. If he suffered taunts by not going, I don't know, but in the end he had no choice in the matter. Uncles and cousins departed for overseas in the army and air force. One of them was taken prisoner-of-war in

Europe, managed to escape and after many traumatic months, found his way back to the Allied lines and lived to tell the tale.

Although the war was at that time a long way away, food and clothing were rationed … and of course, petrol. Ration books became part of our everyday life, as did tasteless food substitutes. And everywhere we went, so too went our ration books. Little coupons were torn out with every purchase. Not too many things could be bought without them.

I remember the day Mum and Grandma pasted strips of brown paper on the windowpanes. (Wendy doesn't remember seeing a clear glass window anywhere until the war was over.) Then there were the thick 'black-out' curtains. There was a terrible fuss if there was a chink of light showing anywhere at night. The air-raid wardens would be banging on the door, threatening terrible retribution. Searchlights lit the sky every night.

I remember one evening when a couple of young sailors came to say goodbye to Mum and Dad. One of them was the son of one of Dad's work-mates. Not long afterwards both were lost at sea when their ship, the HMAS *Sydney* was sunk.

We went to the pictures most Saturday nights and the newsreels were terrifying, particularly to small girls and boys. I would clutch Wendy's hand on the walk home and promise I'd never let anything happen to her. Just what I was going to do, I don't know, but I was determined to protect my one and only sister. There was very little traffic noise in those days and such was the measure of quietness that as we walked home on a still night we would hear the lions roar over in the zoo at South Perth, a fair distance away.

Both Grandma Heywood and Nanna Coupar (mother's mother) belonged to the Red Cross and knitted furiously for the men overseas - socks mainly. I remember one period of time when we were all urged to make camouflage nets. From memory, we were supplied with a type of coarse rope and some sort of large hook. I can't remember this activity as being particularly suc-cessful, but I do know the house smelled horribly of something like tar for the whole of this period. We were all glad when knitting resumed.

Toys were in very short supply and Grandma Heywood made us the most wonderful furniture for our dolls' house. She did this by covering matchbox-es with material scraps and sewing them all together. We had lounges, chairs and beds – and anything else we fancied in the furniture line. It was only limited by imagination.

As the war progressed, our playground at school was dug up and became trenches into which we had to go every time the air-raid siren went, and for lots of practice runs in between. We were all issued with some Wrigley's Chewing Gum which we were supposed to keep for the time when we went into the trenches for real. We weren't quite sure what good this was supposed to do, but in any case it didn't matter, as I never knew one child who had any left after the first few days. We also had to have a large cork on a string that we had to hang around our necks. When the siren went we would leap into the trenches and pop the cork between our teeth, presumably to stop our teeth shattering when the bombs fell!

Most of us had calico bags that hung over our shoulders for these trips to the trenches. I've kept mine. Mum had stitched my initials L H on the flap with coloured material. It looked quite good I thought, and contained the most important things for survival – the above-mentioned cork and a white tin with a red cross emblazoned on the lid. Inside was an assortment of tiny rolls of gauze bandages, suitable maybe for cut fingers, and some tiny pots of salve. Thus prepared, we would leap into the trenches, or if given half the chance, run home as fast as we could. Anyone with less than half a mile to go was always allowed to run home and I was always amongst them if I could get away with it, although we were twice that far – and more.

We were all sitting around the radio, listening to the news the night Singapore fell. Singapore was our last bastion of defence and thought to be impregnable. As long as it was held, we were safe. The news therefore was dreadful. One of my classmates had escaped with her mother at the fall of Singapore. She was understandably terrified when the sirens went. "Just wait till the bombs start falling", she would scream as we raced together up the hill. She was living with her mother at the Broken Hill Hotel where I'd leave her to run (with shaking legs) the rest of the way home.

We had our own air-raid shelter in the back yard. An uncle helped Dad build it and it was really very good. A dug-out all sand-bagged with steps leading down to an area large enough to hold a double-decker bunk bed, small table, two chairs and a cupboard that contained food stuffs to keep us going in an emergency. Wendy and I thought it pretty amazing, although the times we had to use it properly were very scary.

In 1943 the United States Navy set up a Flying Boat Fleet on the Swan River at a place called Matilda Bay. There were between 60 and 70 Catalinas and with all their attendant crew, they added a new dimension to life in Perth. Often as we walked home from school they would fly right over us and we would instinctively duck down. The noise was deafening, but there was something very satisfying about having those big planes close by. In our young minds they meant a measure of protection.

I remember some of the young wives of servicemen revelling in the extra activity caused by the coming of the Americans. There were regular dances and the young women would ignore the frowns of their elders as they dressed up and headed off to catch the train to the city. As a girl, I was conscious of the disapproval; as an adult I understand all too well how lonely those war years must have been for those young women.

Our pleasures and pastimes were simple. One I remember more clearly than most was our collection of film stars cut from the pages of *Women's Weekly*. Every Friday night we'd spread these pictures out on the kitchen floor and play 'swaps' or 'guess who'. This involved one of us giving the initials of one of our favourite stars and the other one guessing which one it was. I don't know why we ever bothered to play this, as such was our addiction, I don't think we ever got one wrong.

With friends, we played hopscotch in squares drawn in chalk on the side road and we followed that road past the few scattered houses until it ran into a large section of bush. Here my sister and I picnicked when the weather was good. Never in summer because of snakes. Spring was our favourite time because it meant picking the wildflowers that grew in abundance. We always picked Mum a bouquet which just made it home before it wilted.

We loved it when Mum took us on the train to the city and almost always we ended up calling in to see Dad at work. Dad was a very good artist, but the thought of trying to earn a living this way never entered his head. It was far too chancy an occupation. He turned his talents to sign-writing and commercial art. We loved the colour and smell of Dad's workshop, but our favourite part was the wall where all the faces of our favourite film stars peered down at us. In those days, all the advertising outside cinemas had to be done by hand and this task always fell to Dad. Larger than life, these posters, once used, were retrieved and attached high up on the walls at work. I guess it was no hardship for the sign-writers to glance up from time to time and see some of the most glamorous film stars of the time gazing down at them.

Guy Fawkes night (5 November) was a big event in our lives. Everyone called it 'Bonfire Night' and for months we saved our pocket money to buy crackers and piled as much rubbish as we could on our own particular bonfire. Some families made a 'Guy' too, stuffing old clothes with straw, or rubbish. The Guy would be put on top of the fire and the whole lot set alight when the time came. It was a grand night and usually friends and family came around. We kids would wave sparklers, and throw jumping jacks at one another's feet and pin Catherine wheels to the trellis and watch them whiz around. Then there were the rockets! The Dads were the only ones allowed to operate these and didn't we shriek when they went sailing up into the air, trailing what seemed to us millions of stars. It was always a night to remember.

The year before the outbreak of WWII Dad bought our first car. It was a great day. In the years to come, the entire family got very used to pushing the car down the street to get it started. The car was a Standard – a small car with a sunroof that lifted off and a front seat that you could lay back to make a bed. During the early war years when we shared a beach cottage at Coogee Beach with friends, my friend Aileen and I would sleep in the car and so safe was it in those days, that we would sometimes get up on a hot summer's night, race through the sand hills and have a swim – only to climb back into our make-shift bed all damp and sandy.

There were only six basic wooden cottages at Coogee – built and owned by the Road Board. These could be rented and for several years running we shared a cottage with another family for Christmas and Easter holidays. We thought it marvellous. I'm sure it was a very mixed blessing for our mothers. There were no washing facilities. We went some distance to the lavatories and showers and all the laundry was kept until we got home.

Washing the clothes was a major production. The copper had to be filled, the soap shaved and added to melt and the clothes boiled: sheets first, any other white clothes, then towels etc. Working clothes were done last. Any dirty marks were scrubbed off on our glass washing board before boiling. Following this, the washing was hooked out with the copper stick, dropped into one of the troughs of cold water, wrung by hand, lifted and rinsed in the other trough and finally wrung and hung on the line. Into the second trough was swirled a knob of Reckitt's Blue in its white cotton bag. This helped whiten the clothes and was widely used.

The clotheslines were held up by wooden props that invariably were bought from tramps that came around regularly trying to earn enough money to keep going. (This happened especially in the years after the Depression.)

In those days, toilets were called W.C.'s (water closets) or lavatories and were simply large pans set in wooden seats. These were emptied through a hole in the back wall by the 'night men' – men who drove horses and carts through the streets (mainly at night). The slang name for lavatory was 'dunny' and these men were usually referred to as 'the dunny men'. They didn't always work at night and on one memorable occasion, we saw a dunny man driving along with his very smelly cargo, placidly eating his lunch as he went!

At Coogee, Mum was paranoid about the public lavatories (with good reason) and devised a plan to keep us free from all the germs she was sure were lurking there. She got a piece of old linoleum and from this she made a seat cover with a large hole in it. Armed with this, Wendy and I would set off. The lino was completely stiff and impossible to roll or fold. There was simply no way to hide it and our embarrassment was acute, but no matter how we pleaded, Wendy and I were made to carry the hated contraption whenever we had to go. It didn't take too long before we got cunning enough to hide it in the bushes to be picked up again on the way home.

As time went by, the rules were relaxed and people were allowed to build private cottages at Coogee. Our friends built one first and shortly afterwards one of my uncles helped Dad build one for us. Ours was only two rooms: a bedroom that we all slept in and a kitchen. The walls inside were of hessian and whitewashed for strength. It was basic, but a lot of fun – except I'm sure for Mum, who had to cook on an old wood stove in the middle of summer in a very hot little house. She must have taken it all in her stride as I don't remember her complaining.

Mum didn't like the beach, never swam and was really frightened of the ocean. But that didn't stop her going out in the boat on occasions. One such occasion I remember was the day we set off across the ocean for a picnic on

Carnac Island, about 6 miles away. There were three boat-loads of us – the boats being small rowboats with outboard motors. The weather was beautiful and my friend and I swam and generally explored the island (which is well-known for snakes), while the adults and younger children swam or sat on the beach chatting. We all ate our picnic with one eye on the flies and another on the ants. Alcohol wasn't a part of our lives at all in those days. The adults drank cool drink and we children usually had cordial.

It was late afternoon when we set off for the return journey, but we hadn't gone far when the most unexpected happened: a thick fog rolled in from the sea, blanketing everything so thoroughly it was impossible to see the boat in front unless we kept really close. Before long, we realized we were lost.

Fortunately, the navy had built a submarine net stretching from Garden Island to the mainland ending up at what we called 'The Magazine'. (This was an ammunition dump and was behind rolled up barbed wire at the end of our beach.) We knew if only we could find the net we would be safe, and we did. It seemed forever before we came close enough to shore to see huge bonfires. All our friends and neighbours, realizing our predicament, had lit them along the beach to guide us home. What a welcome sight that was.

Holidays at Coogee conjure up such great memories. Walking across the railway line to the dairy before breakfast to collect fresh milk in billy cans; trips to the beach shop across 'the green' to spend our pocket money; after-noons and evenings spent playing 'Monopoly' while our parents played cards (usually '500').

There was the wreck of an old ship on our beach. It was extremely derelict and very rusty. We kids would go there often, climbing the rusting iron and jumping from as high up as we dared on to the sand below. I can't imagine why none of us ended up breaking bones or getting tetanus. We certainly had enough cuts over the years.

While we were staying at Coogee, we would sometimes go to the pictures at the Hamilton Hill hall. 'Hammy Hill', as it was called, was notorious for having a projector that was always breaking down. This being the case, the local boys would go prepared with bags of grapes and every time the pictures stopped, the projectionist's box would get pelted. Lots of grapes were grown in the area, so there was never any shortage. Unfortunately it didn't improve the performance of the projector.

Between our house and the river there used to be Chinese market gardens. They ran along the banks of the Swan River from the Rivervale Railway Station to the Causeway. The market gardeners worked very hard. Always, when we went past, they would be there in their gardens, bent over double, planting, weeding, harvesting. In my memory they were never upright – always stooped. In their place there is now an up-market casino set among well-tended lawns and gardens.

We loved the old steam trains. They had carriages strung out behind the engine and each carriage had a whole lot of separate compartments – two long seats facing each other that held about five people, with luggage racks above. Long-distance trains were very different. They had long corridors opening into the seating compartments and one carriage was joined to the next by means of a narrow metal bridge.

During the war, fuel was in very short supply and to keep our home fires burning Wendy and I would be sent off with metal buckets to collect the coal that fell from the engines. We never minded doing this and sometimes when we were walking beside the tracks, a train would puff along, smoke billowing from its funnel. Always the engine driver would give us a friendly wave and sometimes – just sometimes – the fireman would throw us some big chunks of coal. They were the best days.

One day early in the war, a whole company of soldiers on horseback rode by. I guess the young men were off to war, but certainly not with their horses as after WW1 horses never again left Australia to go to war. We children ran to watch them go by and as we watched, one of the soldiers threw us a handful of coins. Soon others were doing the same and I can still remember them laughing and waving as we scrambled to pick up the pennies and halfpennies.

When I finished at Victoria Park Primary School, Mum and Dad sent me to St. Mary's Church of England Girls' School. It was quite a distance from home and involved a long walk down to Albany Road, then a trip by tram across the Causeway all the way to West Perth. It seemed to take for ever, but was well worth the effort and I loved my years there.

A friend of my mother's had married a farmer and gone to live in a small country town called Pingrup. It was during my first year at St. Mary's that I had my first visit to a farm. Wendy and I were excited beyond words. We went by train and it took such a long time that an overnight stop had to be made at a larger town called Katanning. Next morning we then caught a branch-line train out to Pingrup to be met by our host in a vehicle with chains on the tyres. It was the May school holidays. The rains had come early and the countryside was drenched. Pingrup was situated in salt-lake country and getting around the slippery roads was both a challenge and a real experience for us.

I can still remember that first visit. The unforgettable smell of chaff as we fed the teams of work horses: the feel of mud squelching between our toes as we ventured out onto the salt lake below the house. Perhaps most of all I remember the feeling of endless space: just fields and lakes and the huge vaulted sky. To me it was idyllic.

It was on one of our many trips to Pingrup that we heard the news that the war had ended. That was perhaps the best holiday we ever had.

Memories of Childhood

Rupert Wheeler

It is surely an expectation, perhaps subconsciously, in recording memories of one's childhood, that one would do so in chronological order with a reasonable balance between life at home and school. My memories hardly fit into that pattern. With my father working on the Indian railways and also a part time soldier during the Second World War, my early life was somewhat nomadic flitting between east and west India: Pakistan did not then exist. Nowhere did we live in the same place more than a few months.

I was born in Simla, nowadays Shimla, on 28 September 1939 in the Portmore Nursing Home. My mother was so sure that I would be born that morning that she had insisted, she said, going into the nursing home the night before. After a good breakfast and wash, she waited patiently until I arrived mid-morning. The birth was not without its complications, and my father was quickly linked in to give me three pints of blood. Apparently, as I was handed to my mother, the nurse said, "He looks like a Rupert to me." And so, I got my name. Montagu, my middle name, was one that had come down several generations on my great-grandfather's maternal side. Family lore had it that an ancestor was a descendant of noble blood from the Kent region of England. My research years later showed that the name was that of someone, originally from London, who was a clerk for the Maidstone local council, hardly blue blood. My father said that three months after my birth Shimla had such a heavy snowfall that the local station roof collapsed under the weight and teasingly linked the event to my birth. I wonder sometimes whether he was a modern soothsayer warning the world of some impending distress on the Ides of March, or in this case, December.

My younger brother Jeremy returned for a brief visit to Shimla in 2006, and discovered that the nursing home buildings had been condemned and had recently been demolished. It was being replaced by new buildings for the Portmore Girls' School.

The longest stay in any one place that I can recall, or for which I have a record, was two school terms which was at the Miss. Daphne Ross Preparatory Kindergarten & Nursery School. Where that was I cannot remember and the few school reports I have did not carry any clues. It must have been after our life in Calcutta as the average age of the pupils in the class was 4½ years and I was 4 years old. I recall learning how to tie my shoelaces and a most painful lecture and demonstration on ballet. The whole school was assembled to listen to and watch a ballet teacher who encouraged us to try some of the simpler moves including the splits. It was an agonising but determined attempt by me which put me off ballet forever. My end-of-term reports from Miss Daphne Ross show that I was propping up the class, and when watched my behaviour was good although I was rather talkative. Apparently, I enjoyed and was good at singing; nowadays, nobody, including me, would believe that had it not been in writing. I must have returned to the School a second time in 1944, because the size and style of the school term reports had changed. It seems my behaviour had improved and my writing was painstakingly slow but tidy. I am recorded as being by far the best at drawing although nobody realised I was an excellent draughtsman but without the flair needed to be an artist.

Until my last school, the Lahore Cathedral School in 1947, I have no more than a few flashes of memory, and to which school those flashes apply, I have no idea. Even memories about the Lahore Cathedral School are sketchy. I am sure all the teachers were female, but what they looked like, what they taught, or whether they were encouraging, gentle or disciplinarians, I have no idea. My father used to say that I attended seven schools in India between the ages of about four and eight years old. How I ever learnt to read and write is a mystery. The nomadic life also meant that I have no recall of any lasting friendships, children's birthday parties except for one instance, or any social events involving children of my own age, and so my memories are largely limited to home life in general until 1948 when I began to attend school in England.

Only a few weeks after my birth I unknowingly experienced my first move. A formal announcement of my birth records that we had moved to 3B Scotch Corner, Lahore. There is still a building at that address. I doubt whether it is the same one as we lived in as it now appears to be part of the National Institute of Public Administration.

By early 1942 we were back in Simla for the birth of my Brother Jeremy. It was in the travelling back from Simla to see the new-born Jeremy, that my father was involved in the infamous Kalka-Simla Line ambush.

Jeremy was still a little baby when we moved to a flat in Albert Road, Calcutta. There were four flats in the block of which we had one on the ground floor. The layout of the flat, the compound on the far side of which were the servants' quarters, the large side garden, and our own small private garden, are the earliest clear memories I have of life in India. I am still able to sketch the layout of the flat and grounds.

We became friendly with the Mullick family who lived in an upstairs flat. The adults remained friends for life. I became friendly with their daughter Nita who was about the same age as I. I remember her telling me about the need for the servants to check the dogs for fleas, and showing me how the fleas were removed.

It was wartime and the Japanese were edging closer. When the sirens sounded, we quickly shut ourselves in the store room, small but the safest room we had, waiting for the explosions and the shaking to stop, and the 'All clear' to sound. The experience was quite unsettling for a young chap like me. The storeroom was securely locked for it held our food, consumables, and cloths other than our clothes.

My mother was a skilled dressmaker and ordered dress patterns from Vogue. Weavers would stretch the cloth on the loom to increase its length. So, after buying a greater length than was required by the pattern, she would leave it in a bucket of cold water overnight for the cloth to shrink.

I was told that there was a famine in the region at the time, which perhaps explains why we kept chickens and geese. Several years later, my mother recounted that she used to barter some of our rice ration for the servants' bacon ration. Security was in place not just because of the famine, my mother told me later, but because any consumables had a mysterious way of disappearing. A drying up cloth one day might become a pair of shorts for a servant's child a few days later. To guard against unauthorised sampling of drinks such as sherry, whiskey and gin, the levels left in each bottle were marked on the label when the bottle was held upside down, confusing those who did not understand the system. To contain the chickens within the confines of our private enclosed garden, my father clipped their wings to prevent them flying away. The two geese were another matter. They became family pets walking in every morning to greet and be patted by my mother. If she ignored them, she would receive a little nip reminding her to give their necks a tender stroke. Being not quite four years old, I was wary of such large birds, but it did not stop me trying to help them by giving them a bath in the back bathroom. The geese made it clear that my efforts were not appreciated, and taught me never to try that again. I also attempted to train our pet white rabbit, and it too, ensured I left it alone in future by giving me a nasty scratch. As door stoppers we had several cast metal white rabbits one of which I have kept to this day.

I remember that we had gas masks handy but they would have been of no use had the worst happened because the filters were completely blocked, thus preventing one from breathing.

Occasionally, the back door to the house was locked whilst the snake man came to clear the compound of what people called the dust snakes: so called for obvious reasons during the dry season. Otherwise, there were no other natural dangers that were considered significant.

At the end of Albert Road, there was a Paan stall. Paan is a preparation combining betel leaf with areca nut. It is chewed for its stimulant and psychoactive properties. After chewing, people spat it out on the pavement leaving horrible dark red splashes. I never got use to the disgusting sight of peoples' red mouths and fouled pavements.

One day my parents invited two American soldiers to our flat. What made the visit so memorable, was that they brought a large jar of sweets and chewing gum. This was my earliest recollection of tasting sweets of any sort. I had the same feeling of wonderment as I had when I first saw and played with snow. It occurred when we visited my father's home in Leeds in May 1945 just before VE day. I suspect it was through the visit of the two soldiers that I have some coloured cine film, a rare commodity in those days, of the family taken in the side garden.

One day, when everybody was asleep in the afternoon during the hot sun, I wasn't, as was normal. My brother Jeremy was, so as not to wake him, I went outside to make sure that I could play where nobody could hear me. I was on the back lawn and Nita's parents had started arranging her birthday party. There was a bit of a marquee up and a large space of lawn for the children to play on. Whilst I was there, one of the street entertainers called to me through the railings and asked me if there was some sort of party planned. I said it was to be for a little girl's birthday party. He asked me if I knew whether there were any entertainers booked. I said I didn't know but why not come, in fact, why not bring all your friends as well. By the time Nita's parents had woken up from their afternoon sleep, I had arranged all down one side of the lawn, snake charmers, conjurors, bear dancing, a puppet show and one or two other things. I don't think Nita's father was awfully pleased with the cost I had incurred on his behalf, but we had a jolly good party and I still retain the invitation. As a near four year old, it was my first effort at managing a project. I have to say I was quite pleased with the outcome. Not so Mr Mullick. Many years later, during a visit by Mr Mullick to my parents' house at Foxfield near Northampton, he and I recalled the party and he said he had long forgiven me for what I did. He was delighted to report that Nita had become a popular member of Indian society.

I must have had some toys in Calcutta, but our nomadic life and the war meant I had very few. My mother, and sometimes the servants, seem to have made sure I was kept amused. The servants showed me how to catch small birds that had come through the collapsible lattice gates into an open area. I was presented with a set of wooden shapes which could be arranged in a variety of interesting patterns. I still have the pieces which are kept in an old

Gran-Bits cereal tin. Gran-Bits, an Australian version of Grape Nuts, was my favourite cereal, and the only cereal I can remember until we began living in Lahore and Karachi when rice-crispies and puffed wheat appeared.

During our time in Calcutta, I can recall two holidays. The first was of our visit to Puri, a seaside town about 300 miles south of Calcutta that we reached by train. Even today, the journey takes 10½ hours but I have no idea how long it took in 1942. My outstanding memory was of the enormous sea waves. It was essential, even for adults, to use a lifeguard to breach the first set of waves after which the sea was fairly calm. I remember the crabs one could see when the water receded as the next big wave formed.

The holiday in Kurseong could not have been more different. Kurseong is a few miles south of Darjeeling about 300 miles north of Calcutta, and by train, the journey took some 15 hours. As it was quite high in the hills, I recall it taking a couple of days to adjust to the thin air of high altitude. My father pointed out the snow-covered Himalayas, in particular, a high peak which I think must have been Kangchenjunga. It was in Kurseong that I first experienced an earthquake while standing on the lawn. I still recall the deep anxiety I felt, never to be forgotten, when everything appeared to be rocking. We paid a visit to a local tea plantation and factory. We watched the women nipping off the tips of the bushes and throwing the tips into a large basket on their backs. At the factory, the green tips were piled in front of more women who carefully separated the buds and leaves from the stalks. The next stage seemed to involve heating the leaves, which produced an extraordinary and overpowering strong smell of tea. I always considered this the moment I began to dislike the taste of tea. Not so my parents, who for several years afterwards, had tea regularly sent in a small wooden box to wherever we were living, even after we settled in England.

I do not know when we left Calcutta but we did seem to spend life travelling between Karachi and Lahore. One of my father's responsibilities on the railways was to investigate major problems and crashes on the lines. To cover the vast distances we had the use of a carriage which had been fitted out as a mobile home with our bedrooms and bathroom at one end, living and dining area in the middle, then the servant's quarters and finally the kitchen.

In our travels we had continual change of ayahs (nannies). I am told I managed to pick up sufficient grasp of Hindi, Urdu, Tamil to add to my elementary (so said my father) grasp of English, to act as the translator between my mother and the ayahs.

Our first floor flat in Karachi overlooked the railway line that ran not far from the back garden. Goods trains moved rather slowly in those days, and my father showed me how to put a coin on the rail for the engine to flatten out. I also recall the servants occasionally walking out to the line with my father's lunch box to hand to him as the train passed. We had a gardener who was perhaps the first person to make me take an interest in plant propagation.

He rooted small lengths of rose cuttings in an old tobacco tin which he carried round filled with damp moss. Much to my amazement, the high humidity combined with the ever warm weather during the day and his pocket at night, soon made the cuttings produce roots.

Jeremy and I shared a bedroom until I caught measles when I was moved to the spare room for a while. Our bedroom, like all the other rooms, had ceiling fans in the motors which bats occasionally found ideal for nesting during the day. Unfortunately, it was unknown to us when we switched on the fans that the motor housings occasionally contained bats and agonising high pitched screeches were heard.

During one of our spells in Karachi, I must have learnt to swim. We would visit a club which was next to one of the inlets that formed the geography of Karachi. My parents were at first rather anxious when I attempted but successfully swam out to the floating platform. We also used to catch the sailing boat to the beach chalet on Sandspit owned by the railway company. It had two bedrooms and a general living room. We spent the day at Sandspit playing in the sea on a calm day and at the back in what might best be described as a lagoon when it was stormy. Those who stayed overnight usually did so to collect turtle eggs. I had some concern about playing in the lagoon partly because of the mangrove trees with their roots sticking vertically up from the mud, and partly because of the occasional sighting of a Portuguese-man-of-war.. I did once get stung. Camel trains passed along the beach from time to time. When they were sighted we either went indoors or round the back because the camels smelt so awful. Sandspit is today a popular tourist destination, but in those days it was delightfully clear. Fishermen would pull their boats up on to the shore and I would be fascinated by their catch. On one occasion they brought in a swordfish. My father bought the sword for 1½ rupees, a few pence in today's money. This I have today with some grains of sand still adhering to the base.

I do not think we ever owned a car although I can remember one or two car journeys. The car must have been hired by my father or loaned to him. Most of our travelling in town was done in rickshaws and occasional rides on my parents' bicycles. Today's rickshaws have small motors but in our day, they were all pulled by people. I recall how slim they were and amazed at the stamina required to work like this day after day. My father showed me something similar on the railways where one could ride on a small trolley manned by four people who had the ability to match their stride so as to land their bare feet exactly on the wooden sleepers. At any one time two of the four would be pushing the trolley and the pairs changed over without any apparent effect on the speed.

About this time, but where we were living I cannot recall, we visited a place where grapes were grown. To protect the crop men were employed sitting on platforms at head height using slings to fire stones at the birds.

What a crack those slings made when the men fired! I am not surprised that David was able to slay Goliath. I cannot remember whether or not it was the same place, but there was a sacred crocodile pit. I was warned not to get too close to the edge unless I too became a human sacrifice. That really did frighten me.

Cakes were sweet and filling. I was unaware that there was a shortage of wheat flour so all cakes and many pastries were made by the highly skilled cooks using ground almonds. Cakes were kept under cover on a stand in a bowl of water to keep them safe from ants. All water for drinking was boiled, bottled, and kept in the refrigerator.

About April in 1945 my father decided to risk visiting England. We travelled down to Bombay to be met by my brother's godfather Capt. Jack Maloney who saw us aboard our ship which I think was the *Stratheden.* The journey took about three weeks. To keep young children amused, a lady organised a daily programme of activities. I remember her as an attractive young lady with short blond hair who had the rare talent of making each one of us believe she was especially interested in all we did or wanted to say. One day I proudly showed her the new jersey my mother had knitted. She took a keen interest, and paid my mother many compliments before tactfully suggesting I was wearing it inside out. In the evenings, I remember she sometimes sang accompanied by a pianist.

It was a largely uneventful voyage until we reached the southern end of the Red Sea. We had several times practised lifeboat drill and guns fired blank shot. Suddenly it had become much more realistic. We were surrounded by several naval ships and spectacular but frightening depth charges were dropped close enough to rock our ship. I was told that there was a Japanese submarine hovering close to and sometimes under our ship. We were therefore guided towards shallower water so as to expose the submarine. I cannot remember the result. My parents told me later that the Navy had dealt successfully with the submarine.

I was largely unconcerned about an accident I suffered during the voyage, although it shocked my mother. I began descending an outside gangway to a lower deck when I slipped and lost my footing. I remembered someone once telling me that when falling I should relax and wrap my arms round my head. This I did, and tumbled down to the bottom and then slowly rose to my feet bewildered but unhurt. I was embarrassed but only my pride was hurt.

The journey up the Red Sea and Suez Canal was interesting. Somewhere along the canal when the ship was temporarily halted, we were surrounded by men in boats selling a wide range of goods. Ropes were thrown up over the railings of the ship, people bartered, and money and goods exchanged via the long ropes. Fascinating to watch.

The journey through the Mediterranean Sea was uneventful except for the regular lifeboat drills. As we began approaching Malta, I recall quite clearly my parents pointing out in the darkness a distant red glow emanating from a mountain top. I can only assume we must have been sailing near to Mount Etna. This seemed a joyful stop on our way to England but of course I was not fully aware of the effects of World War II. There was no possibility of staying longer than was needed to refuel and take on provisions. I don't know where we docked in England, or how we eventually reached my father's home in Leeds.

My father was anxious to reach that city as soon as possible as his father had died some three years before. To me, this was just another house with a lady who I was told was my grandmother, but having no previous connections with her, I felt no emotional or family attachment. On 8 May we joined a large happy crowd on the town hall steps in The Headrow to celebrate VE day. 14ᵗ May, my mother's birthday, was memorable because it snowed. This was the first time I had seen and played with snow. It was an extraordinary experience. My father delighted in showing me the small patch of London Pride in the back garden: another sign perhaps of my future hobby. We managed a short visit to Didsbury, a district of Manchester, to see my mother's parents. My aunt Peggy lived with them. The adults seemed happy enough but to me it was just another visit to someone else.

My father managed to obtain a car and the family went on a visit to Goathland in the North Yorkshire Moors where my father had heard there was a large patch of wild raspberries. We took a large biscuit tin which he and my mother filled with raspberries. I tried to help until I could eat no more and got rather bored by the time we started to return home. The tin was not watertight so my mother had to stem the leaks with handkerchiefs. We managed to get the fruit home where I presumed my mother and grandmother made some jam despite the rationing of sugar, and lots of stewed fruit.

Having taken so little leave since 1939, my father had earned enough time to be able to take us down to The Headrow again on 2 September to celebrate VJ day. Soon afterwards we were back on board ship sailing from Liverpool to India.

I presume we continued to shuffle between Karachi and Lahore: not that I can remember anything until we came to live in Mughalpura, a district of Lahore. Our bungalow at 101a Canal Bank Road had an extensive garden, and the servants' quarters were at the rear of the back garden. The wide space, rather like an unmade track, ran behind and the length of the servants' quarters. This was where the laundry man (dhobi-wallah) had his large square concrete washtub alongside which was a slightly inclined slab of stone against which used to beat and scrub the washing. At one end was the outside toilet block the first part of which was a raised trough for the men and the second part a similar trough for the women. There were no doors of course. The place was kept clean by the sweeper. I used to spend quite a lot of time watching the people as they worked, and the wives showed me how they ground spices for their curries, and chapatis using a stone roller and shaped stone base. The wives sometimes used wood for their ovens, but more often than not it was animal dung which was scooped up from the road, shaped into thick pancakes and slapped on to a wall to dry in the sun for later use. When we had emptied a food tin, it would be eagerly taken by one of the servants who would turn it into a useful household container for their families.

Our gardener (Mali) was a wonderful character who kept the garden in excellent condition. He had a weakness for nasturtiums and antirrhinums and grew a wide range of vegetables. I took an interest in the vegetables and was particularly attracted by some glossy green pea-shaped pods, and popped one into my mouth. It was the last time I attempted to eat a green chilli. The vegetable garden was watered by flooding each of the little plots by digging out, temporarily, a small section of the artificial stream bank at the far side of the garden. In the back garden was a small swimming pool, probably less than ten yards square which proved a blessing in the hot weather. I was told not to swim in the canal on the other side of the road which only made me want to do so when everybody else was having their afternoon siesta. Again my abilities did not match my ambition, and I struggled to return to the bank after diving in. I never tried again. We had some vultures nesting in the tall trees. My father assured me that I was perfectly safe. When I asked if he had ever shot one, he said it took two pistol shots to kill a vulture. The first shot was into the nest to attract the bird's attention, and when the vulture looked over the edge to see what was happening one could shoot it with the second shot. I found out later that he was, of course, teasing me. The vultures may have been safe from my point of view, but other birds could be a dangerous nuisance. Once, when eating a sandwich outside, which I knew was unwise, a bird swooped down and snatched the sandwich out of my hands. Although frightened I was untouched by the bird.

We were visited by a series of people offering us certain useful services. I remember visits by the knife sharpener and hairdresser. As was expected by the hairdresser, my mother inspected the combs and scissors for cleanliness before allowing the man to cut my hair. Every so often, the pest control team would visit. A room was sealed and the men would create a fog of pungent insecticide with their flit guns in order to kill the mosquitoes.

Prior to our departure from India, my parents decided they needed a new set of dining room chairs. For several weeks carpenters took over the garage where they proceeded to saw by hand large slabs of teak into planks. I now recognise these men were extraordinarily skilful. Straight lines were made by holding a pencil and ruling a line at the correct distance by holding the fingers against the side of the wood or using a plumb line. Then the rough plank would be planed smooth. The chairs were designed to come apart and packed flat for the voyage to England. The leather was tanned in the spare bedroom and the bungalow reeked of chemicals and oils which I found unpleasant.

A typical day began before I woke up with the cook going to the loco works behind the bungalow to collect hot coals to fire the oven, and one of the servants to go to the early market to buy the milk. In addition to the cook and the gardener, we had two servants who carried out domestic duties, the sweeper who also looked after the toilets for us as well as for the servants, a man to do the laundry and ironing, and an overall supervisor who acted something like a butler, but I cannot remember much about him other than that he seemed rather remote. We no longer had an ayah. It was important to respect the caste system and the individual skills. This prevented an overlap of duties and dictated to some extent, how many servants one employed. As we were only living in Lahore for a short while, I assumed they must have been connected with the railways although we paid them and gave them rations.

After breakfast I would stand by the side of the road with one of the servants waiting to catch the bus to the Lahore Cathedral School. As we progressed through 1947, and partition day approached, we began having soldiers on the bus and manning a platform above the school gates. Providing one didn't interfere with whatever might be happening, the Indians never touched a white person. The mornings were cold, probably near freezing point even when the sun shone brightly. We huddled in the sunny niches formed by the sides of the Cathedral and its buttresses. A servant would cycle to school with my lunch, somehow keeping it warm.

During the lunch breaks a man would come with his cart loaded with sugar cane. Those with some pocket money would buy pieces of cane from which the man would skilfully remove the outer skin leaving the pupil to chew the piece and enjoy the sweet juice. There was no question of going outside the school gates nor did the school provide anything approaching a tuckshop. Of the contents of lessons and the teachers I have no memory. I do remember being cajoled into playing the part of a tailor in the school play. Never have I been so embarrassed as I sat near the front of the stage pretending to sew a piece of cloth when there was no thread in the needle. I have never been tempted to act on the stage again.

I would be home early afternoon just when the day was reaching its hottest, and people would have a nap. Then it was playtime for me. Every day throughout our time in India, the house stood still to listen to the BBC World Service and events in Europe. It did not mean much to me at the time as I was too young to appreciate my parents' concern for their families in wartime England.

The servants were patient and instructive in devising interesting things for me to make and do. I remember their showing me how to make simple jigsaw puzzles out of the front of cereal packets, and kites out of a square of paper stretched and held by some thin bamboo sticks to which was attached a long string. The paper was glued with a paste made from flour.

Kite making and flying was a most important skill to acquire especially, I recall, in time for the Hindu Holi festival. The Holi is a spring festival that is celebrated at the approach of the vernal Equinox, and is also known as the festival of colours. The festival signifies the arrival of spring and during the day there is a free-for-all carnival where people chase and colour each other with dried powder and coloured water: vivid yellows and oranges seem to come to mind. During the celebrations kite fighting was a popular activity. The idea was to sever the string holding your opponent's kite after which you rushed to where the kite landed and claimed it as yours. You did this by pulling your string quickly so that you wore through your opponent's string, unless your opponent was quick enough to pull his string at the same time so nullifying the aggressor's actions. Some people cheated by impregnating their string with an abrasive.

Kasim, one of the servant's children, showed me how to play the game of sticks. You created a slight trough in the ground across which you laid a short twig. With a longer twig poked underneath the small one, you flipped the short one in the air and tried to see how far you could hit it. It was a very quick flick of the wrist which I'm sure would be an excellent training exercise for a badminton player.

A favourite game amongst children was spinning tops which you did on the ground. The more skilled managed to lift the top in the air and have it spinning on their open palm.

1947 was our last Christmas in India and was made a memorable for me because I was presented with my first bicycle and a Meccano set. The bicycle was too large for me to start with, so a special low wooden seat was made and wooden blocks screwed onto the pedals. The bicycle stayed with us until well into the 1950s. Jeremy and I were also each presented with a drum similar to that used in a military band. Modern plastic skins had not yet been invented so the drumheads were of traditional animal skins.

We finally left India in January 1948 by ship from Karachi stopping at Malta for provisions and refuelling as we had done in 1945. My father decided that I should have some lessons from him so an hour a day was set aside for teaching. I am sure it did me good but at the time I could not understand the advantages of lessons over playing on deck with my friends. I enjoyed playing deck quoits and other long forgotten shipboard games.

In Leeds we stayed with my father's mother. I think it was on this second visit that I caught a mild dose of scarlet fever. I recall feeling rather warm and flushed but otherwise I was oblivious of the concerns shown by my parents and the doctor. It only lasted about a week before I felt back to normal. Rationing and the cold damp weather took some getting used to. Jeremy and I were each given 6d a week pocket money which was just enough for four ounces of sweets at the local shop in Hyde Park. I was introduced to several of my father's close University friends. One I recall was a fellow gymnast specialising in high bar and who held the then record for the number of times one could swing round in a minute. He ran a China and glass retail shop in the city. There were the Illingworth sisters who lived in Regent Park Terrace, and worked on the administrative side of the University: I presume therefore for my grandfather who was the registrar. The sisters had an interesting collection of succulents in the garden. Then a few doors down in Regent Park Avenue, there was Nellie Bowman whom I got to know a lot better when I attended Leeds University.

I spent two terms at the Headingley Preparatory School about a mile further into Hyde Park where the emphasis seem to be on learning one's arithmetic tables by heart, and being taught an incomprehensible language called French. Hindi seemed a lot simpler to me. During my stay there I took and passed the common entrance examination and was enrolled at St Peter's School, York, as a boarder. I think I was sent there, as was Jeremy later, because my father thought it would provide an excellent education and would provide some stability whilst he found permanent employment. My father chose St Peter's over the nearby Bootham School because, as he said later, at Bootham boarders had to make their beds every morning, and it was a soccer school. We were blessed with an odd-job man who cleaned and polished our shoes. He was terribly bow-legged and we all believed his story that he had been a horse jockey for many years.

Strict rationing was in force when we arrived and was slowly eased over the next few years. The eggs we had were a special treat but not always appreciated. When an American came to stay with us one day, he was given a precious fried egg for breakfast and exclaimed "What, only one egg?" I think my parents were lost for words. On another occasion, there was only one egg left in the pantry and my mother did not know whether to give it to me or Jeremy. When she broke it open, the problem was resolved when she found it contained two yokes.

My parents moved down to 63 Minton Avenue, Norwood Green in London where my father worked for The Metal Box Co. Whilst we lived in London, I made the journey to York by train. At the tender age of nine my parents put me on the train at King's Cross with my trunk and sufficient money to cover the other travel expenses I would incur before reaching the school. At York station I hired a porter to take my trunk from the guard's van and take it to the taxi rank for a tip of one shilling and sixpence, and a similar sum of money and tip to the taxi driver. Coming home at the end of term I would do all these things in reverse until I met my parents at King's Cross. I am sure in today's world parents would not contemplate sending a nine-year-old boy on his own.

About three years later it was on to the British Timken roller bearing company in Birmingham. Home moved to Sutton Coldfield until 1956 when, because Timken consolidated its activities in Northampton, my parents moved to the nearby village of Quinton. All this time I had a term at school then a break wherever home was before another term at school. So my nomadic life continued and friendships were transient.

In Sutton Coldfield, my father encouraged Jeremy and me to take an interest in gardening by allocating us a small portion of the rear garden where we grew a few annuals from seed. To earn extra money, we mowed the lawn, cleared stones from the flower beds, and broke up the concrete lined garden pond. In order to encourage our contribution to the household, my father paid us to perform small tasks. Washing up or wiping up after a meal was re-warded by 1½d (old pence). Mowing the front lawn was 4d and doing the edges was 2d. The back lawn was considerably larger and the equivalent rates were 6d and 3d. I once dragged the yard brush up and down the back lawn to create the impression of a newly mowed lawn and was duly paid for it. I do not suppose I hoodwinked my father. Perhaps he paid me as acknowl-edgement of my audacity. Jeremy was for ever impressed with my deception.

Boarding school was hardly a fulfilling and satisfying experience, but I did develop a sense of self-reliance. I had been brought up to expect an abundance of tropical fruits and foods. To be faced with rationing and a new dietary regime of badly cooked porridge, indescribable mashed potato con-taining lumps of dubious colour, an appalling vegetable called swede and unpleasant blancmange, was a shock which gave me an everlasting adverse impression of the school. To this day, I avoid these foods although mashed potato at home is most acceptable. The school discipline - there has to be some when there are so many boarding pupils - was a mixture of army disciplines and Edwardian standards of behaviour far from the school's defi-nition of *in loco parentis*.

There were two boarding houses in the Junior School. I began in St Olave's under the care of Miss Mason. A year later all the pupils were moved to a nearby house which became The Grove. In my view the housemaster was short tempered and a bully which made life uncomfortable, and probably adversely affected my opinion of boarding schools in general.

We were encouraged to take up hobbies as part of our education as well as to help pass the time. I spent quite a lot of the winter months building model aeroplanes, mainly gliders, because my fingers were not strong enough to fire the EDB 1cc aero engine. In the summer months we were encouraged to grow flowers and vegetables on small plots near the boarding house. Virginia stock was grown by everyone and we received free seeds for salad items such as radishes and lettuce. I was keen to grow the lettuce and made sure that the rows were weeded and plants watered when necessary. Then imagine my disappointment when it turned out that the seeds handed out were for sugar-beet and not lettuce. The other summer pastime was developing a model village. The houses were based on a brick with a mud roof.

The conspirators of the Gunpowder Plot of 1605 contained several old boys of St Peter's School including Guy Fawkes. As the headmaster of the senior school told newspapers annually, the school did not celebrate November 5th as the school did not celebrate failures. However, the junior school was allowed a bonfire. The boarders borrowed a large two wheeled cart from the groundsman, and we toured the neighbourhood for suitable bonfire material. It was quite a crazy process for those involved but we enjoyed ourselves.

On Sundays, we were forced to attend Chapel and expected to put some of our pocket money in the collection plate. As a nine-year-old losing several pence out of my one shilling a week pocket money, I found frustrating and annoying. That added to the general feeling of boredom engendered by the monotonous service.

I found most lessons uninspiring. Perhaps it was poor teaching or perhaps I suffered from Attention Deficit Disorder, probably a bit of both. What I found interesting were the scientific subjects which I tended to be quite good at, but all the others I found tiresome and struggled to make the appropriate grades. The highlight of the week was probably the music lesson during which we were encouraged to learn and sing British folk songs, and listen to some of the more popular classical music played on a large gramophone. The music teacher had frequently to cut the thorn needle in the pickup arm to sharpen the point.

The Latin teacher I found encouraging and much admired his ability to speak pidgin English and Japanese: he apparently acted as an interpreter during World War II. The Junior School Headteacher was feared by all. He taught biology and when I was asked if I could recognise a song thrush, I said no, but I could describe a hoopoe. His favourite pastime was hunting for game which he seemed to do most weekends. On the one occasion I accompanied him and can confirm what an observant man he was spotting and shooting game before any of his colleagues. Monday lunchtime usually saw him sitting outside the changing rooms with a bucket and a bowl more often than not cleaning up the rooks he had shot, showing us what were the edible parts before washing them in their sink to take home for his rook pie. The French teacher had no more success at teaching me French than the teacher in my primary school in Leeds. He was an inveterate pipe smoker and would take a lung full of pipe smoke in the staff room before rushing across to our class room and exhaling a not unpleasant odour.

I did get considerable relief and satisfaction from the stress of lessons through my success in the sporting activities of the school, although the cross-country runs on damp cold days were not my idea of fun, neither did I find soccer to which we were limited for the first year at all satisfying. I breathed a sigh of relief when from the age of 10 we progressed to rugby.

We managed a two-week holiday during the school summer break. My father admitted many years later that he would have much preferred to stay at home. The holidays near Cardigan in Wales were amongst the most enjoyable as we stayed in a hotel which was also the local pub and the locals allowed me to join in the games of darts. I practised hard and was delighted one evening to score two treble 20s and a treble 18. I like to think it was due to my practising and not to the relaxed approach that resulted from drinking half a point of local cider. The landlord employed a delightful, and no doubt grateful, ex-German prisoner of war to help with all the outside tasks which included caring for a few pigs. The landlord's dog proved to be such a nuisance to everyone including car drivers that the landlord eventually put it down.

A holiday at the Farkkegrav Badehotel in Denmark was memorable for several reasons. We went just as Jeremy recovered from a bout of chicken-pox. Shortly after arriving, I developed chickenpox much to the concern of my parents but to the amusement of the hotel staff who treated the malady as nothing worse than a common cold. The weather was sunny and the sea was crystal clear. We enjoyed sampling smorsbrot (a slice of rye bread with a variety of toppings), watching the seahorses, and swimming after overcoming the initial bracing temperature of the water. Jeremy had taken a "Teach yourself Danish" book and by the end of the fortnight he was carrying out simple conversations with the hotel staff.

1953 was the year of the coronation of Queen Elizabeth II, and like many others my father bought a television set. In those days no colour screens were available to the public. Owning a television set was still uncommon so we invited our neighbours to join us. The Arbenz son, his wife and their daughter lived next door with Mrs. Arbenz senior. She had a white Scottish terrier that was the bane of our lives with its constant barking which did not cease even when the dog was sprayed with water from the hose or had a weed thrown at it. Mrs Arbenz senior had a greenhouse in the garden. I assured Jeremy that his harmless pop-gun was so weak that it could not break the glass should he accidentally shoot at the greenhouse. He proved me wrong.

Finally, as I approached the age of fourteen, I moved to the senior school. Long trousers at last!

Childhood Memories to the Age of 12

Wang Gungwu

SURABAYA

When you are Chinese and born outside China, there is a lot to think about. I realize that now more than ever as I recall how my life began. I was born on 9 October 1930 in a Dutch hospital in Surabaya. This was because my father had recently gone to work in that city. When he decided to go to Java in September 1929, he was teaching in two schools in Taizhou, his hometown in Jiangsu, China. Before that, he had spent three years in British Malaya: in Singapore, Kuala Lumpur and Malacca. When he was offered the job as the first principal of a new Chinese High School in Surabaya, he had gone home to marry my mother earlier that year.

My parents did not stay long in Surabaya and I grew up in another town, Ipoh in the state of Perak in British Malaya. I was very conscious of having been born somewhere else and always thought my birthplace had the lovelier name. Surabaya also made me different because, when I first went to school, I was the only boy who had a birth certificate in Dutch. It was only much later that I discovered that the town's name came from the Javanese words for shark (sura) and crocodile (baya), creatures I do not care for.

I remember nothing about the town because my parents moved away when I was just over a year old. My mother had two photographs of me as a baby. One of them had me sitting on a stool with a tall Javanese woman standing beside me. She was the servant who looked after me and my mother believed that I learnt to speak to her in her brand of Malay. The other photo had me in the arms of the gardener of my father's school who apparently was very fond of me and carried me around whenever he could.

I cannot explain why Surabaya meant so much in my life. Perhaps it was because my mother spoke so often about her time there when I was still a baby. The city was where she had her first contact with the non-Chinese world, where she had her only baby in a modern but foreign hospital with no members of her family around. She talked often about her sense of helplessness and bewilderment when the Depression caused the failure of my father's school. She said that this was followed by months of uncertainty as to where they would go if they could not return to China. As far as I can remember, her stories always ended with the refrain about China.

Until my late teens, Surabaya was for me my beginning and, more definitely, China was my end. Because I could remember nothing about Surabaya, I was always very curious about the place and what my life would be like if I knew more about my beginning. But the city remained out of reach and was imagined only through my mother's stories. Every now and then, someone who heard that I was born there would ask if I had family there and what I thought of the people. I would explain that I left when I was too young to know. Whenever that happened, I wished the place could be more than just the place to be born in. What was touching was that the Chinese I met who were originally from Surabaya were very polite and seemed willing to treat me as if I was one of them even though I was not.

When my parents moved to Ipoh at the end of 1931, they saw the unexpected move as a brief stay on their way back to China. Ipoh was a newly built mining town, very different from Surabaya, the historic port city that had once served as the trading port of the Majapahit Empire. Surabaya had in 1930 a Chinese population of nearly 39,000. Although that included many local-born who had been there for generations as well as many more recent arrivals from South China, they were a small minority in the city. Also, the main Chinese dialect was Hokkien. Ipoh Chinese were a different mix of mostly newcomers from China who used Cantonese as their lingua franca. Furthermore, they were the majority people in the town.

IPOH, MY TOWN

The town of Ipoh did not have a long history. When we moved there, it was not even fifty years old. But it was already a great mining town, in the heart of the Kinta valley that had one of the richest tin deposits in the world. With the rise of the global tin industry, the town had grown rapidly. It had started with Old Town on the west bank of the Kinta River where the British built government offices, banks and commercial houses. In 1931, Old Town had a few short streets of shops. It also had the railway station, some churches, the club, and the padang (sports field) where games like cricket and rugby were played. Also, there were two boys' schools run by Christian missions: the Catholic St Michael's Institution and the Anglo-Chinese School of the Methodists and at least two Chinese primary schools.

On the east side of the river was New Town, planned after the turn of the century. It had a new hospital and five large schools: Anderson School established by the state government, the Catholic Convent and the Anglo-Chinese Girls' School that taught in English, and two Chinese high schools, one for boys and one for girls. I knew there was at least one Malay primary school in a kampong on the edge of town. New Town also had a new market and most of the town's cinemas. When I was growing up, it continued to expand, with numerous grand houses built by rich Chinese. On the hospital end of the town, next to the Convent, were government quarters called Green Town. That was where we lived from 1931 to 1941, and again from the end of 1945 to the middle of 1947.

Green Town was built for senior non-European officials working for Perak state. They were a mix of Malays, Chinese, Indians and Eurasians. Among them, our family was an oddity. My father was a graduate of a university in China who worked for the Education Department of a British Malay State. Although his office was at the far end of Old Town, we lived more than a mile away in a place where we were the only ones who spoke Mandarin at home and none of the Chinese dialects common in Southeast Asia. In addition, my father was the only person there who worked with Chinese schools.

The town had over a hundred identical houses, small and built on short stumpy pillars, but they all had large gardens. Ours consisted of a small sitting room and two bedrooms each with a bathroom. A ten-yard long covered corridor with a walled courtyard led to the kitchen where there was also a servant's room and a small storehouse. Our garden had three coconut trees and four fruit trees, two rambutan, one mangosteen and one durian. One of the rambutan trees was very large and tall and I loved to climb it as far up as I dared until I thought the branches were too thin. Every season, all the trees bore fruit, but I never had the chance to eat the durian. The fruit would ripen and drop in the middle of the night, and our neighbours would pick them up whenever they heard the thud of durian dropping. I sometimes woke up and heard the patter of feet. By the morning, there was nothing on the ground. In any case, my mother disapproved of tropical fruit and I was not allowed to eat any of it when I was growing up.

CHINESE HOME

I remember nothing of my first five years there except that a kitten came to the house one day and I was allowed to keep her as my pet. I called her Maozai, little kitten, and she grew up faster than me and had several litters before I was ten years old. My mother told me later that we were inseparable because Maozai was my only playmate in our first years there. Looking back, all I can remember is that I learnt to make the same calls as Maozai and thought that she responded and understood what I said. Another memory was my mother's refusal to let us keep her kittens and how sad I was when my servant, Ah Lan, took the kittens away to give them to friends. Maozai cried for days and I consoled her in what I thought was her language.

My parents had no friends in Green Town, partly because my mother could not talk to anyone because she had no English or Malay. I was conscious, however, that our only family friends were the Wu family who lived on the other side of the Kinta River by the railway tracks. Mr Wu Yuteng was someone my father had known in Singapore when they were colleagues at the Huaqiao High School. He had helped my father get the Perak education job and was my father's boss.

Mrs Wu loved to play mahjong and invited my parents every week to make a foursome. Although I cannot remember much about our early visits, I remember them as happy moments in my life. When we arrived in Ipoh, the Wus had three children, the youngest, a girl, being only a few months older than me and I grew up calling her elder sister. There were three later additions and I enjoyed being called elder brother by the younger ones. I was an only child, and becoming friends with the Wu children was the nearest thing to having brothers and sisters of my own.

Mrs Wu and my mother became good friends. My parents would go to their home in a rickshaw on Sundays and spend the day with them. During school holidays, I was allowed to stay overnight. We would then sleep late and I would act out stories from the English books I read. These stories were new to the Wu children because they went to Chinese schools. One thing I remember that struck me as strange. Why did we speak Cantonese to one another when our parents always spoke in Mandarin and the Wu children could all speak it? At that time, none of us thought it unusual and we took it for granted that Cantonese was what children spoke. We seem never to have asked why.

I became very fond of the short cut we took to get to the Wu home. It meant crossing a small bridge, passing an elegant Hindu temple and a cave in a limestone outcrop that was used as a Taoist temple. Every now and again, we would pass by when there were crowds attending some ceremonies in one or the other. I was very curious about what the people were doing. But my parents never stopped to join them, so I never learnt what it meant to take part in such festivities. It was only later that I understood that my parents regarded such religious activities as no more than superstitious affairs that had nothing to do with us. I noted that none of my parents' friends visited temples or churches and there were no sign of anything to do with religion in their homes. There were also no altars of any kind in our house. My parents spoke reverentially of their ancestors and showed deep respect for their parents and other elders in my father's family. My mother took pains to identify who those elders were and the precise relationship that my father had with each of them. But we did not pray or perform any kind of worship.

My parents did not entertain. The only visitors to our house were a handful of schoolteachers, usually from small towns outside Ipoh, who came to ask my father for advice or help. They were mostly from Jiangsu or Zhejiang provinces and spoke in Mandarin with a variety of accents. I would ask my mother who they were and she would tell me how some of them had problems with the state education office, others with their school boards, and yet others brought their personal problems. Many of them lived far out in small mining villages or rubber estates where their primary schools were located. As my mother explained this to me, she would remind me that we, too, were far away from home and, like most of them, we too would not be staying long but would return to China when the opportunity arose.

Ever so often, she would find reasons to tell me about my father's longer-term plan for us. What she told me became very real when I was six years old. This was when we were preparing to visit my grandparents in China. She wanted me to understand why they lived so far away and why we were not returning to our family home. That was when she elaborated on her own story when she married my father in Taizhou and left for Java shortly after the wedding. She would also tell me how sickly I was in my early childhood, how little she knew about having a baby and how helpless she was in a foreign land living among people whose languages she could not speak.

My mother began to teach me simple Chinese characters when I was only three years old. I cannot now recall what I actually learnt. She had bought a packet of character-cards used for teaching the written language. She told me later that I could remember scores of Chinese characters after a few days and she proudly told my father about what I was able to remember. After a while, my father, the modern educationist, was concerned that she was pushing me too hard and explained to her what harm that could do if children began too early to learn merely by memorizing individual characters. She stopped rather reluctantly and had to be content to know that there was nothing wrong with my brain, proudly concluding that I was intelligent.

Learning in different worlds was never dull. However, it was one thing to be formally taught together with thirty or more other boys in the class, competing for teacher's attention and graded to show how much has been learnt. It was very different when, after my sixth birthday, my father began to teach me the classical Chinese language in the evening. School finished at one in the afternoon and I usually played with schoolmates who lived nearby till it was time for dinner. My father began with the traditional *Sanzi jing* (Three-Character Classic) and then the *Qianzi wen* (Thousand Character Text) but then turned to the *Xinguowen* (New National Language) textbooks devised early in the 20th century. These texts included numerous stories of famous Confucian literati whose behavior when young were exemplary.

They were the Chinese equivalent of Washington who could not tell a lie and King Alfred and the cakes. Language mastery was tied closely to lessons on moral excellence. The names that stuck in my mind came from stories of men like Kong Rong and Sima Guang when they were boys. There were no stories about little girls.

My father wanted me to learn a language that was not spoken and rarely used outside of the texts we used. Much of it was about remembering the characters, how they were pronounced, what they meant in the past and the changes when used colloquially and in a wide range of phrases and contexts. My father did that for several years. He believed that the baihua vernacular commonly taught in modern schools would be easy to use when one has mastered skills in writing classical Chinese. He was therefore reluctant for me to study the standard textbooks used in the Chinese schools. He admired instead the efforts of men who ran private classes in classical Chinese at the time. But he did not send me to study with them because they were teaching the classics in Cantonese.

But it became clear that language learning was not enough. In school, I was learning different subjects five hours each day five times each week. That way, I was building a vocabulary of English words that described ideas and objects not covered at all in the ancient Chinese texts. I also needed modern Chinese words, so my parents finally decided to send me to Chinese school in the afternoons. I was ten years old when they bought me a bicycle so that I could ride to a private school nearby in New Town. There I was introduced to words that better matched those I was learning in my English school. I was introduced to words about mathematics and science and re-member being overwhelmed by many of the new terms now standard to the language.

ENGLISH SCHOOL

When I was five, my father decided that I should go to Maxwell School, a small English school next door to his Education Office. He persuaded my mother that that would be all right because they could teach me Chinese at home. My father had studied English literature and loved it. He regretted that he had started learning the language only when he was in his late teens and thought that this was a good opportunity for me to start early to master this useful foreign language. It was an unusual thing for him to have done. Mr Wu and all his friends working in Chinese education sent their children to Chinese schools. My mother was doubtful and argued with him. But he was confident that he was right. In this way, I started to adjust to life in two contrasting worlds. I now became an oddity in my parents' circle because I was the only child attending an English school. On the other hand, the children of Green Town who had found me odd because my family was so different now thought I was less so. They also went to English schools. Once I could speak English, I could regularly play with them.

Starting at Maxwell School in January 1936 was also convenient. My father rode his bicycle to work every morning and I sat behind him. He dropped me off at the school beside his office. At noon, he would take me home and, after lunch, returned to work. I cannot remember much of the school except that Mrs Francis, a dark-haired matronly English woman, was my Primary One teacher. She taught me the alphabet, corrected my pronunciation and encouraged me to read aloud. She noted that my birth certificate was in Dutch and that I could only speak Chinese. Most of my classmates came from homes where English was spoken. The Chinese boys came from local-born Baba families, the Indian boys were from families who had come from Ceylon or British India and knew English well, while the Eurasians spoke English as their first language. There were no Malay boys because they went to either Islamic or Malay primary schools. I learnt English quickly because everyone spoke it in school all the time.

Later that year, my parents took me to China. They had not been back since 1929 and my grandparents had never seen me. I was away for two months with the school's permission. After I came back, I caught up with the class and, at the end of the year, passed the tests that allowed me to go to Primary Two. By that time, it was decided that Maxwell School should become part of Anderson School, the government English school located near Green Town and thus much nearer to our house. Thus the next year, my father made arrangements for me to be taken to school by one of our neighbours who also happened to be a teacher at Anderson School.

Mrs Navaratnam lived at the other end of our street, Jalan Abidin. She and her eldest daughter both taught at the school and went to work together every morning by rickshaw. I walked to their house and sat in the rickshaw on a small stool at their feet. They had the same rickshaw puller come each morning so the four of us were a regular sight on the way to school. Mrs Navaratnam was eventually also my class teacher when I went on the next year to Standard One. She spoke in English to me each morning and told my father that I was a quick learner. Her youngest daughter Rasamah was about my age and, when we grew up, we became good friends.

My Primary Two teacher was Miss Widowson. She was petite and fair-haired and very strict about speaking correct English. She did not allow us to speak the Malayan English patois that schoolboys used and scolded us if we spoke any of the local languages. My class now included a few Chinese from the town who spoke Cantonese and I remember some of them being fined five cents each time they spoke that language in school. Miss Widowson provided many storybooks for us to read. My English improved but the stories were always about children in England and their lives and exploits were so different from ours. It was one more social layer that I added to those I already had. My classroom world and the worlds of the different communities of Ipoh town were already quite different from the life I shared with my parents and their Chinese teacher friends. The English life I now gleaned from the books I read was one more.

Anderson School had a new building in the 1930s. It was not a large school and intake was limited to one class for each standard and each then had a classroom to itself. The primary school was on the ground floor while the senior standards were on the first floor. In addition, the school had two special classes for Malay boys. They had finished their studies at local Malay primary schools and spent two years learning English before joining Standard Five with the rest of us. They were housed in a large hostel in the school and were supervised by English and Malay teachers. One day a week, there was assembly in the school hall when the principal would address the whole school. Sometimes teachers or senior students would speak about our studies and the benefits of competitive sports. I liked the school and looked forward each morning to meeting my classmates, and even some of my teachers.

The next four years I spent in five classes. My class teachers were either Ceylonese or Indian; in addition, there was one Malay teacher who taught us geography and one Chinese who taught art and carpentry. The teachers I remember were Mrs Navaratnam who taught Standard One and Mr Rajaratnam who taught Standard Two. Later, it was less clear. I was only briefly in Standard Three taught by Mr Krishnan (or was it Mr Sinniah?) before being moved to Standard Four where I think Mr Morais was class teacher. And then I had Mr Narain Singh and some specialist teachers for the year I spent in Standard Five, the class I was in when the war broke out in December 1941. By that time, I had learnt to manage life in my several worlds, of which Anderson School was central to my formal learning. As far as the school was concerned, I was no longer odd.

School was not demanding. Apart from arithmetic and the English language, I never felt I learnt much. We were taught nothing about Ipoh or the state of Perak apart from the fact that there was a Malay sultan and that we were technically his subjects. This was borne out when we showed our respect to the sultan's representative, usually the Raja Muda or the Raja Bendahara, who presided over our annual sports meet and gave away the prizes. For schoolboys, this was a little confusing because such events would sometimes be accompanied by the singing of the British national anthem, at the time, "God save the King". All this was presented to us with no explanation, as if they were the natural order of things. We were not encouraged to be curious, and certainly learnt nothing about the neighbouring lands that were not in British hands. I also do not remember anything about China and Japan ever being taught in class except in passing when we read about British ships going there to trade or fight. What we did know was the extent of the

British Empire and it was marked in red on the maps on display. Apart from that, we were encouraged to take part in athletic sports. I enjoyed that but did not play any game well. I also remember our art and carpentry teacher because he was sorely disappointed to find out that I could not draw and told me so.

Our teachers in the primary school were mainly from British India and Ceylon. There were also British and Chinese teachers in the upper classes. But I do not recall anyone saying that this was unusual. It was well known that most of the Chinese families in town sent their children to Chinese schools and, if they chose to send them to an English school, they sent them to Anglo-Chinese School or St Michael's Institution in Old Town. I later noted that there were more Chinese teachers in the other English schools and that the study of Christian biblical texts was important there. In contrast, our school was secular to the point when I do not remember the word religion ever been mentioned. I thought this was perfectly natural since the word was not in my family's vocabulary either.

It is difficult for me to remember what I thought between the ages of six and eleven, but I think that having teachers largely from India and Ceylon left a deep impression in my mind. While there was no propaganda about great British achievements, our teachers were products of a century of "imperial India". That had coloured their world outlook even if some of them were moved by the growing anti-colonial nationalism in South Asia. I recall mentions of Rabindranath Tagore having visited British Malaya and was aware of the respect several of my teachers had for Mahatma Gandhi and his satyagraha movement. Although I paid little attention to things Indian, my early exposure to India drew me to appreciate its leadership in Asia after the Second World War. One of my closest friends in primary school was a Sikh boy who also lived in Green Town. We played most afternoons after school in his house where his two young uncles would tell us about their support for Indian independence.

I did not learn about the "plural society" in Western colonies until much later but, thinking back, I realise that I had grown up in such a society in Ipoh, with a particular version of it in my early childhood both in my school and within Green Town. This variety modified the plurality by mixing children and families of different origins and connecting them through a common English language. It did little to bring the adults together but was successful in enabling the children to minimize difference and to know one another well. Among the Chinese in school and Green Town, I came to recognize, but without understanding its significance then, another dimension of being Chinese. I was particularly fond of two brothers who were also neighbours. Theirs was a Baba family that had come from Penang. They spoke English as well as Hokkien at home and observed many traditional Chinese customs that I knew nothing about. They were several generations local-born, had no links with China, and did not know read or write Chinese. We became very good friends but my parents and theirs had nothing in common. What puzzled me at the time was why they were not the least interested in going to China when my parents seemed to talk about nothing else. But I learnt from my two friends what it meant to sink roots in one place. As I wandered around in so many places the rest of my life, I think often of them and how they were comfortable to be at home.

CHINA IN THE MIND

I do not remember much about our trip to China in 1936. What I know of it comes mainly from what my mother told me that was reinforced by the few photographs taken by my uncle when we were in Taizhou that she kept in her album. I do have vague images of cities like Singapore, Hong Kong and Shanghai and of being on a large passenger ship. But I cannot recall how we got to Taizhou and what we actually did there. My mother told me how happy my grandparents were to see me and how well behaved I was on the whole when I met all our relatives. But there was an embarrassing incident she has repeated to me several times. This happened in the middle of a solemn ceremony when all male members of the family were kneeling before our ancestral tablets and I climbed on the back of my elder cousin and asked him to play with me. Although my grandfather was indulgent and did not complain about the disruption to the proceedings, my mother felt guilty for having not brought me up properly.

I mention this incident because it was one of the reasons why she told me so much about my father's family thereafter. She was determined that I understood that my ancestors had a distinguished lineage. My father was a taciturn man who never talked to me about family and personal matters. It was left to my mother to tell me where our family came from, whom my ancestors from northern China were, and why my great-grandparents moved south to Taizhou. In contrast, she told me little about her own family and it was many years later that I found out more about their origins. She was content that I knew that hers was an arranged marriage between good families, why she married relatively late and only met my father after all the arrangements had been made for the wedding. I thought all this was normal until much later, when I wondered how my parents had adapted to each other so well and lived together with such affection and mutual respect.

My father worked long days and regularly travelled outside Ipoh to inspect schools far away. I normally only saw him at dinner time, after which he taught me the basic Chinese texts and assigned me reading that he asked my mother to supervise. Now and then, he would take me along when he visited his friend's bookshop in town. He bought me children's books in

Chinese and boys' magazines in English. I noted that, apart from the news magazines in Chinese that my mother looked forward to reading, he also ordered British Sunday papers like *The Observer* and *The Sunday Times.*

While he was happy to hear from my teachers that my English was improving, he never spoke English to me. I knew he could because he worked with English officials in the Education Office but I never knew how well he spoke the language. It was years later that I discovered that he wrote very correct English and had a very fine grasp of English grammar and idiom. But I rarely heard him utter a word in English; that was much later when he met my university friends and talked briefly with them. Those trips I made with him to the bookshop were special treats. There I appreciated that he was comfortable in two complex language worlds and realized that even his English world was in two parts: the public part he used to meet the needs of his office and the private part he turned to in order to follow current literary tastes and trends in Britain.

After we returned from China, the event my parents had feared came to pass. War between Japan and China began in earnest. Shanghai was attacked and Japanese troops pushed towards the capital city of Nanjing. With this war, I became increasingly conscious of being Chinese at school. The contrast between what my parents talked about at home and among their friends and what concerned my teachers and fellow pupils in school could not be starker. Our teachers did talk about Britain and the Empire facing tensions in Europe, but there was almost no mention of the war in China. Even my school friends who were Chinese did not talk about that war.

My parents followed the events in China closely and the Chinese in the town began to raise funds for the war effort. My mother joined the women's organizations that held events to collect money for the cause. I remember listening to my father telling my mother about Chinese schools that were actively supporting the Nationalists in China and about confusion in the community. Among Guomindang members, there were those who supported Chiang Kai-shek and others who sided with Wang Ching-wei. As for those who sympathized with the opposition parties, including the Chinese Communist Party, there was also hesitation about how best to help the Save China movement.

I listened to my parents without understanding the finer differentiations among local Chinese. It was nonetheless my introduction to the elements of politics. I did not know it at the time, but my parents' conversations had laid the foundations of an interest in political affairs that would surface later in my life. The Japanese war on Chinese soil dragged on for years. It did not much affect the time I spent with my school friends, with whom I enjoyed playing. It was only when I was home listening to my parents talking that I felt that the ongoing war was really about us.

My parents began to take me to cinemas to see patriotic films. The turning point for me was late in 1938 when I saw the film on the battle for Shanghai, *The Heroic 800*. I identified with the heroes who bravely defended the city. Thereafter, I listened more carefully to my mother when she talked about going home to China one day. It was now a place that had become more real, one that I began to identify with.

Other films I did not enjoy as much but found *The General*, the story of the Song dynasty general Yue Fei who defied orders to fight the Jurchen invaders of northern China, inspiring. My father taught me Yue Fei's famous poem, "The River is Red", and I was grew to love the song composed for that poem. But I could understand why my mother came to dislike going to most other Chinese films. She thought too many of them were tearjerkers that made the audience very sad and she thought real life was sad enough. But there were films that produced popular songs that I particularly liked, those sung by Zhou Xuan and Bai Guang, and learnt to sing them along with my childhood friends. One of Zhou Xuan's films, *Malu Tianshi* (Street Angel) stayed in my mind for years.

When I saw the film *The 800 Heroes*, war in Europe was imminent. My schoolteachers began to talk about the possibility that, with Britain, France and Netherlands engaged on that continent, Japan would threaten their colonies. I do not recall the discussions being very serious but there were by then some reason for anxiety. Once war began in Europe, adult conversations included the Sino-Japanese conflict. There was concern that it might spread to Malaya.

But the government was determined to keep everything as normal as possible. Local British officials became more openly sympathetic towards China Salvation events and I recalled how my mother was drawn to take part in more of them. My father, however, was not one to engage in political debate in public. He had the task of keeping an eye on school activities that were politicised among different Chinese factions. He kept a low profile while trying to discourage school boards and principals from turning schools into political arenas. He concentrated on the key task of providing good education for all who wanted to study. Although he attended many community fund-raising events and talked to everyone who sought his advice, he rarely spoke about China politics.

When I was older and knew him better, I realized my father was someone with a keen sense of duty and capable of great self-control. His strict Confucian upbringing made him dislike the idea of parties and factions fighting against legitimate authority. As an education officer, he sought to be above all that although I knew he often found it painful to be caught in the struggles going on.

At the same time, he encouraged me to improve my English and also began to take me to see English films. My parents chose those with historical themes. I remember being taken to see *Mary of Scotland* and *The Private Lives of Elizabeth and Essex*, both of which my mother loved. My father also wanted to see films based on famous literary works. He took me to see *A Tale of Two Cities*, *David Copperfield*, *Captains Courageous*, *Elephant Boy*, among others. I remember them well and was most moved by a film called *Lloyd's of London*, which featured the death of Admiral Nelson after his victory at Trafalgar.

SOUNDS OF WAR

Standard Five in Anderson School was equivalent to the 7th year in school, comparable to the first year of secondary school. In January 1941, I was ten years old and eager to learn from the new set of specialist teachers in English and Mathematics. There was more English grammar, and we were asked to recite poetry, read simple one-act plays and make short speeches about everyday topics. The questions we were asked to solve in mathematics needed more thought and calculation but I decided that it was still largely a matter of practice. The geography class was interesting. We were taught about landforms, climate, crops and agriculture, mining and industry, trade following the flag, the location of ports and cities and I was keen to relate them to the globe in our classroom. Some of the teachers urged us to study hard but it was not school policy to pressure us to excel.

Elsewhere, everything was more serious. The Chinese schools my father was responsible for were committed to support the war in China. School assemblies were focused on being patriotic as overseas Chinese and, at dinner every night, my father would update my mother and me about the mood in the community. We talked more about Sun Yat-sen and the role of Chinese abroad in the 1911 revolution and the efforts thereafter to build a modern nation. My mother was an avid reader of Chinese magazines and would tell us about the course of the war, the desperate needs of people in China and the various efforts to raise money. On Sundays, I visited the Wu children, who by that time had been joined by their cousins from Shanghai. They told us how they fled the city and the war seemed to come much closer to all of us. They went to Chinese schools and could also describe their money-raising activities to support China. They talked about classmates whose elder brothers had volunteered to fight and left to join the Nationalist army. We were especially excited when one of them joined the air force to become a pilot.

Late in 1939, the Wuhan Choir from China that had been raising funds from all over British Malaya came to Ipoh and its singing inspired the whole Chinese community. The Wu family got to know some of the singers personally and I remember two of them well. They remained behind after the Choir returned to China to teach in schools in Perak. After we heard the Wuhan choir perform, we wanted to sing more patriotic songs. This included "Volunteers Marching Song" (later to become the National Anthem of the Peoples Republic of China), songs of loss like "On the Sungari River" (about refugees from Manchuria who lost their homes) and "The 800 Heroes". Some evenings, I accompanied my mother to concerts where new songs were introduced and I learnt to sing them as well. I began to know what patriotic feelings were like but I was also conscious that it was only a small part of my response to the events unfolding quickly before us.

PEOPLE AND PLACES

An only child, I had my mother's full attention, and my father was very protective and deliberate about my education. But he never really explained why, as an inspector of Chinese Schools, he decided to send me to an English school. Many Chinese schoolteachers were puzzled at, if not critical of, his decision. At the same time, he was very public about his intention to return to China as soon as he could and my mother never failed to prepare me for that return one day. She even told me, when I asked her why I did not have brothers and sisters as all my friends did, that it was because she wanted us to afford to travel home to China when the chance came.

Thus I grew up thinking that we were not normal. My father had a degree from a university in China. We were the only Mandarin-speaking family in Green Town and I the only one with that background in school. The Chinese in town each had their own organizations, temples and festivals, and held their social activities there regularly. But our family did not join any of them. My parents were Confucian and only believed in rituals that paid respect to their ancestors. We had nothing in the house that could be linked to any religion. And, to cap it all, we were known to be only temporarily living in Ipoh and always ready to leave.

I remember two conflicting thoughts that troubled me now and again. One was that I liked Ipoh. I loved my school and my friends and was not happy at the thought of leaving them. The other was more discomforting. I believed that China was our real home and was therefore keen to master everything I could to prepare myself to return. Yet I was drawn to the images of England in my books at school, especially those that dovetailed with those in the English literary works that my father admired and encouraged me to read.

A temporary resolution came when I was ten years old. This was when my father bought me a world atlas as a birthday present. I had seen such books in school but never thought they would be exciting to read. But when I had my own copy and began to pore through each map, I was overwhelmed by the sense of discovery and wanted to examine every corner of the globe. My father was surprised when he found me so transfixed by every part of the atlas. After going through some of the pages many times, I felt the urge to list every feature of importance, if only to help me remember them. I started with the countries, cities and provinces, then the islands, oceans and seas, the mountains and valleys, and then the peninsulas, bays, gulfs and capes. After a while, I could visualize the better-known places and where exactly they were in the maps.

My mother noticed that I stopped going out to play with my friends after school. Instead, I went straight to my room after lunch and turned to my atlas. I filled my special exercise book with my lists. I no longer felt burdened by being located in any single place. There was so much to learn beyond China and England, so many places far away from Ipoh. And when I related them to the historical films I saw, I found another dimension where there were many interesting times in the past to turn to. With so much space and so much time out there, I was filled with wonder at what the world had to offer.

From then on, every time I felt uneasy about who or where I was, I would think about the atlas and my lists. A calm would descend on my mind. I could think of Shanghai and London, Horatio Nelson and Yue Fei, whoever and wherever. All places and people had become knowable. Nothing could stand in the way of my learning about them. Looking back, I believe I had accidentally found a way to make my oddity easier to bear. Indeed, I began to feel I was not so different after all.

WAR COMES TO IPOH

I soon learnt that war was something far-reaching and disrupting. Years before war reached Malaya, it was the topic of conversation at our dinner table. It was why we were not going home but merely visiting China to see my grandparents. After our return, war did start in China and the subject was never far from every conversation my parents had with their friends. The only notable difference was that, with each year, war seemed to be spreading. By 1939, news about wars reached us every day and eventually the war became something that could reach us in Malaya.

I realized it was serious when my father bought a radio so that we could listen to the war news. This was exciting for me because, with my atlas, I found that I could trace where the fighting was going on. I remember being struck by news of bombings in Chongqing and London on the same day. That had made me aware that the talk of world war was true. Japan would soon expand southwards after its forces took control of Guangzhou and then the island of Hainan. The British knew that the Japanese planned to use French Indo-China to attack other parts of Southeast Asia. Vichy France was help-less to stop Japan, and serious preparations had begun to defend Malaya. By 1941, most people knew that it was only a matter of time before Japan would move. My parents, like many others, remained hopeful that Britain was strong enough to keep the Japanese out. I never sensed any alarm until very late.

The attack came from the north in December. Within days, the bombs fell on Ipoh. In great haste, my parents joined their friends Mr Wu and family to leave the town. I learnt later that arrangements had been made for us to hide in a timber camp and rubber estate outside the town of Tanjong Tualang. The owner was the Board chairman of the local Chinese primary school who knew Mr Wu and offered to help. When we were there, a few Japanese soldiers visited the camp but they were in a hurry to move on and did not harm anybody. I remember little of the fortnight we spent there except that I had high fever from malaria. Fortunately, we had a supply of quinine and the attack was quelled.

We then moved to a hiding-place in a range of limestone caves closer to Ipoh. There were many families there. We felt safer and saw no Japanese troops for another fortnight. By that time, the Japanese had taken Ipoh and a small garrison remained to help the civilian officials restore order and services. Mr Wu and my father went to Ipoh to find us new homes. There was no question of returning to Green Town and we looked for a place in town. We followed the Wu family and my parents rented a room in New Town just beside the market.

I joined the Wu children to help our families. We set up a stall outside the market and sold sundry goods like soap and soya sauce that Mr Wu obtained for us to display. We did that for several weeks. One day, the Japanese came to the market entrance and placed several human heads on a high stand not far in front of our stall. They announced that these were heads of executed looters and warned against any kind of criminal act. We were horrified and our parents decided to close the stall. I then tried riding my bicycle out of town to sell soap from door to door but was totally unsuccessful. Our parents decided to retire us and we ended our brief careers as salesmen. They began to wonder about our going back to school.

My parents found a place closer to a school and we moved again, this time to Old Town where we rented a room from the Fujian Association. My father arranged for me to go to Ming Teh Primary School established by the Hakka Association. I was put into its senior class for 11-year olds. My teachers were Hakka and taught us in their version of Mandarin. It was a new experience and I enjoyed learning subjects like arithmetic, geography and history in Chinese instead of the classical Chinese texts I had read at home. But something irked my father greatly. It was required that the school teach Japanese and two young local teachers were sent to start us on the language. We also had to sing the Japanese national anthem every morning and learn a number of Japanese patriotic songs. After three months, my father decided that he did not want me to do this any more and took me out of the school.

He then organized a private class to teach his friends' children so that he could have me learn with them. Here he taught only classical Chinese. By that time, I was using the *Guwen Guanzhi*, the standard text of famous prose writings and started on the *Tangshi sanbaishou* (Three Hundred Tang Poems). We studied together for more than a year and went on to other selections of prose literature. There was a lot of memory work and we tried our hand at writing classical Chinese ourselves. It was a struggle to do well in all this because everything we learnt seemed so distant and unrelated to the life around us.

I was now twelve years old living among town Chinese in an environment totally different from that of a government officers' compound. No English was spoken at all but every variety of southern Chinese dialects with a few Malay words now and again. For the next three years, I saw none of my teachers and school friends. It was as if one life was suspended and the other darkened by clouds of uncertainty.

Contributors

ELIZABETH ARNDT worked busily and travelled widely before marrying and settling in Eire. Now retired, she teaches silk painting.

JAKE DALEY. After service in World War II and the Korean War Donald ['Jake'] Dailey became a successful businessman in Mount Ayr, Iowa. He became County Recorder for Ringgold County and continues to serve the community though the American Legion and as a hospice volunteer.

GEORGE DIBLEY spent much of his life in tertiary education administration in Australia and New Zealand. Somewhere in the years of pleasure parenting his son and later his daughter, his father's watch stopped and was lost. His altar boy years formed a lifelong interest in painting, literature and music.

PAUL G. HALPERN. After graduation and military service, he completed a PhD at Harvard in 1966, then spent his entire academic career at Florida State University. His specialism is naval history.

B.A. HUSSAINMIYA. After completing a Bachelor's degree at Peradeniya University in Sri Lanka, he obtained a scholarship to Monash University. Much of his subsequent career in historical research and teaching was at Universiti Brunei Darussalam.

PRADEEP KANTHAN served as an officer in the Indian army. On migrating he became an administrator at the University of Auckland and then Finance Controller with the New Zealand Property Council. He now runs a business in trading and financial services in Sydney.

COLIN MACKERRAS has worked as a China specialist at Griffith University, Queensland, since 1974, and has taught frequently in Beijing. His research is on Chinese musical theatre, ethnic minorities, and Australia-China relations.

RUTH MALCOLM has spent her adult years mainly in teaching, first her six children, and after that, through involvement in prison education, basic literacy and numeracy for the long-term unemployed. During a spell in Brunei Darussalam she was an English language teacher. The common thread is her belief in the value of every individual and her or his potential.

SHAKILA ABDUL MAMAN, a former professor of English at Universiti Sains Malaysia, is now an independent researcher, writing on issues related to language and the formation of identity in multicultural Malaysia.

OOI KEAT GIN is currently a professor of history at Universiti Sains Malaysia, coordinator of its Asia Pacific Research Unit and founding editor of the International Journal of Asia Pacific Studies. Travel and enjoying various cuisines are among his hobbies.

HAJAR ABDUL RAHIM completed bachelor and master degrees in the US. Back in Penang she worked as an English schoolteacher before going to the UK for her doctorate. For over twenty years she has been teaching at the Universiti Sains Malaysia.

KENELM ROBERT declined a university place after completing his secondary education and in 1972 began a 40-year career at London's Royal Festival Hall, where he held a number of positions. In 2009 he was awarded an MBE for services to the arts, and for being the first athlete to represent Grenada at the World Masters Swimming Championships and at World Masters Squash.

GEORG SCHMID studied philosophy, history and philology and taught mainly at the University of Salzburg. Retiring early for reasons of health, he continued to give occasional seminars, mainly in Vienna. He has published both novels and scholarly books, the most recent being *The Mind Screen* [2016].

SIGRID SCHMID-BORTENSCHLAGER studied German, English and Comparative Literature. She taught mainly at the University of Salzburg but also at Graz, Utrecht, Paris VIII and Paris XII. Now retired, she lives in

France. Her research and publications are in experimental literature, women writers and semiology.

KOBKUA SUWANNATHAT-PIAN spent over forty years in academic life in universities in Thailand and Malaysia. Now retired, she is a free-lance writer on historical topics of personal interest.

NICHOLAS TARLING (February 1931–May 2017) was an academic historian specialising in Southeast Asia. After getting a doctorate in Cambridge, he taught at the University of Queensland. For the last half-century he was at the University of Auckland, and for the last twenty years he was an honorary fellow at its New Zealand Asia Institute.

LORRAINE WHEELER, née Heywood, married a farmer, Robert Gerald Wheeler, from Mt Hardey, Western Australia. They raised three sons and a daughter. Lorraine taught in local schools and wrote three children's books. On retirement they moved to nearby York, and enjoy grandchildren, gardening and travel.

RUPERT WHEELER spent most of his career in the computer industry ending up as a joint founder and director of a computer services company before retiring. He and his wife Fiona have two children and three grandchildren.

WANG GUNGWU went to the University of Malaya in Singapore and later became Professor of History at the branch in Kuala Lumpur. From there he moved to the Australian National University and subsequently became Vice-Chancellor of the University of Hong Kong. The National University of Singapore now benefits from his leading role in the study of China, as do many others.

www.ingramcontent.com/pod-product-compliance
Lightning Source LLC
Chambersburg PA
CBHW021814270326
41932CB00007B/180